"Well written and insightful. I don't think there's a similar book that provides the reader with such a masterful overview of sustainable design and building practices. Dykstra makes a compelling economic argument as well as an environmental case. This is a fascinating introduction to a crucial topic that affects all of us—a must-read."

—Lawrence Sweeny, Solstice Enterprises, Inc., commercial and residential contracting and project management

"Once again, Alison Dykstra has done a great service, through her unique focus on the green construction industry. This book is a great introduction to the field and represents a powerful argument for an increased focus on green construction. Dykstra's writing is clear, concise and well informed by decades of experience in the field."

—Jerry Yudelson, PE, LEED Fellow, author and speaker, founder of the Yudelson Associates consultancy

"This book is very comprehensive, from the topics the author has chosen to cover to the way the parts are broken down. It identifies all the component parts and provides a really good picture of what green and sustainable building means. The sections are concise and clear on important topics that we should all know about as CMs—this is something I would suggest as reading to Sciame employees—or at least portions of it because it is so well organized and informative."

—Robert E. DaRos Jr., Vice President, Sciame Construction, construction managers, consultants, builders

"This is a terrific book for anyone who works in construction. More and more of our projects are 'green' and it's important for everyone to understand what that means and how it impacts the trades."

—J. Scott Thomas, Project Superintendent, Wright Contracting, Inc., General Contractor

"Alison Dykstra—a long time advocate of intelligent building design—gives us a clear picture of green construction and how it can improve our lives and the health of our planet."

—Sim Van der Ryn, Professor Emeritus UC Berkeley, former California State Architect, President EcoDesign Collaborative

"This lucid and very readable book brings focus and clarity to the often misunderstood term 'sustainable design'. It delineates the burgeoning construction industry trends of designing and building 'green' and the critical need for doing so in a world of limited resources. Essential reading for the student, the designer, the builder and the 'guys' in the field."

—*Richard Wolfe, AIA, LEED AP*

"With existing buildings accounting for nearly 40% of greenhouse gas emissions of cities, this book is a welcome and important contribution. Its easy to call out new building standards, such as zero net energy, but to achieve them and do it well, requires training and real knowledge. Dykstra's book is an important contribution in providing that missing link."

—*Stephanie Pincetl, PhD, Director, California Center for Sustainable Communities, Institute of the Environment and Sustainability, UCLA*

"I have always said 'there are different shades of green'. Alison Dykstra has approached this important subject in a way that will help architects, engineers, builders, and owners decide as to which shade of green works best for their project and budget. It could have been titled—How to get the most green for your dollars."

—*Frank J. Sciame, Jr., CEO/Chairman, Sciame Construction, construction managers, consultants, builders*

"It's about friggin' time somebody wrote this book! An in-depth study of the green building practices of today, and tomorrow. Invaluable!"

—*Lawrence Sweeny, Solstice Enterprises, Inc., commercial and residential contracting and project management*

"The book is well organized and touches on many of the important matters concerning green construction. The chapter on green construction and the trades is especially effective—it discusses each of the trades and their role as they pertain to the scope of work for green projects.

This is a very practical way to look at it; construction managers deal with these type of issues on a daily basis."

—*Robert E. DaRos Jr., Vice President, Sciame Construction, construction managers, consultants, builders*

Green Construction

An introduction to a changing industry

Alison Dykstra

Also by the Author

Construction Project Management: A Complete Introduction
LEED Certification: An Introduction to Certifying a Green Building

Library of Congress Control Number: 2015960690

Printed in the United States of America 10 9 8 7 6 5 4 3 2 1

ISBN: 978-0-9827034-2-7

Cover design and cover photograph by Andrea Young Arts, Berkeley CA
Interior design by Lauren Woodrow Design, Chicago IL

Kirshner Publishing Company
Production Offices:
PO Box 14132
Santa Rosa, CA 95404
Editorial Offices:
San Francisco, CA
www.kirshnerbooks.com
www.kirshnerpublishing.com

For Andrew, Marisol, and Matthew

Thank you to the many people who generously gave their time to offer guidance and feedback as this book was taking shape; it benefited immeasurably from them all. In no particular order, heartfelt thanks to:

Jerry Yudelson—Yudelson Associates Consulting

J. Scott Thomas—Job Superintendent, Wright Contracting Inc.

Brian Smith—NREL/National Wind Technology Center

Douglas Kirk—Director of Environmental Education, IAPMO (International Association of Plumbing and Mechanical Officials)

Lawrence Sweeny—President, Solstice Enterprises Commercial and Residential Contracting

Sim Van der Ryn—Professor Emeritus, UC Berkeley, President, EcoDesign Collaborative

Ted Tiffany—Assoc. Principal, Guttmann & Blaevoet Consulting Engineers

S. Scott MacLeod—Co-Chief Operating Officer, Skanska USA Building, Inc.

Cam S. Fitzgerald—Mechanical Engineer, Energy Opportunities/7 Group

John Guill—Principal, DTR Consulting

Tom Javits—Vice President for Construction, the Metropolitan Museum of Art

Christina D. Mead

Jay True—Partner, Jim Murphy & Associates Builders

Blaine Brownell—University of Minnesota

Bruce King—Sustainable Design and Engineering

Jan Stensland—Inside Matters

Gretchen Dykstra—Writer-in-Residence, New York Public Library

John Shurtz—Consultant and Green Jobs Trainer

Tedd Benson—Founder and Owner, Bensonwood High-Performance Buildings

Stephanie Pincetl, PhD—Director, CA Center for Sustainable Communities

Andrew Truitt—Director of PV Operations, Dividend Solar

Alison A. Bailes III, PhD—Energy Vanguard Education and Green Services

Doug McKenzie—Owner, LightsOnSolar

Thanks to a wonderful production team: Lauren Woodrow for her clear, readable, and beautiful interior design and Andrea Young for a perfect cover, Stephanie Marohn for her willingness to copy edit even as her community was battling wildfires, and to Joseph Ward, Denise Collins, and Troy Mott for assistance and research. A special thank you to my husband, Andrew Schulman for his invaluable blend of skillful editing, sharp-eyed criticism, unfailing support and good humor; once again, I couldn't have done it without you.

Contents

Chapter 10: Renewable Energy and the Trades   **187**

Introduction

Background

Many of us know from personal experience that the construction industry is changing. There are multiple reasons for these changes—demographics, technology, financing—but behind many construction-industry changes is the increased understanding among the general public, government agencies, businesses and others that what and how we build may cause problems for people and for the environment. This is translating into new—greener—construction practices, and it is becoming harder and harder for contractors to sit on the sidelines and not actively participate.

As a result of the links between a healthy economy and a healthy building sector, there is growing worldwide understanding that we need to change the way we build. The United States and the global community have been adopting more sustainable building practices that include how projects are conceived and constructed, what materials and systems are specified, and how projects are managed, operated, and decommissioned. This transformation of the construction industry means new ways of thinking and enhanced skills, which impacts builders, designers, engineers, suppliers, manufacturers, owners, and users.

Green construction is gaining prominence in the United States and globally. Although much of the growth in the green market is occurring in the commercial sector, the application of green design and construction principles are not specific to one building or project type but cross all sectors; residential, institutional, and infrastructure projects now boast green credentials. The growth of green construction is reflected in the data: according to McGraw-Hill Construction's 2013 *Green Outlook*, the value of new green building in the United States grew in 10 years from $10 billion in 2005 to almost $250 billion.[1] Green construction is becoming so common that *not* seeking some sort of green certification is noteworthy.

The numbers from McGraw-Hill and others represent both a challenge and an opportunity for those in the construction industry. As the field has matured, it is clear that green building is here to stay, and evidence points to it becoming the new industry norm. As a consequence, it is increasingly important for contractors and others in the industry to prepare themselves for this reality.

This book comes out of the author's experience teaching construction project management at a community college in northern California. At the start of each new class, with a student body that ranged from young people recently out of high school to experienced contractors, a recommendation that students explore green construction was typically met with yawns. There was skepticism in both the classroom and among many in construction that "green" was anything more than a passing fad.

After 2008 and 2009, attitudes were changing. The recession, unemployment in construction and other industries, increasing scientific evidence regarding emissions and climate change, continued instability in the Middle East, President Obama's emphasis on renewable sources of energy,[2] and other factors were contributing to a shift in public attitude about energy and green jobs. Almost overnight, jobs in a new green economy didn't seem so farfetched and the author's students (among many others) began to ask, "What do I need to do to take advantage of this opportunity?"

Workers in a changing industry

Figuring out how to compete in the new and still evolving green economy is not necessarily straightforward; perhaps more than at any time in the past, success is dependent upon the acquisition of a variety of new skills, knowledge, and attitudes. It's challenging for workers in many industries to sort through the chatter and figure out what's going on and how to respond. This book provides guidance for those trying to figure out how to be successful in this shifting world, and is intended to provide critical information to those transitioning within the industry as well as those just starting out.

This book does not focus on the practical skills that will be required by some: for example, how to install flat plate solar collectors, specify high performance energy systems, or repair wind turbines. The intention is broader: to help contractors, designers, students, and others move forward in an industry that is changing. Although the information contained in this book will be useful to anyone in the building industry—owners, developers, designers, and users—the emphasis will be on the contractor's team: the general contractors, project managers, and superintendents, specialty contractors, and tradespeople working in the field.

Organization of the book

The book is organized in two parts: Part 1 (Chapters 1–6) provides context. Chapters 1 and 2 begin the book with background information. Chapter 1 describes the ways in which our conventional approaches to design and construction create problems. Chapter 2 defines green construction and reviews how the application of green principles addresses these problems.

Why has the industry embraced green, what are the implications for workers, and what does this changing industry look like? These are some of the questions we'll look at in Chapter 3. Chapter 4 delves into specifics regarding changing standards and codes and introduces the reader to several of the systems used to "rate" green buildings and energy, including LEED, Green Globes, Energy Star, and more.

Green building assumes the use of healthy, durable, and efficient products. Chapter 5 explores the challenges both designers and builders face when choosing materials and products, and looks at several resources available to help sort through often conflicting information.

Chapter 6 completes Part 1 with a discussion of the short- and long-term benefits derived from a shift into green building models: the creation of jobs; tax and other incentives on the front end and, on an ongoing basis, reduced energy and water costs; lower maintenance costs due to system durability; improved health; and environmental benefits.

Part 2 (Chapters 7–12) focuses on how the changes outlined in Part 1 affect the men and women who work in construction. Chapter 7 opens this section with a discussion of how green construction impacts owners, architects, and, especially, general contractors. The role of the GC—from the design phase through construction—has changed dramatically. This chapter explores the ways in which this is due to green construction requirements. Chapters 8 and 9 look at the specialty trades and how their roles have changed, and Chapter 10 reviews renewable energy systems and the opportunities they present to workers.

Success in a new, green economy relies on a skilled work force. Chapters 11 and 12 explore the variety of green credentials, classes, workshops, and other tools available to those in the industry. We'll look at several professional credentials as well as programs designed to enhance skills. Chapter 12 also discusses, briefly, how to find work, the continuing changes in the industry, and how workers can keep abreast of these changes.

Terminology in bold is defined in glossaries at the end of each chapter, and in the glossary toward the end of the book.

The appendices provide helpful, expanded information, including a history of the green movement, a more extensive discussion of our energy sources and uses, an overview of the LEED building certification process, and an alphabetized summary of the URLs in this book.

The book concludes with a glossary, endnotes, bibliography, and comprehensive index.

Part 1

Setting the Stage: An Industry in the Midst of Change

Our Buildings: Fabulous but Flawed

Our **built environment**—human-made buildings and parks, transportation systems, energy and water infrastructure, and the other constructed physical components that form our surroundings—is astonishing in its complexity and purpose. The process of building it can be spellbinding. Some readers may understand what it takes, for example, to turn an empty lot downtown into an office building or house. For those less familiar with the process, peering through a sidewalk peephole might make it appear magical: hundreds of activities happening simultaneously, cranes and scaffolds, flat-bed deliveries of steel beams and columns, machinery and equipment pounding and lifting and cutting, concrete trucks rumbling down the street, and floors being poured. A din is likely to accompany the bustle: the hiss of welding torches, the whine of drills and saws, the rumble of trucks, the voices of the workers as they do their jobs.

Workers in dozens of trades often arrive before dawn, lugging enormous lunch boxes, wearing hard hats and boots. All day these workers, mostly (but no longer exclusively) men, use their hands, special skills, and a variety of tools, equipment, and machinery unfamiliar to those outside the construction industry. Their offices are temporary, and often cold and wet.

It's not hard to understand the thrill embodied in the multilayered, complex, and time-consuming work of building our communities. At the end of the day, there can be justifiable pride: the architect and engineers design our structures, the owners use them, but it's the contractors who *build* them!

This built environment isn't just interesting, it's also valuable. In 2012, its dollar value in the United States, (including machinery and equipment, infrastructure, and land) was close to an almost unimaginable 40 *trillion* dollars.[1] Our buildings have asset value beyond their bricks and mortar, too: millions of people are employed, directly and indirectly, in the trades that build, supply, and maintain them and by those who live and work in them. We can appreciate, if only intuitively, that buildings have broad impacts on almost every aspect of our lives: our productivity, our health and sense of well-being, our ability to work and learn and raise our children, the cleanliness of our air and water, and our use of resources. Our buildings are marvels of design and construction know-how, but we've learned that they're also flawed.

The problems with our buildings

We in the construction industry have come to understand, in specific terms, that the approaches we currently use to plan our communities, the way we design and construct our buildings, and the materials, products, and systems we specify have unintended effects on the people who build and use them, and on the broader community. There is growing consensus based on decades of data collected by multiple agencies and industry organizations that, while our buildings and infrastructure are valuable assets, they can also negatively impact human health and the environment. The way we have been doing things does not typically create places that are resilient and durable, healthy, or self-sustaining, nor does it use resources effectively and prudently.

Our buildings can negatively impact human health and the environment.

One of the primary ways we are addressing these problems is through the use of **green construction,** a process for creating and operating buildings and communities that strives to reduce their environmental impact and to maximize social and economic value. An objective is to develop buildings whose construction and operation assure the healthiest possible environment, while incorporating the most efficient and least disruptive use of land and natural resources. The eventual goal is for this way of building to become the new standard.

For this to occur, it will be necessary to change the materials we use, the way we manufacture many of our building products, how we design our structures, the skills and practices used to build them, and how structures are operated, maintained, and decommissioned. These changes are already happening, but although there are more and more green projects being built every day, old patterns die hard and changing course is challenging.

This is not surprising; our development patterns have been in place a long time and we're used to doing things a certain way. Building habits in the United States were shaped by early experiences with what appeared to be limitless land and resources. Later, Americans embraced the exuberance of the post World War II world, with building habits linked to inexpensive energy. This has impacted our lives in many ways. The design of buildings, the layout of towns, the size of our houses and vehicles, the food we eat, the water we drink, the air we breathe, the clothes we wear, the products, equipment,

Conventional office building

Carter Dayne

and machinery we use—all are, to one degree or another, linked to cheap fossil fuels. Inexpensive fuel has meant that inefficient and oversized building systems, such as heating and air-conditioning systems, could be installed without concern, that insufficient insulation was okay because occupants could crank up the thermostat, or that housing millions of Americans in neighborhoods located at a distance from school, work, and services wasn't a problem because gasoline didn't cost very much.

This dependence on cheap fuel has made it difficult to slow down and heed the warnings that, in the long term, our course is unsustainable or unworkable. Over the years, we have built structures and communities that use too much energy and water, are built from materials that can make us sick, and that cause harm to the environment.

Policy makers, designers, businesses, the general public, and builders are responding to these problems. The growth of green construction, a process designed to address these issues, has taken off both in the United States and globally and is increasingly viewed as a long-term economic necessity. In fact, green construction is becoming so common that *not* seeking some sort of green certification or recognition is sometimes noteworthy. A recent news headline, "Casino Developers not Pursuing Green Certification,"[2] is an interesting indication of current attitudes.

Before we move into a more detailed discussion about what green construction is and how it is influencing the industry, it will be helpful to better understand the problems driving this significant change in the construction industry.

The challenges created by our buildings and land use patterns may be grouped into several broad impact categories: energy, water, human health, waste, and the environment. Let's look briefly at the links between these impacts and our buildings.

Energy

It takes lots of energy to build our communities. It's not surprising that, once buildings are occupied, it takes still more energy to power computers and table lamps, to pump water, to operate heaters and air conditioners to keep us warm or cool, to cook our food, and to wash our clothes. Oil, natural gas, and coal—**fossil fuels**—plus a relatively small amount from nuclear, renewable energy, and other sources provide this energy. The energy that is delivered directly to the buildings where we live and work is equivalent to around six billion barrels of crude oil every year[3] and costs consumers approximately $400 billion.[4] About a third of this energy is wasted due to inefficiencies.[5] Given the problems we're having finding, processing, and delivering fossil fuels safely and affordably, this situation is expensive and untenable.

As noted, the direct costs consumers pay for this energy is many hundreds of billions of dollars a year. These costs don't include the indirect costs such as transportation, health costs related to poor air quality, and environmental impact costs.

Energy and efficiency

Energy is the ability to do work and comes in various forms: **radiant** (light), **motion**, **electrical**, **thermal** (heat), and more. A characteristic of energy is that it can be transferred from one form into another. For example, some solar installations convert radiant (light) energy from the sun into electrical energy; hydroelectric dams convert motion of water into electrical energy; and fossil fuel power plants convert the heat energy of combustion into mechanical energy, which is turned into electrical energy. (Please note: there is a difference between energy and power which will be discussed in Chapter 10, but the terms are often used inter-changeably and the author will do so in this book.)

One of the problems with our buildings is their energy inefficiency. **Energy efficiency** refers to the ratio of energy that can be used versus the amount of energy consumed. For example, an 80% efficient natural gas furnace delivers 80 units (typically measured in BTUs) of useful heat energy for every 100 units of natural gas energy consumed, with the remaining 20 units of energy lost as exhaust through the flue; a 90% efficient furnace delivers 90 units of heat and loses only 10% through the flue and so on. In construction, there are two common terms used to describe energy: the **BTU (British Thermal Unit)**, a unit of energy that describes the heating capacity of fuels and equipment such as furnaces and air conditioners, and the **kilowatt** (which equals 1,000 watts), which measures the rate at which electricity flows.

Historically, cheap energy meant that those who designed, built, and owned our buildings did not have an economic need to be concerned about efficiencies. The 1973 oil embargo, along with several other events, was a wakeup call and initi-ated a movement toward more careful attention to the materials consumed in the generation of power (**energy sources**); the percentage of total energy consumed in useful work (and not wasted) relative to the amount of energy supplied (energy efficiency); and the amount of energy consumed by a product, process, or system (**energy consumption**). Concerns over energy sources, efficiencies, and consump-tion are central to green principles. A more in-depth discussion of energy can be found in Chapter 10 and Appendix B at the end of this book.

In recent years the construction industry has greatly improved building and equipment energy efficiencies. Heating and air conditioning systems typically use significantly less energy than in the recent past. Improved insulation, more efficient pipes and valves, and increased understanding of the role of operations and maintenance all contribute toward this positive trend. The challenge is that *overall* energy use in the building sector continues to grow. There are several reasons for this, including that there are more of *us,* people who need places to live and work and play. In order to accommodate all of this, we add around 5 billion square feet of new space every year in the United States alone.[6] It's not just that we're adding structures, however. Our expectations for personal space have changed. The average single family house built today, for example, is more than 60% bigger than it was in 1975.[7] Larger buildings require more energy to build and to operate.

The vast majority of our energy comes from the fossil fuels—oil, natural gas, and coal. (We get a relatively small amount from nuclear and renewable energy sources.) We have discovered that using fossil-based fuels, in our buildings and elsewhere, has multiple negative impacts, among them:

- **National security:** despite a dramatic increase in recent U.S. energy production, our continued dependence on foreign oil makes us vulnerable and reduces national security.

- **Risks to our energy infrastructure:** the pipes, trucks, and rail lines that transport oil and natural gas, the electricity transmission lines, even the facilities that turn raw ingredients into useful forms of power—the energy infrastructure—is vulnerable to terrorist attacks both here and abroad. For example, two-thirds of Saudi oil (which supplies a significant amount of U.S. imports[8]) flows through just one processing plant and two terminals; an attack on any of these could seriously disrupt

Damian Gillie

Alaskan oil pipeline

supplies and increase the cost to U.S. consumers. And it's not just the overseas processing and delivery systems that are at risk. A Pentagon study found that it would be feasible for a small group of terrorists to cause major disruption of gas and oil supplies right here at home, too.[9] When considering the vulnerabilities to our energy infrastructure, it's important to note potential impacts caused by severe events such as fires, snow, and wind, all of which can damage power lines and other infrastructure components.

- **Accidents resulting from drilling and transporting domestic fuels:** accidents associated with the exploration for and transportation of fuel cost people jobs, money and, sometimes, their lives. The 2010 explosion on the Deepwater Horizon oil-drilling rig off the Louisiana coast that killed 11 workers is one extreme example. Accidents happen on land, too; natural gas pipeline explosions and derailments of trains carrying oil are growing concerns. Trains hauling North Dakota oil have been involved in major accidents in Virginia, North Dakota, Oklahoma, West Virginia, and Alabama, and in 2013, 47 people were killed when a train hauling crude oil exploded in Lac-Megantic, Quebec.

- **Emissions:** air pollution, acid rain, and the carbon that causes climate change are by-products of burning coal, which is a major source of the electricity used in our buildings and elsewhere. Coal-powered plants emit toxic particles such as mercury, arsenic, and other heavy metals. Among other impacts, pollution is bad for our health and causes about $120 billion per year in health-related costs both to workers and the general public.[10]

Although we're supplying increasing amounts of our energy needs through natural gas, this, too, has its problems such as groundwater contamination, greenhouse gas emissions, and the quantity of water used in the process of harvesting natural gas. Many natural gas wells are located in drought-prone areas and the process of hydraulically **fracking** a well—injecting water and sand at high pressure to release the gas and oil—can use millions of gallons of precious water. When gas wells are located in areas with serious droughts, they can greatly worsen conditions. Texas is an example; some counties with intensive fracking operations have declared water emergencies.[11]

Water

There are few things we take for granted as much as our ability to turn on the tap and get water. Even during droughts, and in spite of advertisements about shortages and conservation, most of us treat this resource as "free" and endlessly available. In fact, our water supply, like oil, is finite and precious and becoming more expensive to get.[12] The extraction, processing, and delivery of water typically involves an enormous infrastructure: pumping stations, treatment facilities, and distribution lines. This system is costly, inefficient, and, not insignificantly, uses a lot of energy.

Paying for our water

For several reasons everyone is paying more for their water. Some price increases are due to rising infrastructure expenses such as replacing dilapidated pipes. But utilities are also shifting their rate structures by altering how much they charge for access to municipal systems and how they charge consumers for water. In many places water utilities, unlike other businesses, are urging their customer to use less, not more, of their product and are charging more per gallon as use increases. To stabilize revenues, some utilities are also putting more of their rate increases into fixed monthly charges, fees paid regardless of how much water is used. Austin, Fort Worth, and Tucson are three examples. This increase in fixed fees means that even those who use water sparingly are paying more.[13]

Green construction emphasizes efficient use of all resources and, as we do with energy, we waste a lot of our water. If equipment and systems, such as plumbing fixtures and HVAC assemblies, aren't diligently maintained, inefficiencies such as leaks can persist and unnecessarily waste water. The EPA estimates that leaks from worn toilet flappers, dripping faucets, and valves can account for thousands of gallons of wasted water every year for the average home.[14] In commercial buildings, systems that are designed according to conventional standards can result in oversized equipment that uses more water than necessary. This can be a consequential problem not only because oversized systems have higher initial and maintenance costs, but also because the increased use of water can then require a bigger waste treatment infrastructure.[15]

There is a relationship between energy and water, and a growing recognition that saving water saves energy. This link is showing up in municipal systems around the country; when they institute water-saving policies, municipal energy costs go down.[16]

Toilets and water use

Because our plumbing systems don't separate water delivery according to usage, the quality of water delivered to our bathrooms, boilers, and garden hoses is all the same. Every single day, we flush more than a billion gallons of expensively treated, potable freshwater down the toilets in our homes alone![17]

In the United States and around the globe, there are increasing water crises due to a combination of factors such as demand, contamination, and droughts.[18] We have multiple examples here at home: in Arizona, so much water has been extracted from groundwater sources that sections of land have subsided; in 2014, California declared a state of emergency due to severe drought and several rural communities are in danger of running out of water; and Florida, Georgia, and Alabama have been engaged in an ongoing conflict about allocation of water in two major river basins that cross their borders.[19] Predictions are that conflicts over water are going to grow both here and abroad.

U.S.G.S. / Devin Galloway

Land subsidence due to groundwater pumping

Reduced human health

We spend most of our time indoors and it makes sense that we want the places where we live, work, and shop not only to look beautiful and function well, but also to be healthy. Unfortunately, the air quality inside our buildings often does not meet this expectation. Astonishingly, the U.S. Environmental Protection

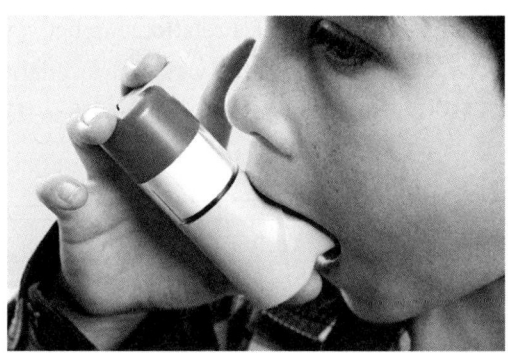

aphrodite74

Agency has determined that indoor air pollution may sometimes be higher than outdoor pollution.[20] This is due to multiple factors, one of which can be the materials used during construction or incorporated into the building.

All materials emit gases; the concern is with the types of emissions that can result in poor air quality. Materials used in buildings may include chemical ingredients that are not safe for people to breath. They can be found in everything from adhesives and sealants to carpeting, roofing, pipes, thermostats, and paint. There is a troubling list of potential ill effects for both builders and end users coming in contact with some of these products and the gases they emit.[21]

To gain an appreciation of the importance of good indoor air quality, let's look at a few problem substances and at why their use can be dangerous for builders as well as for end users:

- **Volatile organic compounds (VOCs)**—elements used in the manufacture of paints, solvents and adhesives, petroleum products, refrigerants, flooring, and more. The chemicals in this group are volatile because they don't want to stay in a solid state and can vaporize—called "off-gassing"—sometimes over several months and enter the air where they are inhaled and may cause a variety of short- and long-term health problems. Off-gassing can occur when a product is applied, when it is drying, and, in some cases, when it is stored.

- **Vinyl chloride**—a chemical component used primarily to make polyvinyl chloride (PVC) pipes, vinyl siding, vinyl flooring, and other products. Short-term exposure to high levels of vinyl chloride in the air has resulted in central nervous system problems such as dizziness, drowsiness, and headaches in humans, and long-term exposure (through inhalation, for example) can result in liver damage and sometimes a rare form of liver cancer. The Environmental Protection Agency has classified vinyl chloride as a Class A human carcinogen.[22]

- **Polyurethane**—a manufactured material that comes in different forms and is found in rigid foam, coatings and paints, adhesives, sealants and elastomers (such as wood sealers and caulks), window treatments, resin flooring, gaskets, and other thermoplastics. Its main ingredients can cause allergic reactions; irritation of the eyes, nose, throat, lungs, and skin; and respiratory and other health problems.

- **Heavy metals**—metallic elements that are toxic, including lead, mercury, and chromium. The inhalation of the vapors from heavy metals, even in low concentrations, can cause damage; prolonged exposure can cause harm to every organ in the body.[23]

In addition to the problems caused by emissions, buildings that don't adequately deal with moisture and humidity can end up with mold. HVAC ducts that leak and ventilation systems that inadequately control moisture are two of the causes of mold.

It's not just building occupants who can become sick; builders are also at risk. Many of the materials used in buildings, such as sealants, adhesives, and paint, are applied wet and emit contaminants as they dry in place.[24] Other examples include plywood, particleboard, and carpet, which are typically made with potentially harmful adhesives and/or use adhesives during installation that can be harmful to workers handling them. Sanding and cutting have the potential to release contaminants into the air and that may be hazardous to builders.

Making buildings healthier and keeping people safe requires the specification of **nontoxic materials and products** (those that are not harmful to people and animals) and installing appropriate ventilation systems during construction and beyond. We'll look at materials and products in more detail in Chapter 5.

Construction and demolition waste

Construction and demolition (C&D) waste is the discarded material from the renovation of existing buildings, the demolition of old buildings, and the construction of new buildings. It can be nasty stuff, including asbestos, asphalt, brick, concrete, masonry, shingles, glass, plastics, aluminum, drywall, insulation, wiring, plumbing and electrical fixtures, vinyl, and more. Typically waste is hauled to separation and transfer facilities or to permitted landfills. Some construction and demolition (C&D) facilities separate materials on site for further processing and recycling; others simply add the materials to the heaping piles of waste in the landfill.

According to the National Institute of Building Science, most C&D waste currently generated in the United States is lawfully destined for disposal in regulated landfills, at great cost. Many landfills are reaching capacity, however, which means the construction of new facilities for either recycling or disposal. Siting these facilities can be very expensive and contentious within communities, and between waste-exporting and waste-importing states. In addition, in some areas, all or part of C&D waste is unlawfully deposited on land, or in natural drainages including water, potentially causing contamination and other problems.

As early as the 1980s, solid waste management issues began to pose potential crises in many areas of the country because of increasing solid waste generation, shrinking landfill capacity, rising disposal costs, and strong opposition to new solid waste facility siting. This problem was illustrated by the much-publicized Mobro garbage barge, which traveled, in 1987, on a six-month odyssey of over 6,000 miles, including six states and four countries, before the cargo was finally disposed in New York, where it was originally generated.[25]

Development patterns

Although how and where we develop our communities may not seem directly relevant to contractors, their design and construction impact many of the issues we've just reviewed: energy, water, infrastructure, and the environment.

One of the defining characteristics in post World War II America has been the construction of millions of square feet of residential and commercial buildings in areas well beyond transit and other services. There were multiple reasons for this, including a "baby boom" after the war, cheap energy, government involvement in housing and development, and a change in demographics and American culture. While many Americans still like the idea of suburbs, their expansion, and the associated explosion of automobile use, depends on the consumption of oil and electricity, which, as we've seen, has multiple negative environmental, health, and other impacts.

The reader may be familiar with examples of developments such as the Colorado subdivision project shown here that appear to be unconcerned with geography, hydrology, natural solar or wind patterns, or existing ecosystems. Locating buildings in areas that require occupants to drive long distances, that involve the destruction of natural habitat, or are in a flood zone or another sensitive environment are characteristics that we now know can have negative impacts on human health and well-being.

David Shankbone

Suburban development in Colorado Springs CO

The natural features of the site shown have been obliterated and biodiversity has been greatly disrupted. The expanse of impermeable, hard surface areas poses a challenge for managing the excess runoff caused by storms (stormwater), and makes it almost impossible for rain to seep into the ground to recharge groundwater. Limiting the ability of soils to naturally filter runoff contributes to water pollution, increases erosion and flooding, and impacts water quality.[26]

Summary

Construction in the United States is dynamic and creative and is a global leader in the development of new construction technologies, materials, and systems. Our built environment is a marvel of engineering, design, and construction; the millions of miles of infrastructure and billions of square feet of structures in the United States is awe-inspiring. But the ways we plan, design, and build come at a heavy cost. The conventional ways of building use unsustainable amounts of fossil-fuel-based energy, too often leave water sources depleted or contaminated, harm the environment, and cause health problems for builders and users. The construction industry now understands that, among other concerns, there is a financial cost to be paid for these problems. But, as we'll see, the problems outlined in this chapter, and their solution, represent an extraordinary *opportunity* for those in the industry. In the next chapter, we'll why this is so and discuss some of the ways the industry and the public is responding.

Glossary

BTU (British thermal unit)—a unit of energy equivalent to the heat produced by a single kitchen match and measured in watts

Built environment—human-made buildings and parks, transportation systems, energy and water infrastructure, and all the constructed physical components that form our surroundings.

Construction and demolition (C&D) waste—the materials that are discarded from the renovation of existing buildings, the demolition of old buildings, and the construction of new buildings and infrastructure.

Electrical energy—the energy made available by the flow of a charged particle through a conductor.

Energy—the ability to do work. Different forms of energy (for example, heat or light) can be converted to other forms, but the total amount remains the same.

Energy consumption—the amount of energy used by a product, process, or system.

Energy efficiency—the percentage of total energy consumed in useful work (and not wasted) relative to the amount of energy supplied.

Energy infrastructure—facilities required to turn raw ingredients into useful forms of power and deliver it to users, including the pipes, trucks, and rail lines that transport oil and natural gas, and the transmission lines that move electricity.

Fossil fuels—non-renewable forms of energy that were formed hundreds of millions of years ago and including coal, oil, and natural gas; carbon is their basic element.

Fracking—the process of injecting water and sand at high pressure into shale rock in order to release gas and oil.

Green construction—a process for creating and operating buildings and communities that strives to reduce their environmental impact and maximize social and economic value.

Heavy metals—metallic elements such as lead, mercury, and chromium, among others.

Kilowatt—a measurement of the rate at which electricity flows (equal to 1,000 watts).

Motion energy—the energy something possesses due to its movement.

Nontoxic materials and products—those that are not harmful to people and animals.

Polyurethane—a manufactured material that comes in different forms and is resilient, flexible, and durable. Polyurethane is found in rigid foam, coatings and paints, adhesives, sealants and elastomers (such as wood sealers and caulks), window treatments, resin flooring, gaskets, and other thermoplastics.

Radiant energy—the energy that is transmitted by waves, especially electromagnetic waves. Light is a form of radiant energy.

Renewable energy—fuels that are not diminished when they are used, such as solar, wind, geothermal, and others.

Stormwater—an abnormal quantity of surface water arising from rain or snow.

Thermal energy—energy in the form of heat.

Vinyl chloride—a chemical component used primarily to make polyvinyl chloride (PVC) pipes, vinyl siding, vinyl flooring, and other products.

Volatile organic compounds (VOCs)—elements that contain carbon and can vaporize at normal temperatures and enter the air. VOCs lead to the formation of air pollution.

Paul Keheler

The Green Alternative

As discussed in Chapter 1, even **conventional buildings,** ones that meet but do not exceed basic code requirements (this is the majority of U.S. building stock[1]), are in many ways astonishing, but they are also problematic. There is increased understanding among the general public, government agencies, businesses, and others that what and how we build may not be good for people or the environment and that those failings create a growing financial cost. This understanding is translating into new practices in virtually every aspect of the industry: the way that projects are conceived, designed, and built; the practices used and skills required to construct buildings; and even (after construction is "completed") their operation, maintenance, and eventual deconstruction. Although these new practices present challenges to the industry, they are also opportunities for workers.

The practice of creating buildings and neighborhoods that reduce or (ide-ally) eliminate the use of fossil-fuel-based energy, that carefully use our finite supply of freshwater, that are made from nontoxic materials, and that conserve the natural environment is called **green construction**. The physical outcomes of using these approaches are referred to, often interchangeably, as **green**, **high-performance**, or **sustainable buildings**.

Green construction, which up until recently was looked on with amuse-ment as a mere fad, is on its way to becoming the new standard. In 2000, there were approximately 30 million square feet of green buildings. By 2010, this number had grown to more than a billion square feet, and today it is three times *that* number. All the foundations, framing, drywall, roofing, and the

Larry Lee

equipment needed to construct them and keep them operating, translate into work for architects, engineers, and builders. Millions of people work directly or indirectly in green construction[2] and, if projections are correct, their number will rise. Industry employers certainly think so: McGraw-Hill Construction reports that a majority of architectural, engineering, and construction firms expect that their work in green construction will grow.

Contractors on international projects benefit, too, as green construction has become a global phenomenon. From Germany and the United Kingdom to Singapore, Brazil, South Africa, and the United Arab Emirates, there are growing applications of green construction techniques. The volume of new projects and the economic rationale has convinced many that the green trend in construction is "extremely unlikely to reverse itself."[3] As a result, it is increasingly hard for those in the industry to ignore the numbers; unless they want to sit on the sidelines, contractors need to adapt to this new reality.

Defining green construction

What exactly *is* green construction? How do green buildings differ from "conventional" buildings? What are the criteria used to determine whether a building is truly "green," and how can practitioners sift through the hyperbole to choose genuinely green products and materials?

In the United States, we have been exploring the use of green techniques for over 30 years. As new language emerges—such as "high-performance," "green buildings," "zero net energy use," and "renewable energy systems"—we need to develop common definitions for the terms.

The early definitions of what makes a building "green" were narrow and focused on individual components or systems. A house that used an "alternative" heating system (such as solar) was considered green. Switching to longer-life light bulbs was called green. An office building that specified very efficient windows might identify itself as a green building. Improved insulation, low-flush toilets, use of recycled materials, and more meant green.

Though it's true that these measures are all on the right track—indeed, they *are* green—it is now considered insufficient for a building to be labeled "green" based on isolated components. For example, can a very large and material-intensive single-family residence be considered "green" even if it has solar flat plate collectors on the roof? Is a building that has a very efficient mechanical system but poor insulation green? Does a solar-heated building that has destroyed existing biodiversity during its construction qualify? Green principles now require that all parties—owners, designers, and contractors—broaden their thinking to incorporate a more complex, integrated way of approaching design and construction.

> Green implies more than a single, efficient building component.

The new way of defining green is to think in terms of the interconnectedness of systems—**whole building design.** This broader approach assumes that individual systems can be leveraged for greater performance. For example:

> *...the choice of a mechanical system might impact the quality of the air in the building, the ease of maintenance, global climate change, operating costs, fuel choice, and whether the windows of a building are operable. In turn, the size of the mechanical system will depend on factors such as, the type of lighting and controls used, how much natural daylight is brought in, how the space is organized, the facility's operating hours, and the local microclimate. At the same time, these same materials and systems choices may have an impact on the aesthetics, accessibility, and security of the project. A successful Whole Building Design is a solution that is greater than the sum of its parts.[4]*

Conventional buildings

In this book, the author contrasts green buildings with "conventional buildings," but what does that mean? A helpful summation is that conventional buildings, which make up the vast proportion of our buildings, are designed and built to meet but typically not to exceed current minimum code requirements. For example, if code requires that an exterior wall have an R-19 thermal resistance value then, on a conventional building, the contractor's concern might end once R-19 insulation is installed in the framing. (The **R-value** is a measure of resistance to heat flow: the higher the R value the greater the insulating value.) Water consumption in plumbing fixtures is another example. Toilets have become more efficient and federal plumbing standards specify that new toilets can use no more than 1.6 gallons of water per flushing cycle. Conventional buildings typically are built to this standard.

Green buildings (whether officially certified as such or not) are different. Their systems are designed and built to *exceed* minimum code requirements, sometimes by significant amounts. So, in the previous examples, Instead of using R-19 insulation per the local building code, a green building might use an insulating material much higher than R-19 and also take other measures, such as an upgraded **building envelope**, to further increase insulation values. R-values on a green building might be R-30 or R-49, or R-60, for example. And, instead of installing toilets that use 1.6 gallons per flush, the designer might specify dual flush or pressure-assist toilets that use 1 gallon or less, or composting toilets that use no water at all.

Today's green buildings require that all the members of the owner, design, and construction team look at the project objectives and building materials, systems, and assemblies from many different perspectives in order to maximize performance.

Whole building design, and the design and construction of buildings that meet today's broader definition of green, depends on a highly cooperative working relationship among the players: the designers, engineers, builders, and owners. Beyond the normal working relationships that create good projects, green projects require a deeper commitment to meeting performance goals and a willingness to work together to meet them. This cooperation extends from the design phase through construction. (The next chapter, on changes in the construction industry, covers this aspect of green construction in more detail.)

There is no one absolute way to design a green building; they come in all sizes and shapes; they have different uses and occupant loads; some are steel frame, others are made of straw bales; buildings in a cold climate such as Minnesota will have different heating requirements from an otherwise similar building in San Diego; an office building in New Jersey will have different design parameters from a building in Phoenix. Despite this, green construction operates within a set of common principles and objectives in six broad categories:

1. **Location and Environment**
   - Conserve and protect natural environments.

2. **Orientation**
   - Situate a structure on a site to take advantage of natural features such as sun, wind, views, and shade.

3. **Energy**
   - Minimize or eliminate the use of fossil fuels.

4. **Water**
   - Conserve water both inside and outside a structure.
   - Use natural systems to manage stormwater.

5. **Human health**
   - Create nontoxic and comfortable indoor environments.

6. **Durability, operations, and maintenance**
   - Use durable and recyclable materials and products.

Let's look at each of these in more detail to see how they contribute to a green building alternative.

Location and environment

Green projects conserve and protect natural environments.

One of the first major decisions for any owner is the project location: where will the project be built? A site is a piece of land on which something has been or will be located. Every building or neighborhood, whether a single-family house or an office building in a complex, has an impact on its site and, conversely, site characteristics affect the operation and efficiency of the community and its structures. There are endless examples of poorly located buildings and communities, such as we saw in Chapter 1.

Modern **zoning ordinances**—regulations that determine how a site can be used—typically isolate functions from each other so that businesses, shopping and services, housing, and so on are separated. This isolated zoning, plus low-density automobile-dependent growth, contributes to traffic-congested, unhealthy, and inefficient urban sprawl. Careful siting of buildings and rethinking how construction affects our communities—both urban and rural—is fundamental to sustainability.

There are many factors that affect a piece of land's suitability for development: existing site characteristics, access and utilities, regulatory requirements such as zoning, building codes, size, and appropriateness. In a conventional project, all of these are weighed primarily against short-term cost. Projects that strive to have green characteristics will require a developer to consider several additional issues, among them:

- Is the site appropriate for development; does it avoid disturbing natural ecosystems, sensitive and pristine areas, or prime agricultural areas?

- Can the location contribute toward resiliency when faced with natural events such as storms, droughts, or social and economic change?

- Will a project on this site provide walkable access to work, schools, and shopping, and is it close to transit services?

- Will the location enhance human health and satisfaction?

The Rio Vista Apartments in Los Angeles is a compact, multi-family housing project developed on a vacant parking lot within walking distance of a park, public transit, basic amenities, and schools. Locating a new development on a previously under-used or abandoned parcel (called **infill development**) is a highly valued green principle, and this certified green project scored high marks because the site is a former **brownfield** (a term used to describe property that contains hazardous substances, pollutants, or contaminants from an earlier use.[5] The Rio Vista site went through an environmental clean-up to enable safe reuse.)

Infill apartment project in Los Angeles

In addition to location, this project benefits from the use of solar power for space and water heating, the use of municipal recycled water for irrigation, and the inclusion of an edible-plant garden that sits atop the roof.

The issues surrounding location and environment extend beyond a single project to the development (and redevelopment) of entire neighborhoods and districts. In Chapter 1, we saw an example of a suburban development that is representative of modern suburban sprawl. These developments are often located without concern for existing ecosystems, mass transit, and accessibility to services, work, or schools, and ignore natural systems such as solar, wind, and natural features. Developers, designers, and builders are moving beyond the individual green buildings to create entire communities or districts that address regional water, energy, transit, and public health and economic goals.

Sonoma Mountain Village is an example of such a community. Located on a 200-acre business campus formerly occupied by the Hewlett-Packard Company in Rohnert Park CA, the site was closed and locked and 3,000 jobs were lost when H-P's successor company, Agilent Technologies, vacated the site. The Sonoma Mountain Village project is reclaiming not only the site, but the jobs as well. When completed, the community will include over 4,000 residents, businesses, schools, and recreation and hotel facilities.

Orientation

A green building is situated on its site to take advantage of natural features such as sun, wind, views, and shade.

Energy performance starts with how a building is oriented on its site—particularly how it is sited relative to the path of the sun, or natural breezes. Ideally, a structure is oriented on its site to take advantage of energy from the sun and wind, and to minimize heating and cooling needs. Two otherwise identical buildings facing different directions will perform very differently and the amounts of energy each requires to maintain interior comfort can also be very different. Proper orientation and design should enable winter sun to flow into the interior, adding natural light and warmth, and keep out unwanted summer sun through shading or vegetation.

The Lorry I. Lokey Graduate School of Business at Mills College, in Oakland CA, is an example of a building that is well situated on its site. Oriented to take advantage of both sun and wind direction, its design uses these resources to advantage. The main lobby, for example, captures breezes that naturally flow through the building to provide cooling and ventilation. In a conventional building, ventilation is provided by fans, dampers, and controls that move air

Nic Lehoux/Bohlin Cywinski Jackson

Manually operated windows and sensor controlled clerestories cool the lobby of the Lokey Graduate School

into and out of the building. At the Lokey School, manually operated windows and sensor-controlled high windows (called a clerestory) offer natural ventilation.

A small, single-family house in Belfast ME (see photo), is another example of effective orientation. This house, located in a cold northern climate, can satisfy 100% of its energy needs by taking advantage of solar thermal power through windows that face south and solar panels on the south-facing roof that convert light energy into electricity.

A highly efficient single family residence with windows concentrated on the south side and solar panels on the roof

Careful orientation on a site also strives to take advantage of other conditions such as views and natural features including topography and landscaping, all of which can contribute to the comfort and pleasure of users. Orientation can even benefit the health and vitality of the surrounding community, by orienting courtyards or other social spaces to connect to street life, for example.

Fallingwater (see photo) is an example of a single-family residence from the 1930s that is oriented around an existing creek and waterfall.

Exterior view of Frank Lloyd Wright's Fallingwater in Mill Run PA

We don't typically think of this Frank Lloyd Wright masterpiece as an example of green building principles, but the brilliant way in which the design responds to and respects its immediate environment is. Light, views, and the sound of water surround the house and, from the living room, there are not just views of the creek but direct access.

Energy

A green building minimizes or eliminates the use of fossil fuels.

Reducing the amount of fossil-fuel energy we use has multiple positive impacts. One is that it's good for the economy. As we saw in the previous chapter, the extraction of raw materials, the manufacture of products, and the construction, operation, and demolition of our buildings takes massive quantities of energy. Because it costs less to operate more durable, high-performance buildings, green construction is now primarily driven, not as it was until recently by the notion of "doing the right thing," but by market demand.[6] This shows up in the numbers: green approaches have saved building owners billions of dollars, money that businesses didn't have to spend to heat and light their buildings.[7]

> ### *A high-performance building*
>
> The word "performance" refers to the process of operating or carrying out a function or action. In construction the term "high-performance" is often used to mean superior energy efficiency. It is also used to refer to entire building characteristics: energy, water, durability, etc. The Energy Policy Act of 2005 defines a high-performance building as one that optimizes energy efficiency, is durable, meets high-performance standards throughout its life (from the extraction of materials through decommission), and contributes toward occupant productivity.[8] Many sources, including this book, use the terms "green," "sustainable," and "high-performance" interchangeably.

Immediate cost savings in **delivered energy**—the amount of energy consumed at the end point (a home, office, or school, etc.)—is only one of the benefits gained by reducing our dependence on fossil fuels. Improved air quality, increased national security, and environmental health are all impacted by our energy-intensive buildings.

How does green construction approach the problem of fossil-fuel-based energy use? There is no single solution but rather a collection of design principles that may be incorporated to reach, at minimum, a dramatic reduction of fossil-fuel energy use, and ideally, its elimination. These approaches include:

- As already indicated, orienting a building on its site to take maximum advantage of the sun to provide warmth and natural breezes to cool the structure with no (or minimal) additional energy consumption

- Improving insulation to minimize heat loss through the building envelope (the foundation, the roof, and the walls)

- Using very efficient, durable equipment, appliances, pumps, lighting, and other products

- Right-sizing HVAC and plumbing systems to reflect actual anticipated use patterns so that equipment sizes can be reduced (thus using less power and water)

- Designing ways to draw natural lighting into the interior of the building in order to reduce artificial lighting requirements

- Installing occupancy sensors for HVAC, lighting and other systems, and controls for building shading and ventilation

- **Commissioning**, prior to (and, ideally, after) completion of construction to verify that all assemblies are working optimally and as intended

- During occupancy, effective and ongoing operation and maintenance of systems and assemblies to ensure ongoing efficiencies

The many benefits derived from reducing fossil-fuel-based energy have convinced many jurisdictions to issue strict energy codes. Municipalities and other jurisdictions around the country, and all but seven states, have done so. As a result of these requirements and the increased use of green building rating systems such as **LEED** (a suite of building rating systems developed by the U.S. Green Building Council, see Chapter 4) with even stricter standards, there are many thousands of examples of such buildings. Energy-efficient buildings can be found in every state and every climate zone; they come in all sizes, and all occupancies, are represented in both new and renovated construction, and are owned by private parties and public entities.

The single-family house in Emlyn KY, shown here, represents an effort to meet a more challenging energy performance goal than is currently required by any codes. This rather conventional-looking house is anything but: the designers and builders utilized multiple strategies (including a rooftop solar array) to create a home that is extraordinarily efficient and generates as much power on-site as it requires annually.

Michael Hughes/CSC Design Studio

A neighborhood of high-performance 1200 SF residences in Emlyn KY

Many believe that improving efficiencies and reducing the use of fossil-fuel-based energy is insufficient and that a higher standard should be used: to completely eliminate the use of fossil-fuel-based energy sources. The Kentucky home represents this high standard. A **zero net energy** (ZNE) building produces, on average, as much energy as it uses and achieves this through a combination of reduced energy loads and renewable energy sources. ZNE buildings use batteries to store power, or are connected to an existing energy grid, and provide power to the grid when excess is generated and draw from it when necessary. There are multiple private and public efforts around the country (and globe) to encourage the more challenging ZNE standard. In the United States, California and Massachusetts are state leaders in this effort. California, for example, has an Energy Efficiency Strategic Plan, with the goal that all new residential construction in the state be ZNE by 2020, and that all new commercial construction be ZNE by 2030.[9]

Another, quite different, example of a zero net energy building is the David and Lucile Packard Foundation in Los Altos CA.

This 50,000 square foot building is, of course, much bigger than the Kentucky home, but it uses a similar approach to meet a ZNE goal: the reduction

The David & Lucile Packard Foundation ZNE headquarters in Los Altos CA

Jeremy Bittermann/Packard Foundation

of energy loads (such as heating, cooling, and lighting requirements) through careful design, including an emphasis on natural lighting, triple-glazed windows, automatically operated exterior shades, and extensive energy monitoring,

Net energy isn't the whole story

The term "zero net energy" is something of a misnomer, as it does not take into account all the energy required to build and operate a building. The extraction and processing of materials and the manufacture of them into products that then get transported to a building site and installed take enormous amounts of energy and other resources. Steel, concrete, and drywall are particular examples; the production of cement alone consumes 1% of the total energy used in the United States.[10] All this energy—what it takes to get a product into a building *before* it's used—is called a product's **embodied energy**. This means that everything we use—the chairs we sit on, the roofs that shelter us, the pens we write with, the clothes we wear—has energy within it. Reducing a structure's total embodied energy in addition to the delivered energy required to operate, maintain, and decommission it is a goal of green construction and green product selection. (As noted elsewhere, buildings that claim to be zero net energy mean that they don't consume more delivered energy than they generate on-site; the embodied energy is not, however, factored in.) The durability of a product is an important consideration. For example, sometimes a material with very high embodied energy (such as aluminum) may be a more appropriate choice than one with a lower embodied energy (such as timber or steel). This would be true if the durability of the product or material means that its embodied energy can be amortized over a long useful life.

sensor, and control equipment.[11] A one-year post-occupancy commission phase showed that the building was performing 40% better than anticipated.[12]

Skeptics might ask, "Isn't the cost premium for building zero net energy buildings prohibitive?" In a recent study, dozens of high-performance construction projects in New York state and similar climates were analyzed to answer this question. The study found that the average estimated price using cost data from the RS Means Company, for similar buildings in similar locales, was actually slightly *higher* than construction costs for the ZNE buildings. How was this possible? According to Mike Rovito of Energy & Resource Solutions, "The short answer is load-reducing design...that leads to down-sized mechanical systems and less demand from lighting equipment. This makes the building cheaper to build and operate." In addition, some features, such as orienting the building to minimize thermal changes, had no cost at all, while others, such as shrinking or eliminating a heating system, can pay for super-insulation and very efficient windows that reduce heat loss. Often bigger up-front costs are offset by the savings wrung from installing smaller equipment.[13]

The rebound effect

There's an unfortunate situation that shows up in some buildings, called the "rebound effect." Some newer, more energy-efficient buildings have been shown to use **more** energy than similar buildings. What's going on? It may be as simple as human nature: when efficiencies are higher and energy costs less, there is a tendency to use more. The rebound effect points out that efficiency and **conservation** are different. For example, LED lights have much higher efficiency ratings than do incandescent lights, which means the units produce more light from less power. But even these very efficient lights may not *conserve* energy if they're left on for a longer time. Although studies have shown that the rebound effect is potentially consequential, evidence suggests that the benefits of energy-efficient products still greatly exceed the increased use.[14] The potential for a rebound-effect can be managed: for example, the installation of occupancy sensors that turn off lights when no one is in the space. Maximizing both efficiency and conservation are two important components of green buildings.

Energy use and building retrofits

Energy efficiency isn't only for new construction. There is a vast, untapped market for the renovation of poorly performing existing buildings. Upgrading this stock will be a cost-efficient way to address energy consumption. Among other benefits, adapting existing buildings (as opposed to building new) has been shown to save the energy used to produce a building (embodied energy), reduce immediate and long-term energy costs, avoid environmental impacts over a building's life cycle, and avoid generating waste from building demolition.[15]

Although many of our older buildings were not designed with energy efficiency in mind, until recently, there has been little emphasis on how to improve, adapt, and reuse these buildings to reduce overall energy use. This is changing. The industry knows that energy cost savings of around 20% can often be achieved by tackling the relatively straightforward, least invasive "low-hanging fruit" such as equipment upgrades. Although there are multiple obstacles (primarily financial), it is possible to realize even more substantial savings. (Efforts that result in energy savings of 50% or more, as measured against a pre-renovation baseline, are referred to as **deep-green retrofits**.)[16] In addition to HVAC upgrades, these energy-efficiency measures include: adjustments to the building envelope; lighting and electrical systems upgrades and controls; the replacement of doors, windows, and skylights that are thermally-leaky; strategies for increasing the amount of daylight in a space (to reduce lighting requirements); energy auditing; commissioning services; and more.[17]

Water

Green construction maximizes the conservation of water both inside and outside and uses natural systems to manage exterior water.

As we saw in Chapter 1, fossil fuels aren't the only finite, non-renewable resources. Freshwater is another and it is becoming increasingly difficult and costly to find and deliver. Like energy, water is often wasted. Efficient use of water—both inside and outside a building—and effective management of stormwater are important principles of green construction.

Where does our water come from? As part of the hydrologic cycle, our freshwater originates from precipitation that falls as rain or snow and seeps into aquifers in the ground or flows, as surface water, into lakes and rivers. This water is pumped, treated, and delivered to the user, in most cases, by a municipal water provider. Once delivered, in residential applications, energy is used to filter and soften water and to heat it for use in certain appliances; in commercial, industrial, and institutional situations, energy is used to produce hot water and steam for heating, to cool water for air conditioning, and to generate hot water needed to manufacture or process materials. In addition to the direct expenses for the delivered water (and the energy associated with its use), there are enormous infrastructure expenses incurred by water providers who must hire contractors to build pumping stations and treatment facilities and install distribution lines.

The increased difficulty in getting sufficient freshwater supplies and the resulting increase in water prices is of concern to water managers and building owners. In recent years, there has been a significant tightening of national plumbing codes and other regulatory initiatives. The Energy Policy Act of 2005, for example, established tighter federal standards for plumbing fixtures and many states have mandated improved water efficiency in buildings. Multiple code bodies, such as the Association of Plumbing and Mechanical Officials and the International Code Council have recently revised their codes to reflect more water-conserving approaches. Local jurisdictions around the country have mandated tighter restrictions on landscape irrigation, and other water uses. For many consumers, green building rating systems such as LEED (discussed in detail in Chapter 4) have set benchmarks for even higher levels of water conservation.

Green construction is concerned with water use and management in four broad areas:

- Use reduction

- On-site rainwater collection

- Alternative waste management

- Exterior water use and stormwater management

Let's look briefly at each of these areas:

Water use reduction

There are multiple ways to improve water efficiency and increase conservation in both the interior and exterior space. Alternative plumbing equipment and products such as **dual-flush toilets** (toilets that are based on the standard toilets but have two buttons that allow for different flushing options) or **waterless toilets** (such as composting toilets) that use no water at all, **metered-valve faucets** that use a predetermined amount of water, and electronically controlled fixtures are all commonly available.

Engineers typically design systems according to conventional standards that may not take into account likely use; this can result in oversized, wasteful systems. Sizing HVAC and plumbing systems to reflect actual occupant loads can mean smaller, less costly, systems that conserve both water and energy.[18]

> Systems designed for actual use can save water and energy.

Wastewater that has not been generated by toilets or urinals—called **greywater**—can be diverted through different pipes and used for non-potable purposes such as flushing toilets and landscape irrigation. Greywater recycling can be used in small applications from car washes to single-family homes as well as in much larger buildings.

The link between water and energy

Water and energy are resources that are linked and so are their costs. Water, often in large quantities, is necessary for fuel production (for example, natural gas fracking and hydropower) and, in turn, energy is needed for the pumping, treatment, and distribution of water and the discharge of wastewater. It stands to reason that saving water also saves energy. According to a 2013 report to the U.S. Congress, water-related energy eats up as much as 13% of the nation's total electricity generation.[19] Water-related energy costs (which can absorb a significant amount of a municipality's budget) are reflected in the costs consumers must pay for their water.

On-site rainwater collection

The collection of rainwater (called **rainwater harvesting**) is used to make buildings all or partially self-sufficient for non-potable water needs such as landscape irrigation or toilet flushing. Rain is collected (typically from a roof) and stored in a cistern sized for anticipated use and rainfall. Systems are as simple as storage drums connected to downspouts on a single-family home to complex systems for commercial buildings that use sophisticated storage and filtration systems.

Municipalities are using rainwater harvesting to meet part of their water needs. In Santa Monica CA, for example, this community of 90,000 (with around 12 inches of rain a year) has set a goal of water independence. One approach to meeting this goal is to encourage rain harvesting by the public and to install rainwater collection systems on public buildings. Other efforts include treating excess urban runoff that is then used to water parks, school grounds, and a cemetery. Since 1997, the city has required that certain new construction and remodeled homes install rainwater harvesting systems.[20]

How much water can we collect from rain?

Lots, it turns out. Every time it rains an inch, a 40 × 70 foot roof, for example, gets pelted with more than 1,700 gallons of water. According to the U.S. Geological Survey, one inch of rain falling on one acre of ground is equal to more than 27,000 gallons.[21] Depending on annual rainfall, over the course of a year this could be a substantial quantity. If we look at a whole city, the numbers are dramatic. In Atlanta GA, for example, with an area of 130 square miles, one inch of rain falling over the entire city translates into more than two *billion* gallons of water. If the rainfall in a single year could be collected and stored without evaporation loss, it would supply the needs of about five times as many people as currently live in the entire city.[22] Especially in areas with low rainfall, it makes sense to capture and use rain. As a result of this logic, the design, installation, and maintenance of rainwater harvesting systems is becoming more common.

Alternative wastewater management

Wastewater is any used water (including human waste, also known as **blackwater**) as well as runoff from streets, and contains dissolved or suspended matter. Purifying wastewater so that it can be reused or discharged is a complex process. Typically, municipal wastewater is conveyed in a sewerage system to a facility where it is treated using physical, biological, and chemical processes before being discharged. (In some urban areas, sewage and runoff from streets are conveyed in a single system; in other areas, they're separated.) Rural areas treat wastewater on-site, usually in septic systems.

There are alternative treatment systems including engineered **wetlands** specifically designed to treat wastewater (a wetland is an area that is regularly saturated by surface water or groundwater with vegetation that is adapted to these conditions); floating rafts of plants and systems that use bacteria, protozoa, and other aquatic microorganisms to clean and condition wastewater for reuse. Some systems are appropriate for application in a single building; others are municipal-scale systems.

Exterior water use and stormwater management

A substantial amount of our water is used for irrigating landscapes, such as watering lawns, and, in dry climates such as the Southwest, it typically represents a majority of per capita water use. Inefficiencies are high: some experts estimate that as much as half of the water used in landscape irrigation is lost to evaporation and poor irrigation techniques.[23] Green projects reduce the amount of water used outside by, in part, eliminating water-intensive lawns and plantings and instead using native plants that are acclimated to the local weather conditions. The installation of **drip irrigation** systems that deliver water directly to plant roots instead of overhead sprinklers that result in water losses due to evaporation, are common. Drip systems typically require contractors who install them to understand controllers and pressure-regulating valves, remote-control valves, and electrical connections.

Green construction is also concerned with exterior stormwater management. When it rains, impervious surfaces like roads, roofs, sidewalks, and parking lots can deliver huge amounts of water to streams either directly or through stormwater drains. This water is not clean: as dirty surfaces are flushed by rainwater, oil, chemicals, fertilizers, and other toxic materials are swept along, causing contamination, increased sedimentation, and the degradation of local streams.[24] Because it isn't practical to eliminate hard surfaces, many municipalities are turning to green infrastructure as a way to mitigate this problem. **Green Infrastructure** uses vegetation, soils, and systems that mimic natural processes to slow down and manage excess runoff, and then infiltrate it into the ground, evaporate it into the air, or discharge it slowly.[25] In addition to managing contaminated runoff and reducing the impacts of storms, green infrastructure systems increase wildlife habitats, beautify neighborhoods, improve water quality, recharge groundwater, and reduce sewer overflows.

Green infrastructure projects vary depending on needs and can take many forms. Many urban areas are using techniques such as permeable paving that will allow rainwater to soak into the ground instead of funneling it to distant, expensive, and high-maintenance treatment facilities, **bioswales** (vegetation-filled depressions), planters, and other landscaping techniques to manage runoff on-site.

An example of a municipality that has made a commitment to using green infrastructure to manage water is Portland OR. Over one-third of the city's 2,500 miles of sewer pipes are more than 80 years old. The City manages runoff by directing it into planted areas where it slows down and seeps into the ground. These infrastructure approaches help the aging system operate more efficiently by keeping excess stormwater out of sewers.[26]

Kevin Robert Perry/City of Portland Bureau of Environmental Services

Sustainable stormwater management project in Portland OR

Another water management tool (particularly in wet climates) is the use of "living" or green roofs. A **green roof** is one that is partially or completely covered with vegetation. Typically, shallow-rooted, low-maintenance native plants are planted in a growing medium over a waterproof membrane on a flat or low-sloped roof. There are multiple reasons for installing such a roof, including tax incentives, reduced building energy loads, and a reduction in stormwater runoff. Using the same principle as we see in Portland, rain that falls on a green roof reduces runoff and the load on conventional stormwater management infrastructure.

Green roofs require considerations beyond the inclusion of plant material, and contractors who install and maintain them need to be aware of the implications for increased roof loads, techniques for eliminating the potential for moisture infiltration, considerations regarding wind and exposure, fire restrictions, and safety and code regulations.

Human health

A green building is nontoxic and comfortable for its users.

Dust, chemical fumes, off-gassing materials, and moisture can all cause health problems both during construction and following occupancy. Conventional buildings, with an emphasis on controlled environments without **natural ventilation**, can result in a potentially toxic interior environment.

Green projects avoid using materials that are toxic: solvent-based finishes, adhesives, carpeting, particleboard, and many other building products release formaldehyde and volatile organic compounds (VOCs) into the air (called off-gassing). These chemicals can affect the health of both construction workers and building occupants and can contribute to smog and ground-level ozone pollution outside. Green designers and builders carefully choose materials and products free from harmful chemicals, and install effective ventilation systems.

An example of a building that uses green principles to create a comfortable and healthy environment is the Bechtel Environmental Classroom at Smith College in Massachusetts, shown here.

Ethan Drinker Photo courtesy
Coldham & Hartmar Architects

A comfortable, healthy interior space at Smith College

This 2,500 square-foot facility includes materials chosen for their low toxicity and ease of maintenance. Operable windows allow natural ventilation and are a useful part of maintaining healthy indoor spaces. The introduction of toxic materials such as cleaning products have been reduced or eliminated. (See Chapter 5 for more on nontoxic products and materials.)

Durability, operations, and maintenance

Materials and products in a green building should be durable, made from recycled materials, and be recyclable or compostable at the end of their lives.

Green buildings take into account the useful life of the structure as well as the durability of materials and products. **Durability** measures the anticipated useful life of a system or product before it must be removed and replaced, and requires careful installation and maintenance. As with many aspects of buildings, system durability is often linked to other products or installations. For example, even a very durable exterior cladding might not be as long lasting as anticipated if windows or other openings are improperly weatherproofed.

One of the key characteristics of a sustainable building is that it operates as a total "organism." Components are designed to work together, and failure in one part of the structure can negatively impact the performance of the entire structure. A common example is the failure to properly maintain systems following occupancy. A building may have high-performance characteristics—proper orientation, built to minimize heat loss, the use of highly efficient equipment and systems—and yet, if users make unauthorized changes, or if a leak is unnoticed or a pump is malfunctioning, performance characteristics may be significantly reduced.

> **Watch out for tight buildings**
>
> As high-performance buildings are well insulated and tight, they are prone to moisture being trapped in walls. This can cause damaging and unhealthy mold and fungus. Moisture can also reduce durability. Very well insulated and tight buildings require special attention by both designers and builders to ensure proper ventilation.

As noted, durability is linked to efficient operation and maintenance programs. Green buildings are designed and built with an appreciation that highly efficient systems can lose much of their advantages if not properly used and maintained. **Commissioning**—the process of verifying that a product or system is working properly—has been shown to be a key element in reaching and *maintaining* performance standards.

Sustainable vs. green construction

The terms "sustainable" and "green" are often used interchangeably, including in this book, but there is a difference the reader should understand. In Chapter 1 and in this chapter, green construction is defined as a process for creating and operating buildings and communities that strives to reduce their environmental impact and maximize social and economic value. The assumption here is that the term "green" is more than a feel-good buzzword. This is not always the case and the word is often used to describe something (typically a product) that *may* be green but not sustainable. While there is no one accepted definition, **sustainability** generally refers to the ability of something to contribute toward long-term environmental and social endurance. Its meaning is nicely summarized by perhaps the most quoted definition of sustainability: the ability to meet the needs of the present without compromising the ability of future generations to meet their own needs.[27] In other words, don't mess things up for those coming behind you. Implicit in the definition are long-term biological, environmental, social, and economic impacts. A system (whether it's a building or a community or a wetland) isn't sustainable if it doesn't support and maintain the ecosystems (human and other) that are dependent upon it and upon which it depends. In general, sustainability incorporates a "future factor."

How does the concept of future sustainability relate to green and to construction? Take the beautiful wood floor you've just installed. Wood is a renewable product, and is therefore "green." But because sustainability is concerned with a deeper set of issues beyond renewability, the particular wood chosen may not be a sustainable choice. There are several characteristics that would make the wood unsustainable, such as it was harvested from a clear-cut forest or it had to be transported long distances to get to you, thereby using large amounts of fossil fuels, or it was treated with a product that is hazardous to human health. These are not sustainable characteristics.

The term "green" typically implies manufacturing, planning, designing, and constructing just as we always have, just doing it more efficiently. There are many respected members of the construction community who are dismissive of "green" because of concerns that it implies incrementalism in the move toward sustainability. The author understands (and respects) this concern. The

Andrea Young

reality in the field, however, is that the majority of us are in the early stages of a revolutionary shift in our thinking about the built environment. As the public, and the industry, gains a broader understanding of long-term needs and goals, our behavior (and the language that describes it) is changing and being refined. Our conventionally designed and constructed buildings are problematic in part because most of us are just beginning to appreciate that they often include elements that are not sustainable in the long-term. The goal is for true sustainability to become the new standard as rapidly as possible.

Summary

Whereas Chapter 1 showed that the conventional way of planning, designing, and constructing buildings causes a variety of problems, this chapter has shown that owners, designers, builders, and the public are grappling with ways to counter these problems. This chapter explored how green construction principles are being adopted to create cost-effective, healthy, and durable buildings and communities.

The incorporation of green standards and practices is driving changes throughout the construction industry. In the next chapter, we'll look at green's impact on jobs, materials, and products as well as on construction operations and practices.

Glossary

Bioswales—vegetation-filled depressions used to manage runoff.

Blackwater—wastewater that includes human waste.

Brownfield—a site that has hazardous substances, pollutants, or contaminants from an earlier use.

Building envelope—the physical separators between the parts of a building that are heated and cooled (conditioned) and those parts that are not.

Conservation—the act of trying to protect or preserve something or the limiting of how much of a resource is used.

Conventional buildings—a building that meets but does not exceed basic code requirements.

Deep-green retrofits—efforts that result in energy savings of 50% or more, as measured against a pre-renovation baseline.

Delivered energy—the amount of energy consumed at an end point.

Drip irrigation—systems that slowly deliver water directly to the root zone of a plant, with almost no water loss through surface runoff or evaporation.

Dual-flush toilets—toilets that are based on the standard toilets but have two buttons that allow for different flushing options.

Durability—a measure of the anticipated useful life of a system or product before it must be removed and replaced.

Embodied energy—the energy required to extract, process, manufacture, transport, and install a material or product.

Green construction—the practice of creating buildings and neighborhoods that reduce or (ideally) eliminate the use of fossil fuel-based energy, that carefully use our finite supply of freshwater, that are made from nontoxic materials, and that conserve the natural environment. The physical outcomes of using these approaches are referred to, often interchangeably, as **green, high-performance**, or **sustainable buildings**.

Green infrastructure—the use of vegetation, soils, and systems that mimic natural processes to manage excess runoff, and then infiltrate it into the ground, evaporate it into the air, or slowly discharge it.

Greywater—wastewater that has not been generated by toilets or urinals.

High-performance building—a building that optimizes energy efficiency, is durable, meets high-performance standards throughout its life (from the extraction of materials through decommission), and contributes toward occupant productivity. Many sources, including this book, use the terms "green," "sustainable," and "high-performance" interchangeably.

Infill development—the placement of a new development on a previously under-used or abandoned parcel.

LEED (Leadership in Energy and Environmental Design)—a suite of building rating systems developed by the U.S. Green Building Council and certified by the Green Building Certification Institute (GBCI).

Living roof—a roof that is partially or completely covered with vegetation; also called a green roof.

Metered-valve faucets—fixtures that use a predetermined amount of water.

Natural ventilation—the process of supplying and removing air through an indoor space by natural means, without the use of a fan or other mechanical system.

Orientation—the way a building is situated on a site and the positioning of windows, rooflines, and other features.

Rainwater harvesting—the process of intercepting rainwater from a roof or other surface and putting it to beneficial use.

Rebound effect—the condition whereby a green building performs poorly due to human actions.

R-value—a measure of resistance to heat flow; the higher the R value the greater the insulating value.

Sustainability—the ability of something to contribute toward long-term environmental and social endurance. In construction, sustainability, high-performance, and green are often used interchangeably.

Tight building—a building with an envelope designed to greatly restrict air, heat, and moisture flow from conditioned to unconditioned spaces.

Wastewater—any used water as well as runoff from streets.

Waterless toilets—toilets, including composting toilets and urinals, that use no water.

Wetland—an area that is regularly saturated by surface water or groundwater with vegetation that is adapted to these conditions

Whole building design—a design approach that analyzes system interdependencies and how they can be leveraged for maximum benefit.

Zero net energy (ZNE) **building**—a building that produces, on average, as much energy as it uses.

Zoning ordinances—regulations that determine how a site can be used.

Erick S. Holmes

A Changing Construction Industry

The construction industry is in a state of flux, due not only to the increase in green construction, but also to other long-term changes—in costs and the way projects are financed, in technology and the types of materials used, in the way projects are organized and delivered, in globalization. Industry demographics are changing too: the work force is aging and includes more women and minorities and, unlike in the past, fewer workers move up in the ranks without academic education. Workers interested in advancing their careers must be proficient in reading, writing, and computer skills, and today's project superintendent or manager is likely to have a degree in management or business, as well as years of field experience. Increased regulatory and health and safety requirements and the use of technology and other conditions have resulted in significant changes.

These and other trends are the result of both internal and external forces and affect virtually all aspects of the industry. One of the most important drivers of change is the growing emphasis on energy efficiency and the broader concerns addressed by green construction. In the last chapter, we looked at the ways in which green principles address flaws in the way we create our built environment. In this chapter, we'll explore how the incorporation of these principles is impacting the construction industry and its work force.

The impacts of green construction

Multiple studies show that buildings designed and built using sustainability as a standard cost less to operate, are healthier for the workers who erect them and those who use them, and provide significant benefits to the broader community and to the natural environment. Consumers are paying attention: every year the number of buildings that are certified under building assessment programs, such as **LEED** and Green Globes, grows substantially. During 2011, for example, floor area that was registered with a LEED green building rating system saw a 45% increase over 2010.[1] This statistic is, not surprisingly, reflected in the work of contractors and others in the industry: the number of architects, engineers, and contractors involved with green projects is growing substantially.

It's not just consumers who are demanding high-performance buildings; so are government entities. As we saw in the last chapter, one of the forces behind the increase in green construction, and the changes that accompany it, is the civic sector. Federal, state, and municipal governments own or lease more square footage of real estate and spend more on construction than any other entity. Because multiple economic arguments can be made for green construction, government entities are demanding high performance buildings and this demand is shaping construction practices in other sectors.[2]

High-performance buildings are all around us: green construction in the United States is now measured in billions of square feet and this figure is growing by more than 800 million square feet each year.[3] If we look at this in terms of building share, that, too, is impressive: by 2016, more than half of commercial and institutional and 38% of residential construction is expected to be green.[4]

Ethan Drinker, courtesy of
Coldham & Hartman Architects

These numbers represent a lot of building activity—enough to exert significant influence on the entire construction industry. Our understanding

*Bechtel Environmental
Classroom, Smith College*

about materials and products, the way we design and where we locate our buildings, the role and skills of general and **specialty trade contractors**, and construction procedures and attitudes about waste and efficiency are all shifting to accommodate this new type of building. The challenge for the American construction industry and its work force is to understand the opportunities presented by these changes.

Even if buildings aren't formally green—in other words, they aren't rated as such by a recognized organization such as the U.S. Green Building Council— green standards are influencing perceptions about buildings and their relationship to the health of people and the environment. Importantly, green standards are providing a new, higher benchmark for best practices in the industry. Both of these conditions—the increase in certified green buildings and the shift in public perception—are influencing industry change in everything from workforce skills to construction practices.

Green construction is affecting several aspects of the industry, including:

- Changes to industry jobs
- Changes to construction operations and practices, including:
    - Project delivery
    - Site procedures and pollution control
    - Waste management
    - Close-out and green documentation
    - Tightening codes and standards
- Technology
- New materials, products, and systems
- Changes to liability concerns

Let's look at how each of these aspects of the industry is changing.

Changes to industry jobs

Typically, about seven million people in the United States are directly employed in construction as carpenters, electricians, plumbers, and so on. The shift to green construction requires varying levels of adjustment by workers. On most green projects, most of the occupations involved already exist but require enhanced skills; HVAC installers, electricians, and plumbers are examples. Due to the emphasis on energy and water efficiency, and the installation of new types of assemblies and systems such as solar photovoltaic arrays, these specialty workers are likely to require additional skills. Sustainable buildings have requirements beyond the installation of solar or wind systems, however, such as the use of nontoxic or locally sourced materials. Most workers will need to perform tasks in new or different ways, often using new systems or materials. Even some off-the-shelf products such as adhesives, joint sealants, and drywall compounds may be disallowed and require alternatives with which the worker is unfamiliar.

> Green construction requires workers to perform tasks in new and different ways.

It's not just specialty contractors with direct involvement in green systems who are affected. All builders on green jobs need to be up-to-date on changing building and energy codes, proper installation techniques for high-performance products, new site procedures, and recycling requirements. Beyond those in the field, estimators, product specifiers, facility managers, maintenance workers, manufacturers, and many others are also affected.

In addition to impacting industry jobs, green construction is changing the way projects are organized and run.

Changes to construction operations and practices

Maximizing performance and meeting green goals for either a renovated or newly constructed building are dependent upon effective construction operations and procedures. How the work is organized, coordinated, and carried out in the field is not the same on green and conventional projects and these differences occur in several areas:

- Project delivery
- Site procedures
- Waste management
- Close-out and green documentation

Let's look briefly at each of these.

Project delivery

Project delivery describes the organizational structure for completing a project. There are many ways that projects can be organized and successful projects of any kind require teamwork. (See Chapter 6 in the author's book *Construction Project Management: A Complete Introduction*.) On a green project, however, project delivery is marked by a level of cooperation at all levels—from design through construction—that is significantly higher than it is on most conventional projects. For many in the industry, the level of required cooperation may be unfamiliar and perhaps even uncomfortable.

Integrated Project Delivery (IPD) is a type of project delivery often utilized on green projects and which employs a highly collaborative approach (see *Project delivery*). The components that make up a project—durability, aesthetics and space planning, materials, assemblies and systems, the construction process—are conceived as a whole. Although it is true that every project requires teamwork, meeting stringent efficiency goals requires that collaboration begins early in the design process and continues throughout construction. On projects that utilize IPD, everyone's experiences and skills contribute to finding the best ways to meet the building goals. Conventional assumptions may be revised as the team analyzes and considers multiple ways of approaching a design problem.

How might such a collaborative process work? In a conventional approach, an upgraded building envelope (roof, walls, and foundation) that has increased insulation and air barriers, for example, might be rejected based only on up-front cost. But if the team is working together, with clear performance objectives, the mechanical engineer and contractor might determine that the upgraded envelope allows a smaller, more efficient HVAC system, with total cost savings that justify the envelope upgrade. Or the lighting consultant might determine that decreased artificial lighting—and reduced up-front and operating costs—will be sufficient if the designers can develop a way to get more natural light into the space. Similarly, the HVAC engineer and contractor might determine that a shift in how the building is oriented on the site will maximize solar thermal gains and therefore reduce heating loads and, consequently, the size of the heating equipment.

Technology has made collaboration easier through **Building Information Modeling (BIM)** software and several web-based management tools. The information provided by BIM, for example, allows team members to make smart design decisions early in the process, identify problems before construction starts, schedule efficiencies into construction sequencing, and get accurate cost estimates up front.

On buildings with high performance goals, poor execution by one trade can compromise the entire project. For example, insulation that is not meticulously installed, has gaps, or is stuffed too tightly into walls will not provide the expected resistance to heat loss and may compromise the energy efficiency of the building. Similarly, the drywaller who slashes a vapor barrier with a utility knife to make drywall installation easier or the framer who leaves gaps in the sheathing that he assumes can just be covered by siding might be making their own lives easier but risking weather and air leaks that could cause moisture or mold problems later. When everyone on the team understands building performance goals, it helps create a collaborative environment that can result in project refinements and improvements all along the way.

This kind of collaborative project delivery is in sharp contrast to the conventional "silo" process, in which each participant works primarily in isolation. On a typical project, a designer and engineer draw up plans to meet an owner's requirements, the plans are turned into detailed construction drawings, and a **general contractor** is hired (typically after bidding on the drawings) and, in turn, hires **subcontractors** to complete most of the work. As buildings become more technologically complicated and costly, this isolated approach has been changing. High-performance projects magnify this change.

Site procedures

As with project delivery, site procedures may be different in green and conventional projects. Construction always includes some disturbance to the existing site; cutting, grading, paving, and the processes involved in constructing the building itself, plus many other activities, have the potential to cause severe damage. The general contractor should develop a management plan (which will include a catalog of existing vegetation and site features, such as creeks and trees) to minimize the negative impacts of construction activities such as:

- Traffic, including access and on-site parking
- The location of the field office
- Materials and equipment storage and staging

- Recycling area access

- The use of heavy equipment

Conservation of natural features extends to the protection of water both on and adjacent to the site. Stormwater runoff needs to be managed to prevent toxins from migrating off the site and contaminating lakes, rivers, and bays, and erosion control measures should also be installed to prevent the loss of topsoil and the build-up of soil sediment in water. Simple control measures, such as silt fence barriers, can be installed at the time of construction to reduce runoff both during and after construction, can effectively limit the entry of pollutants into surface water and groundwater, and protect water quality, fish habitats, and public health.

> Conservation of natural features extends to the protection of water.

Green projects emphasize minimizing construction-generated pollution and providing a healthy work environment during construction. Pollution can be anything that is harmful and should be managed both for the safety of the workers and of the adjacent properties and neighbors. In addition to water contamination, there are multiple pollutants such as dust, noise, vibration, and airborne particles such as exhaust soot from heavy equipment that may be toxic and irritating to both workers and neighbors.

Some toxins also come from additives as a result of construction, such as heavy metals, oils, and debris from construction traffic and spillage. Pollution control efforts can include revising schedules to avoid work during sensitive hours, spill prevention and cleanup procedures, redirecting lighting, dust control, and more.

Site procedures on green projects extend to the management of indoor air pollution. Emission contamination such as through volatile organic compounds can be hazardous for workers as well as end users and requires ducting to bring in adequate outside ventilation. Air should also be forced through the finished building at the end of construction so that any pollutants will be flushed out, reducing future air quality problems.

Waste management

We know from Chapter 1 that building construction, renovation, and demolition generate large amounts of waste, some of which can be toxic and which

Tom Lee

Recycling station at a construction site

ends up in landfills or elsewhere. In addition to their traditional roles during completion of the physical work, contractors play a central role in meeting green goals through the reduction and proper handling of waste.

Waste management on green jobs begins with reducing or eliminating waste. This includes using fewer materials, recyclable materials, and materials that are durable and therefore produce less waste over the long term. The general contractor is responsible for developing a waste management plan including sorting instead of comingling waste to maximize the amount that can be recycled. Everyone working on a green project will be involved with responsible waste management procedures and expectations.

Close-out and green documentation

An important aspect of construction is **close-out**, the tasks at the end of construction (that must be tended to before the contractors can all get paid and move on. These tasks include ensuring that all items are complete, the site is clean, and paperwork has been properly submitted. On a green job (and increasingly on others), a process called is typically completed as well.

Commissioning is the process of measuring and verifying that all systems and equipment are installed as specified and that the building is operating at optimum performance. Although we're discussing this as part of close-out, commissioning can occur throughout the life of a building: starting at design, extending through construction and close-out, and, ideally, during the functioning of the building to resolve problems and keep the systems fully functioning. A commissioning agent is hired early in the design process and works with the architects, engineers, and builders to ensure that systems are max-imized for performance. The agent assists in developing performance goals and a quality assurance process that delivers preventive and predictive main-tenance plans.

In addition to fewer product and installation errors, commissioning is recognized as a mechanism for saving operating costs for owners as well as providing buildings that perform as expected. Failures to com-mission have resulted in multiple examples of "green" buildings that don't operate as intended (or advertised) and there is now an understanding of the important link between commission-ing and performance. Commissioning is required for build-ings being certified under several of the green building rating systems and, increasingly, federal and state governments are requiring commissioning services for their projects.

> Commissioning ensures that a building operates at maximum performance.

Documentation of green measures and procedures, called **green doc-umentation**, may be required. If a project team decides to pursue green certification (or it is taking advantage of incentives tied to meeting green com-mitments), the contractor, as well as subcontractors, will have to provide vary-ing degrees of verification that the building and its materials, products, and systems meet the green program requirements.

Documentation processes are varied: some certification information is submitted during the design phase and might consist of a drawing to iden-tify where the recycling area will be located, for example; some information may be required during construction to show, for example, that stormwater is being appropriately managed; other documentation is submitted at close-out to verify the recycled content of materials, that wood was properly sourced, or that the HVAC system is sufficiently efficient. For some rating systems, per-formance data must be compiled and submitted for a predetermined length of time after the building is occupied as post-occupancy performance data.

A discussion of liability issues follows, but it is worth noting here that green documentation can become grounds for dispute. A case filed in a California court is an example. In 2014, the City of Palo Alto fired the gen-eral contractor responsible for construction of a local library, a project that was supposed to be certified as a green building under the voluntary LEED assessment program. The parties ended up in court; Palo Alto contended that the terminated contractor failed to turn over the documentation that was necessary for the city to pursue LEED certification. Included in the documents that were allegedly withheld was documentation verifying the source and types of materials, and the methodologies employed by the contractor to reduce waste. This case highlights the potential conflicts over and importance of documentation.

Another critical close-out task is owner education. A green building is likely to have special features with which the owner or facility manager may be unfamiliar, for example, a solar photovoltaic array or a high-performance heat pump. The **Operations & Maintenance (O&M) Manual**, put together by the contractor, provides the owner with product data, maintenance, repair, and cleaning information. Comprehensive manuals provide guidance for operating facilities in a sustainable manner by reducing the use of energy, water, and toxic chemicals. The O&M manual helps facility managers identify any special handling and tracking requirements (such as for chemicals), equipment maintenance and operation procedures, and any other special record-keeping protocols such as the requirement for post-occupancy performance data). Inspection requirements and warranty information are also included in the manuals. In buildings with complicated or unfamiliar systems, the general contractor will be responsible for training facility managers. Educating maintenance personnel on the long-term care of materials and systems will be part of the procedures at the conclusion of construction.

There are several other areas, in addition to jobs and construction operations and procedures, that are changing: codes and standards, technology, materials and products, and liability.

Tightening codes and standards

As broad understanding of the flaws in current building practices has grown, so too have the number of related **codes** and regulations designed to address these flaws, particularly energy and water inefficiencies. As discussed in detail in Chapter 4, codes define minimum standards for many aspects of construction; plumbing codes, electrical codes, and building codes are examples.

The adoption of new codes and tightening of existing codes, especially related to energy and water use, are happening rapidly. Sometimes these codes are in conflict with voluntary green building certification programs or existing regulations. For example, San Francisco had to reconcile the existing requirements for certification of commercial buildings through one of the voluntary green building assessment programs with new state-mandated building codes.[5] This incompatibility can lead to confusion and conflicts among designers, builders, and owners. (See the later discussion on liability.)

Andrew Schulman

The federal government is in the forefront of efforts to tighten **standards** (guidelines developed to establish best practices), and has issued multiple rules, regulations, and policies related to green design and construction. Some federal initiatives are mandatory (such as protection of natural habitats and wetlands and the reduction of energy use in buildings) and some are guidelines (such as the adoption of a green building assessment program for federal buildings). Federal regulations are likely to tighten further. *The Strategic Sustainability Performance Plan,* from the General Services Administration, for example, commits to designing buildings that produce as much, or more, energy than they use—zero net energy buildings.[6] (The reader is urged to review the concept of ZNE in Chapter 2.)

It's not just the federal government that is issuing new regulations: states, municipalities, and local jurisdictions are also adopting green codes and regulations. California is leading efforts at the state level; in 2014, its updated Green Building Standards Code (CALGreen), a statewide green building code, went into effect. The majority of states and many local jurisdictions have adopted energy codes, although none are as comprehensive as California's efforts.

As always, construction workers are responsible for understanding how codes, regulations, and best practices impact their trade. With increasing efficiency requirements, this understanding must extend to green regulations, codes, and incentives.

Technology

New technology enters the workplace almost daily and has impacted many aspects of the construction industry. Changes in how information flows on a jobsite, the ability to design and construct very complex forms, and the development of **smart buildings** and sophisticated systems controls are just some examples. Various types of building modeling software (Building Information Modeling or BIM, noted previously) that create 3D models from which both graphic and non-graphic information can be extracted have been in use for 20 years. As designers and builders have gained familiarity with modeling software, its use has increased. Drawings can be produced quickly and accurately, and embodied data let designers and contractors analyze code and installation requirements, including the optimum sequence for installing building components. Manufacturers' specifications, cost data, and scheduling information are embedded in the software and when changes or adjustments are made, the model and the accompanying data change too. This has resulted in more effective communication, better work flows, tighter cost control, and more.

Technology is also playing an ever-increasing role in the development of new materials and products. Buildings are becoming "**smart**": computers can control access, lighting, and communication and make it possible to incorporate green components, including recycled products, into structures of all sizes. Technology has also made it possible to create buildings that, until recently, would have been impossible to design or construct. The massive curvilinear buildings by Frank Gehry are examples of structures defined by innovative forms and materials that did not exist or would not have been possible to utilize in the pre-computer world. The Walt Disney Concert Hall shown here is an another example. New types of materials and unfamiliar application of existing materials are requiring changing work-force skills.

Exterior elevation of Walt Disney Concert Hall in Los Angeles

PD Photos

Technology has also revolutionized management: how designers and contractors plan and organize for construction, and then manage, track, and control the process. There are software programs for developing estimates and monitoring costs, preparing and updating schedules, standardizing information, tracking labor and other performance indicators, and communicating with those working to complete the job. The tendency for each trade to operate isolated from other trades is changing because of technology. BIM, cloud computing, mobile apps, and more are creating interconnections among those on a project resulting, ideally, in improved decision-making, creativity, and speed.

The wide use of electronic technology in construction has made it mandatory for today's construction managers to be computer literate. The rapidly changing nature of systems and products in the industry also requires informed and sophisticated builders. The days are fast disappearing when the contractor was just a guy with a tool belt.

New materials, products, and systems

New green products and materials are flooding the market. This is in response to growing consumer demand for sustainable products, changes in technology, expectations regarding best practices, and regulatory requirements. Some of these new materials are upgrades to familiar products such as high-performance windows and plumbing fixtures. Other products are entirely new and others are futuristic: solar arrays, light-weight high-strength carbon materials, energy-harvesting glass, panels made from sorghum stalks, and paint that helps clean the air are examples. There are even building materials, such as bricks, that are being produced by 3D printing.[7]

The choice of materials and products that perform successfully in the field and truly meet sustainability goals can be a challenge. While sustainability criteria are increasingly part of the product-specification decision process, sorting through all the contradictory information can be both complex and confusing. There are certain principles that are used to assess the environmental value of materials and products, including:

- Product durability

- Embodied energy contained in the product

- Percentage of recycled content

- Source

- Product's ability to be recycled after useful life

- Whether a product has been certified by a third party

There is no agreement, however, regarding how to weigh these (sometimes contradictory) criteria. For example: you want to use a pair of beautiful, used French doors in your new house addition. The problem is that the doors will either require extensive and expensive upgrades or, once installed, they will be drafty and energy inefficient. Is it better to reuse the old doors or buy new, tight, doubled-glazed doors?

Beyond the issue of product selection are the estimating challenges presented by new and unfamiliar materials and products. Designers and contractors need to project accurately what something is going to cost, usually in dollars or time, before a project is built. The builder's goal is to predict costs accurately and still have this estimate low enough to be awarded a contract. As is true of any construction project, the best estimates are derived from experience: how long it's taken in the past to install a certain assembly or product, what is the expected lead time, special warranty issues or costs, and so on. With new products and materials, it's more difficult to assess purchase and installation costs accurately.

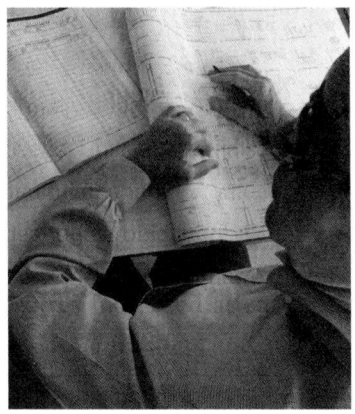

Andrew Schulman

The multiple issues around green materials and products will be covered in detail in Chapter 5.

Changes to liability

Contractors should be aware of the legal issues that can arise on green projects, where new materials, products, and construction processes are used. According to the American Bar Association,[8] so-called green risks are similar to issues traditionally associated with construction projects—uncoordinated drawings, construction delays, and noncompliant construction, to name a few. But other risks can be specifically related to sustainable design and construction practices, primarily because of the use of green materials, systems, and procedures. These risks include:

- **Failure to meet client anticipations regarding operating costs or comfort.** If a project fails to live up to the expectations of the owner, this can cause disputes and possibly litigation. For example, an owner may have expectations regarding long-term energy savings that are not realized. This situation is more likely with products or assemblies that are new to the market and, sometimes, experimental. Another risk is higher-than-projected operating costs due to inadequate design, construction, operation, or maintenance.

- **Problems associated with conflicting standards.** As noted previously, public codes are changing rapidly and may not be compatible with voluntary certification requirements of a building assessment program such as LEED. If conflicting standards or requirements exist at the time a project is undertaken and they are not identified and resolved until after construction is under way, the potential for delays, significant cost overruns, and accompanying litigation is heightened.

- **Risks due to project delays.** Although delays are common sources of conflict, these risks are increased on green projects, sometimes with unexpected consequences. For example, a contractor in Maryland was sued because project delays (not necessarily directly linked to the green nature of the project) resulted in the loss of a green tax incentive for the owner. Other risks can include delays caused by green material shortages or lack of familiarity with green practices such as commissioning guidelines that may be required as part of a building certification program. (See Table 4.2 for examples.)

- **Failure to meet green certification standards.** Because most green standards are new, there is increased risk that designers and builders may fail to meet program requirements. In a case in New York, for example, the owner was forced to pay back taxes because the completed project failed to meet the green commitments on which tax-exempt bonds were issued.

- **Performance or durability failures of materials and equipment.** Some products that are configured with nontoxic materials to meet stringent air quality standards may not hold up as well as the product they replace. A goal and expectation for green construction is an *increase* in durability, not a reduction. Another risk is potential moisture problems arising from air-tight buildings, which may cause warranty and other problems for the contractor. Other risks for contractors include potential delays caused by installation of unfamiliar products or processes required by green codes, and how the installation of a high-performance system might interfere with existing warranties. For example, you're a contractor who has been hired to install a solar photovoltaic array on an existing roof. There are multiple issues that will need to be addressed: will the array impact the existing roof warranty? Are you going to penetrate the existing roof and assume liability for future roof problems? Will the array impact the existing drainage or will its maintenance reduce the life of the roof?

- **Conflicts over documentation.** Legal issues can surface regarding the ownership of green documentation such as with the city of Palo Alto as discussed previously. This case highlights the importance of contract language that clarifies all documentation related to green building certification.[9]

Summary

We have seen in this chapter that the construction industry is in the midst of change in the way that buildings are conceived, planned, designed, and built. An older work force, globalization, higher costs, and new technology are some of the forces exerting stress on the industry. The concern in this chapter has been the increased constraints brought about by economic forces, regulatory requirements, and public demand, especially constraints related to energy and the environment. The consequences of these constraints impact how workers must approach their jobs, and the skills they require; the rapid (and sometimes confusing and conflicting) tightening of codes and standards; the specification of unfamiliar materials and products; and new expectations for what constitutes best practices on a jobsite.

The reader has been introduced to the role of regulations and standards. The next chapter will discuss these in more detail, as well as the emerging importance of green building assessment programs. These programs, such as the U.S. Green Building Council's LEED, seek to develop standardized measures of the ongoing environmental and social impacts of a product or building.

Glossary

Building Information Modeling (BIM)—a process of gathering and managing information that uses 3D virtual models as a tool for design, construction, and facilities management.

Close-out—the process of completing the terms of a contract; includes completion of the physical work (construction close-out), completion of fulfilling the terms of the construction contract (contract close-out), and final evaluations by the contractor (contractor close-out). On a green project, close-out includes submittal of required documentation.

Codes—laws put into place to promote safe practices in design and construction; compliance is enforced through whichever agency has jurisdiction over the project.

Commissioning—a process of verifying that a building systems and equipment are installed as specified and the building is operating at optimal performance. Commissioning can occur during design, construction, and operation.

Construction Management project delivery—a delivery method in which a contract manager (CM) is hired early in the process and acts as the owner's representative. During construction, the contract manager may either manage (but not physically complete the work) or perform as a general contractor.

Green documentation—verification that a building and its materials, products, and systems meet green program requirements.

General contractor—an individual or firm hired by and responsible to an owner for coordinating the completion of a project. The GC hires subcontractors and suppliers.

Integrated Project Delivery (IPD)—a project delivery system that is based on a highly collaborative approach to project design and construction.

LEED (Leadership in Energy and Environmental Design)—a voluntary green building certification program developed by the U.S. Green Building Council and administered by the Green Building Certification Institute (GBCI) that recognizes best-in-class building strategies and practices. LEED includes a suite of green building rating systems as well as professional credentials.

Operations & Maintenance (O&M) Manual—A manual provided to the owner at the completion of the work that gives critical operation, maintenance, repair, and replacement information.

Project delivery—the organizational structure for completing a project. Also called delivery method.

Smart building—a building that uses technology to integrate its systems to optimize services, costs, and operation.

Specialty trade contractor—a contractor who is an expert in a specific area of construction.

Subcontractor—an individual or firm that has a contract with another contractor. In construction, subcontractors are typically specialty trades.

Waste management—the processes of dealing with and controlling construction and demolition debris.

Ichijo

zHome, Issaquah WA

Green Standards, Codes, and Rating Systems

Codes, regulations, and standards are used in all aspects of construction, fabrication, manufacturing, and inspection. These are the rules and recommendations that specify or recommend minimum acceptable procedures or quality. Some rules are legally mandatory, and are typically called codes; other rules, known as **standards**, are voluntary. As market demands increase for the application of green principles (especially regarding energy and water conservation and efficiency), codes and best practices are adjusted to incorporate these principles, and contractors and others in the industry face a constantly shifting regulatory environment. In addition, an increasing number of voluntary assessment tools have been developed to measure energy and building performance.

Green characteristics are commonly identified as best practices and there is an expectation that those working in the industry have green credentials or training. As a result, there is a growing need for designers, engineers, and builders to understand the basics of green construction, including how the regulatory environment is changing.

This chapter defines standards and codes (what they are and how they differ), considers the emerging green standards and codes, analyzes green rating systems, and reviews some of the most commonly used systems such as LEED and Green Globes.

Standards

Standards are guidelines developed to measure the quality or characteristics of something. Standards establish best practices for manufacturing processes, testing procedures, material composition, physical properties, and more. They may be published as recommended guidelines or adopted as mandatory codes that are required by municipal building departments and other jurisdictions.

Virtually every product and material that goes into a building is identified with a standard: a window might be built to meet the North American Fenestration Standards, welding procedures for structural material might be required to follow standards set by the American Welding Society, and electrical wiring is likely to be covered by standards from the National Fire Protection Association, and so forth.

There are hundreds of industries, agencies and organizations, nonprofits, and manufacturers that establish product and material standards: the North American Fenestration Standards, the American Welding Society, and the National Fire Protection Association just noted are three. Among others that issue standards for the construction industry, the reader may be familiar with the following:

- **ASTM International** (formerly American Society for Testing and Materials, *www.astm.org*) develops standards for a wide range of products, materials, and systems, including iron and steel products, paints, and more. ASTM standards include specifications for anchoring systems, piping components, steel rails, high-strength steel bolts, and many similar products.

- **ASHRAE** (American Society of Heating, Refrigerating and Air-Conditioning Engineers, *www.ashrae.org*) is a source of technical standards for the HVAC industry. Examples of ASHRAE standards include: refrigerants, ventilation standards, heat pumps, compressors, and whole-building energy performance.

- **UL** (Underwriters Laboratories, *www.ul.com*) writes testing standards and certifies products for safety. For example, a remote control wire for an irrigation system might be specified as being UL approved for underground burial, or a lighting fixture might come with the UL-approval stamp.

> ### ANSI
>
> The reader might be familiar with the acronym ANSI and might have noted the term "ANSI Approved." ANSI, which stands for the American National Standards Institute, does not develop standards or model codes but certifies those developed by other organizations and thus plays an important role. (It also coordinates with international organizations, so that American products can be used worldwide.) ANSI, affiliated with the International Standards Organization (ISO), serves as a "watchdog" for standards development and conformity and it accredits standards-developing organizations that operate in accordance with certain procedures. Because it only approves standards that are, among other things, developed through a consensus process that is open to public scrutiny (transparent), ANSI approval is highly regarded.

Here's how standards from these and other agencies might be used: If galvanized pipe needs to be specified for a project, the designer might call for the pipe to conform to ASTM standard A53. This standard, for galvanized steel pipe, identifies the pipe's grade, how it has been welded, and more. Everyone on the team will know what type of pipe is called for and the contractor should be assured of getting the correct product that meets project specifications. All galvanized pipe specified to meet the A53 standard shares characteristics. PVC pipe, on the other hand, would be specified as conforming to a different standard with different characteristics. When standards such as these are used, everyone on the job should understand exactly what product is called for.

Standards define best practices, but, unless adopted as a code, compliance is voluntary. As you'll learn in the following section, codes are often based on existing standards.

Codes

Codes define minimum requirements; they are different from but complementary to standards. When standards are adopted by jurisdictions (such as municipalities or states) they become codes and represent minimum *mandatory* requirements. Codes are not flexible and compliance is enforced through whichever agency has jurisdiction over the project (called the **authority having jurisdiction** or AHJ, which reviews and approves projects). Typically jurisdictions do not actually *write* their own codes but use or adapt them from those developed and maintained by model code- and standard-writing organizations.

Many construction-related codes are adopted from published standards developed by organizations such as ASTM, ASHRAE, or UL. But the most common codes are adopted from model codes written by an organization such as the International Code Council (ICC). All 50 states and the District of Columbia have adopted codes written by ICC, including their Green Construction Code (IGCC).[1]

The most commonly applied codes are **building codes**, which promote safe practices in the design and construction of buildings. Building codes include requirements regarding the strength of concrete used in a foundation, the type of welds on structural steel, the size of framing members, or the number of exits in a room. Most building codes are similar to each other, but differ depending on type, use, and location of a project. The codes for a residential project will differ from those for a school or an office building. Codes are variable from state to state and jurisdiction to jurisdiction, as well as among building types. A requirement in Tucson AZ, may not be required in Golden CO, or Detroit MI.

Other codes and regulations might include local or state health, fire, and transportation department requirements, and utility, water, sewer, and environmental quality laws and other codes or regulations. The National Fire Protection Association, the American Society of Civil Engineers, and others typically develop model codes that may be adopted by jurisdictions. There are also federal regulations that can impact new and renovated projects and are typically responses to congressional legislation such as the Clean Air Act. Federal regulations operate similarly to codes in that compliance is mandatory.

Green standards and codes

As understanding about the benefits of green construction have grown, so too have the number of green standards and codes that address high performance

*National Green
Building Standard™*

materials, products, and systems. Some of the organizations that write these are the same ones that write conventional standards and codes, such as ASHRAE and the International Code Council. As with other standards, they may or may not be adopted as mandatory codes by local jurisdictions and often are adapted to meet local needs.

Table 4.1 identifies some significant green standards and model codes that are available for jurisdictions to adopt.

Green standards and model codes such as those in Table 4.1 are being adopted as mandatory codes primarily at local levels. This is particularly true with energy codes: New York City; Seattle; Charlottesville VA; Boston; Tucson AZ; and Austin TX are among the dozens of municipalities, both large and small, from across the country that have adopted mandatory energy codes. The majority of states have energy codes in place, and the number without codes is rapidly dwindling. As of December 2013, all but seven states had adopted statewide commercial energy codes, and all but eight had residential energy codes.[4] Current codes do not address how buildings use energy once they are occupied, and the lack of outcome-based codes is an obstacle in the effort to improve efficiency. As you'll learn in the following, some building rating systems, such as the Living Building Challenge, address this weakness by requiring post-occupancy data.

States are also adopting broader green codes. In January 2011, California became the nation's first state with a mandatory green building code. The California Green Building Standards Code (CALGreen), part of the State's Title 24 California Code of Regulations (CCR), establishes minimum green

Table 4.1 Examples of Green Codes and Standards

Name	Developer	Characteristics
ASHRAE 90.1—Energy Standard for Buildings Except Low-Rise Residential Buildings	American Society of Heating Refrigerating and Air-Conditioning Engineers (ASHRAE) *www.ashrae.org*	Provides minimum requirements for energy-efficient design of most buildings, except low-rise residential. For new and existing buildings, systems, and equipment. This is often cited as a baseline for codes. For example, in 2010 Alaska passed a bill calling for all public facilities to meet or exceed current ASHRAE 90.1. Standards 90.1 is updated every three years.
ASHRAE 189.1—Standard for the Design of High Performance Green Buildings Except Low-rise Residential Buildings	ASHRAE, U.S. Green Building Council (USGBC®), and Illuminating Engineers Society (IES) *www.ashrae.org*	Comprehensive green building standard that is the basis for many codes. Complements existing green standards and rating systems and is more stringent than ASHRAE 90.1, which it is not intended to replace.[2] Covers site sustainability, water and energy efficiency, indoor air quality, and building's impact on the atmosphere, resources, and materials. 189.1 Is a compliance option for the International Green Construction Code.
International Energy Conservation Code (IECC)	International Code Council (ICC) *www.iccsafe.org*	The International Code Council develops model standards and codes that are used worldwide. The 2012 IECC is its model energy code and calls for a 30% increase in energy savings compared to the 2006 code. Adopted by many state and municipal governments for the establishment of minimum design and construction requirements for energy efficiency for homes, schools, and commercial buildings.
International Green Construction Code (IgCC)	International Code Council (ICC) *www.iccsafe.org*	First model code to include sustainability measures for an entire construction project and its site. Offers jurisdictions several levels of compliance and is adaptable to fit local needs.
ICC-700 National Green Building Standard (NGBS)	International Code Council and the National Association of Home Builders (NAHB) *www.iccsafe.org* *www.nahb.org*	A green building standard developed by the ICC and the National Association of Home Builders. The NGBS is also a third-party building certification program. Dozens of regional and local green initiatives use ICC-700 standards and the International Green Construction Code (IgCC) requires compliance with the ICC 700 for certain residential projects.[3]

building standards for the majority of residential and commercial new construction projects in California. Other standards and rating systems have been developed in California, too, including the Green Point Rating System for new and existing homes, and CHEERS, the California Home Energy Efficiency Rating Services.

There are also organizations that develop narrow or trade-specific green standards and model codes. For example, the International Association of Plumbing and Mechanical Officials (IAMPO) offers the *Green Plumbing and Mechanical Code Supplement,* which is a model code developed to standardize sustainable residential and commercial plumbing and mechanical systems *(www.iampo.org).* There are standards for solar systems such as those developed by the Solar Rating and Certification Corporation (SRCC, *www.solarrating.org*), standards for wind power developed by the American Wind Energy Association (AWEA, *www.awea.org*), standards for ground source heat pumps from the International Association for Ground Source Heat Pumps (IGSHPA, *www.igshpa.okstate.edu*), and many more.

Codes and plug-loads

It is estimated that a substantial percentage of the energy consumed by buildings is from products that are powered by ordinary AC outlets such as those found in homes. The energy drawn by computers, monitors, kitchen appliances, speakers, fans, space heaters, televisions, and so on is called the plug-load and, given the use of such products, is emerging as an increasing concern. While codes and standards have steadily mandated reductions in energy use, plug loads remain unregulated and the total energy they consume is largely unknown due to the lack of measurable data. Not surprisingly, as regulated loads are reduced, unregulated products are claiming a larger proportion of total energy use in buildings. Although appliance efficiency standards such as Energy Star developed by the U.S. Environmental Protection Agency and the Appliance Efficiency Regulations in California are helping to drive the manufacture of efficient products, there remains a gap between measured and unmeasured energy loads. Understanding this gap can help create an impetus for managing *total* energy use.[5]

Green building rating systems

Standards and codes have a major limitation: they do not provide any way to determine how a building is actually *functioning* and, prior to the development of LEED (see the following), there were no criteria for determining what components determine the "greenness" of a building. **Green rating systems** are designed to address this limitation by providing criteria for judging the environmental and social impact of products, systems, and buildings.

Green rating systems are relatively new in the industry. In the 1990s **BREEAM** (Building Research Establishment Environmental Assessment Method) was launched in Great Britain. This system provided the impetus (and model) for the development of the U.S. Green Building Council's LEED rating system, which was launched in 2000. Others have followed, including the Green Building Initiative's® (GG) launched in 2004, and the most demanding of all the North American assessment systems, the Living Building Challenges (LBC). Although rating systems for products, such as the Environmental Protection Agency's Energy Star program, were already in use, LEED marked the first U.S.-based program for assessing the impact of entire buildings.

A rating, or certification, system or program is a tool used to demonstrate that a product, system, or building has met certain performance criteria. Some rating systems such as Energy Star are *single-attribute*, and focus solely on water or energy, for example. Other programs such as LEED are *multi-attribute* and address a range of issues including location, energy and water use, material toxicity, and more. Some focus on residential buildings and others on commercial properties. LEED and the Living Building Challenge even have rating systems designed to assess entire neighborhoods. The goals for the building rating systems are similar, however: to create more environmentally sustainable, cost-effective structures that are healthy and comfortable for the people who use them.

Major building rating systems used in the U.S.

Typically, green building rating systems use a point system to evaluate design and performance in a number of areas such as energy and water use, project

location, materials, and indoor air quality. In order to receive green certification, a project must earn a minimum number of points or percentage of
applicable points as defined by the particular rating system. Rating systems
typically require that projects receive certification through a third party. For
example, certification of buildings in the Green Globes assessment program is
through the Green Building Initiative (GBI), and LEED buildings are certified
by the Green Building Certification Institute (GBCI™), an organization distinct
from USGBC.

GBCI administers more than LEED

The Green Building Certification Institute is a body that administers green profes-
sional credentials and certification programs, of which LEED is the best known.
But they administer multiple other programs as well, including: PEER (Performance
Excellence in Energy Renewal), designed to measure and improve sustainable
power system performance; WELL Building Standard, which addresses and certifies features of the built environment that impact health and well-being; SITES
(Sustainable Sites Initiative), which measures and rates landscapes; and GREBS
(Global Real Estate Benchmark), which assesses sustainability performance of real
estate portfolios globally.[6]

The use of a building rating system is voluntary and project teams decide
early in the development process whether or not to pursue certification
through one of the programs. Although there is no restriction on meeting the
criteria for and being certified through multiple assessment programs, owners typically select just one. The choice of rating system is made based on the
type of project, ability of the project to meet prerequisite requirement of the
particular rating system, cost of acquiring certification, and availability of local
incentives.

Green rating systems are not currently designed to be model codes, as
the International Code Council's model codes are, for example. But governments often adopt pieces of green rating systems such as LEED. Although
there are examples of jurisdictions adopting the LEED Green Rating System
for New Construction in its entirety (the federal government and the City of

San Francisco are two), most choose to adopt portions of it, such as an energy performance requirement or exterior water use.

There are two major building assessment programs used in the United States: LEED and Green Globes. With almost 80,000 registered and certified projects,[7] LEED is by far the most prominent and the one that has had the greatest impact on the market. I will therefore describe it in some detail. Green Globes is newer and less widely used but has been identified by the U.S. General Services Administration (GSA) as one of two programs (along with LEED) to be used across the federal government, and this is expected to increase its use. Building certification through a third program, the Living Building Challenge, is considered the most difficult to attain but is gaining considerable interest.

LEED® green building program
www.usgbc.org/leed

Understanding the links between buildings and resource use was the impetus for the 1993 founding of the private nonprofit U.S. Green Building Council (USGBC and the related logo is a trademark owned by the U.S. Green Building Council and is used with permission; *www.usgbc.org/LEED*). USGBC's goal is to promote and encourage the development of buildings that are environmentally responsible, economically profitable, and healthy for the users and the natural environment.

USGBC recognized that the lack of consistent terms and standards for "green building" was creating confusion and was an obstacle to the widespread application of effective green approaches and systems. In the absence of clear and universally accepted definitions and minimum standards, developers, contractors, designers, and the general public tended to view sustainable development skeptically. Due to the impediments posed by this confusion, the focus of USGBC became the development of a green rating system for buildings that would:

- Establish a common standard of measurement for defining what makes a building "green"

- Promote integrated, whole-building design practices

- Recognize environmental leadership in the building industry

- Stimulate green competition

- Raise consumer awareness of green building benefits

- Transform the building market

A committee of men and women from a variety of disciplines—construction, architecture, real estate, manufacturing, and development—assessed the current technology and needs, and studied other rating systems (primarily BREEAM) and, in 2000, launched a system called the Leadership in Energy and Environmental Design (LEED) green building program.

This first system operated as a pilot program and was partially funded by the U.S. Department of Energy. After extensive public feedback and modifications, the LEED Green Rating System Version 2.0 was fully launched in 2000 for new commercial construction and major renovation projects for buildings. Version 2.1 followed in 2002 and Version 2.2 in 2005; a major update to the rating systems was released in 2009 and the latest version (LEED v4) rolled out in late 2013 (effective for all projects started after October 2016). Today LEED includes five separate rating systems covering multiple building types.

Although there have been criticisms of LEED, it has, by most accounts, been spectacularly successful. Today LEED offers rating systems for all building types and even neighborhoods and it's easy to look around and see examples of its popularity: there are LEED-certified government buildings, LEED-certified skyscrapers, LEED-certified private homes, LEED-certified offices, and LEED-certified municipal and state buildings. There isn't a state that doesn't have a LEED building and, as of 2013, there were 45,000 LEED registered and certified buildings in the United States alone, and many state and local governments across the U.S. are adopting LEED standards. In addition, LEED is represented in more than 100 countries around the world, including the United Arab Emirates, Canada, Brazil, China, South Africa, and India.[8]

As noted, LEED has five separate rating systems that address multiple building and project types:

- **Building Design and Construction (LEED BD+C)** for buildings that are being newly constructed or are going through major renovation. LEED BD+C includes 10 building/project types, including new construction and major renovations, core and shell development, schools, retail, and others.

(continued on next page)

- **Interior Design and Construction (LEED ID+C)** for projects that are a complete **interior fit-out** (the process of making interior space suitable for use). This category includes commercial, retail, and hospitality project types.

- **Building Operations and Maintenance (LEED O+M)** applies to buildings that are undergoing improvement work or little to no construction, including existing buildings, data centers, warehouses and more.

- **Neighborhood Development (LEED ND)** applies to new land development projects or redevelopment projects containing residential uses, nonresidential uses, or a mix. Projects can be at any stage of the development process, from conceptual planning to construction.

- **Homes Design and Construction (LEED Homes)** applies to single-family homes, low-rise multi-family homes (one to three stories), or mid-rise multi-family homes (four to six stories).

Every project team that decides to pursue LEED certification must select one of these rating systems and follow its individual requirements.

LEED certification is not awarded only for a particularly efficient HVAC system, or superior insulation, or the use of recycled materials, but instead is concerned with a building's overall performance in different impact categories. Although every project must meet certain prerequisites, the project team is not required to design and construct a project to meet every standard in every category; there are multiple options from which the team can pick and choose.

Although there is variation in each rating system, all of them include three components:

- Mandatory prerequisites

- Performance credits

- Points

Prerequisites set the minimum standard that all buildings must meet (for example, minimum energy performance) and are requirements; they do not earn a project points. Performance credits are the heart of the LEED programs and are what earn a project points. Unlike mandatory prerequisites, owners can pick and choose the credits they want to pursue. There are several credit categories and, within each category, multiple ways for earning points. See Table 4.2 for an example of how points might be distributed, and earned, in the Energy and Atmosphere credit category for the Building Design and Construction rating system. Points are awarded and a single total score determines certification under four progressive levels: LEED Certified (40–49 points), LEED Silver (50–59 points), LEED Gold (60–79 points), or LEED Platinum (80+ points).

Table 4.2 Credits and Points: Energy and Atmosphere for the LEED Building Design and Construction Rating System (LEED BD+C)

Credit	Possible Points	Focus
Fundamental commissioning/ verification	This is a required prerequisite	Project team must follow ASHRAE guidelines for commissioning services
Minimum energy performance	Required prerequisite	Must exceed an ASHRAE energy benchmark (based on performance projections)
Building-level energy metering	Required prerequisite	Must install metering devices to enable post-occupancy energy consumption for five years
Fundamental refrigerant management	Required prerequisite	No use of chlorofluorocarbon (CFC)– based refrigerants or complete a phase-out plan for existing equipment
Enhanced commissioning	Maximum 6 points	Commissioning beyond what is required as a prerequisite
Optimize energy performance	Maximum 18 points	Energy performance beyond what is required as a prerequisite
Advanced energy metering	Maximum 1 point	More detailed metering than what is required as a prerequisite
Demand response	Maximum 2 points	Project reduces energy demand during certain periods
Renewable energy production	Maximum 3 points	Project meets a percentage of energy use through renewable sources
Enhanced refrigerant management	Maximum 1 point	Select refrigerants that minimize ozone depletion
Green power and carbon offsets	Maximum 2 points	Actions that reduce greenhouse gas emissions

(continued on next page)

In addition to the required prerequisites, all LEED rating systems (except for Neighborhood Development) identify eight credit categories that include the following:

1. **Sustainable sites**

   This credit category focuses the environment surrounding the building: on restoring project site elements, integrating the site with local and regional ecosystems, and preserving the biodiversity upon which natural systems rely.

2. **Water efficiency**

   This category addresses indoor and outdoor water use, specialized uses, and metering systems.

3. **Energy and atmosphere**

   This category addresses energy use reduction, energy-efficient design strategies, and renewable energy sources.

4. **Materials and resources**

   This category focuses on minimizing the embodied energy and other impacts associated with the extraction, processing, transport, maintenance, and disposal of building materials.

5. **Indoor environmental quality**

   Indoor environmental quality is concerned with indoor air quality and thermal, visual, and acoustic comfort.

6. **Location and transportation**

   This category addresses site location and access: compact development, the use of previously used or disadvantaged sites, alternative transportation, and connection with amenities such as restaurants and parks.

7. **Innovation**

   This category is designed to recognize projects for innovative building features and sustainable building practices and strategies that exceed those identified by LEED.

8. **Regional priority**

   Points are earned for approaches that address regional environmental priorities and concerns.

Each category is subdivided into a variety of optional credits that vary depending on which LEED rating system is being used. Each credit is assigned a maximum possible point score and the project team may pick and choose which options they wish to pursue. As noted, certification requires a minimum of 40 points and teams will strategize the best way to achieve the desired certification level (Certified, Silver, Gold, or Platinum).

As one example, Table 4.2 shows the credits and points available in the category "Energy and atmosphere" under the LEED for Building Design and Construction (LEED BD+C) rating system (version 4). As noted, this performance credit category addresses energy use reduction, energy-efficient design strategies, and renewable energy sources.

In addition to program prerequisites and optional credits, LEED has a separate set of Minimum Program Requirements (MPRs) that define project characteristics, such as occupancy rates, permanency, and more. The MPRs restrict the types of projects that can apply for certification (no mobile homes or yachts, for example.) Without satisfying MPRs, a project cannot even apply for certification.

Keeping it all straight

LEED can be confusing and keeping its components and data straight isn't easy. Here's a summary that may help:

There are **4** progressive levels of LEED Certification based on the total number of points earned:

- 40+ points = LEED Certified

- 50+ points = LEED Silver

- 60+ points = LEED Gold

- 80+ points = LEED Platinum

LEED has **5** different rating systems, each of which has subsections for different building and project types and with different program requirements:

- **Building Design and Construction (LEED BD+C)** applies to buildings that are undergoing new construction or major renovations.

(continued on next page)

- **Interior Design and Construction (LEED ID+C)** for projects that are involved in complete interior fit-outs.

- **Building Operations and Maintenance (LEED O+M)** for existing buildings that are undergoing improvements or little to no construction.

- **Neighborhood Development (LEED ND)** for new land development projects or redevelopment projects containing residential uses, nonresidential uses, or a mix. Projects can be at any stage of the development process, from conceptual planning to construction.

- **Homes Design and Construction (LEED Homes)** for single-family, low- or mid-rise multi-family residential to six stories.

All rating systems are made up of three components:

- Mandatory prerequisites that must be met in order for a project to be eligible to apply for LEED certification.

- Credit categories that are divided into optional tasks or goals, each of which has a point value.

- Points awarded for successfully meeting optional tasks or goals. The total number of points determines the LEED certification level.

Credits are at the heart of all the rating systems and each of them (except for LEED for Neighborhood Development, which is unique) has **8** performance credit categories including:

- Sustainable sites
- Water efficiency
- Energy and atmosphere
- Materials and resources

- Indoor environmental quality
- Location and transportation
- Innovation
- Regional priority

Each credit category is made up of multiple credits, which have point values. The total number of points earned determines the LEED certification level. (For information on the steps required to LEED-certify a building see Appendix C.)

LEED has shown the market that green buildings don't necessarily mean new construction. There is a vast, untapped market for the renovation of existing buildings and many owners recognize the potential for cost-saving opportunities in implementing upgrades. Buildings across the nation use LEED to certify these upgrades. The Empire State Building, built in 1931 and perhaps America's most iconic building, is an example. This 2.5 million square foot building was awarded a LEED Gold certificate for efforts to improve its energy performance. The replacement of windows, the addition of variable speed drives on existing air-conditioning chillers, barriers at radiators to reflect heat back into the space, and opening up subdivided spaces to increase natural light were methods used to gain energy cost savings in excess of 30% per year. See Chapter 9 for additional information on this project. (It's interesting to note that the Empire State Building is a youngster compared to the Sede Centrale, at the University of Venice in Italy. This Gothic palazzo overlooking the Grand Canal was built in 1453. It received LEED certification in 2013 and, at more than 550 years, is the oldest building in the world to have done so.[9])

Residential properties are candidates for renovation as well. A 100-year-old single-family house in Venice CA, was renovated with the goal of reducing its footprint through energy, water, and material efficiency and restoring natural habitats.

Augusta Quirk/Duvivier Architects

Before and after shots of a renovated 1912 Craftsman Cottage that received a LEED Platinum certificate

The first floor of this LEED Platinum house was opened up, with an increase in natural light. Features such as high-efficiency appliances and lighting, 2x6 framing and high-performance insulation, and solar panels on the roof to generate electricity make it substantially more energy efficient than the average California residence. It also incorporated extensive use of reclaimed and recycled materials, two cisterns for rainwater collection, and a greywater recycling system. (As noted in Chapter 2, greywater is wastewater that does not contain human waste.)

Although LEED is the most widely used green building rating system in the United States and, until 2013 was the only third-party certification system used on federal buildings, it is not the only one. Green Globes, a newer building assessment program with many fewer certified buildings, is making efforts to increase its profile. The program has a narrower focus than does LEED, and focuses primarily on commercial and institutional buildings.

 **Green Globes®**
www.thegbi.org/green-globes

Green Globes (GG) was developed in Canada and launched in the United States in 2004 and is distributed and managed by the Green Building Initiative (GBI), headquartered in Portland OR. GG is an online assessment tool and building rating system with three programs used in the United States:

- Green Globes for New Construction (NC) for new construction and major renovations

- Green Globes for Existing Buildings (EB) for capital improvement projects or the implementation of best practices and including CIEB Healthcare for the Healthcare Industry

- Green Globes Sustainable Interiors (SI) for interior fit-outs

The Green Globes rating systems use a 1000-point scale that assesses buildings in several environmental assessment areas with criteria weighted according to impact on the environment. Similar to LEED, each assessment area has an assigned number of points that vary depending upon the program being used. Third-party Green Globes assessors work with project teams to review documentation, answer questions, conduct on-site building assessments, and offer suggestions.

As an example, Table 4.3 identifies the seven environmental assessment areas used for buildings rated under Green Globes for New Construction.

Green Globes does not use prerequisites as does LEED. This means that an approach that might be required in LEED gives points under Green Globes. For example, it is a LEED prerequisite that indoor water use be reduced by 20% from code-regulated fixtures; this is not required in Green Globes, which awards a

Table 4.3 Assessment Areas—Green Globes New Construction (NC) Rating System*

Environmental Assessment Area	Possible Points	Focus
Project Management	50	Focused on several management issues including integrated design, performance goals, environmental management during construction (e.g., indoor air quality), and commissioning
Site	115	Location of the project, ecological impacts, stormwater management, landscaping, exterior light pollution
Energy	390	Building performance, metering, measurement and verifiction, envelope, lighting, HVAC systems and controls, equipment efficiencies, renewable energy sources,energy efficient transportation (e.g., public transit, bicycles)
Water	110	Consumption and equipment, treatment, alternate water sources, metering, irrigation requirements
Materials and Resources	125	Building assembly, interior fit-outs, reuse, waste, building service life plan, resource conservation, building envelope
Emissions	50	Heating, ozone-depleting potential for cooling system, global warming potential
Indoor Environment	160	Assessment of ventilation, source control and measurement, lighting design and systems, thermal comfort, acoustic comfort

* For detailed information, see Green Globes for New Construction Technical Reference Manual v. 1.3.

maximum of 24 points for reducing water use from a specified baseline. Or LEED projects are required to develop and implement a construction and demolition waste management plan that includes waste diversion, but there is no prerequisite for Green Globes; project teams may choose whether to earn points for diverting waste from a landfill.[10]

Where it is impossible for a project to meet certain criteria or where assessment areas are not within the scope of the project, these can be marked "not applicable." For example, if a project has no oil-fired furnace (as part of the heating

(continued on next page)

compliance pathway under the emissions assessment area) then points related to oil-fired furnaces would be non-applicable. Green Globes certification is based on the percentages of base points adjusted for any non-applicable credits, and it has four certification levels, one Green Globe (35–54%), two Green Globes (55–69%), three Green Globes (70–84%), and four Green Globes, with four being the highest with 85–100% of available points being earned.

Unlike most LEED projects, in which a project completes its documentation and then submits it online for review by a team without direct contact with the project, Green Globes works with a Green Globes Assessor who reviews all construction documents, conducts a site visit, writes a 15–20 page report and recommends a certification level. GBI then reviews all the documentation and provides the actual certification.[11]

Comparing LEED and Green Globes

LEED and Green Globes are both building rating systems. There are similarities but also differences between them. Both use third-party certification and are based on the Building Research Environmental Assessment Method (BREEAM) developed in Great Britain and Canada. Both aim to deliver healthy, comfortable, sustainable buildings that consider a range of factors such as environmental impacts, energy and water use, day lighting and natural ventilation, indoor air quality, and other factors. The differences between the two systems center primarily on process, transparency, cost, and criteria. LEED offers rating systems for a broader spectrum of project types than does Green Globes, including homes and neighborhoods. LEED has many more certified buildings than does Green Globes and a significant worldwide presence; Green Globes is used in the United States and Canada. The U.S. General Services Administration and the U.S. Department of Defense have identified both Green Globes and LEED as the only two recommended third-party certification systems for the buildings owned and operated by the federal government; this will likely result in an increase in the number of buildings using Green Globes. Green Globes NC is the only system based on an ANSI standard, GBI/ANSI-2010 Green Building Assessment Protocol for Nonresidential Buildings, and is currently being updated via an ANSI process. (As noted earlier, ANSI certifies standards and codes that are developed according to a set of procedures such as accountability/transparency and consensus.)

Both systems have their critics. Green Globes has had to defend itself against concerns that it was undermining sustainable practices through its accommodation to the timber and chemical industries, members of which were involved in its founding and several of whom sit on the GBI Board of Directors. These criticisms are focused on concerns regarding what some view as maneuvering to get LEED banned at both the state and federal levels because of its more stringent sustainability requirements and incentives.

Despite LEED's success in bringing green approaches into the marketplace, it has its critics too: some people accuse it of being more about earning points than achieving actual environmental performance. The point system for LEED can reward projects for doing the "easy stuff" that makes it possible to game the system. For example, in the LEED 2009 version, restoring a formerly contaminated "brownfield" is worth one point; so is providing bicycle storage.[12] To address this concern, changes in the point totals from version 2.2 to version 3 and additional advances in version 4 have placed more weight on points with higher environmental impact.

LEED has been criticized for being cumbersome and costly. Green Globes has to date done a better job of simplifying the certification process, reducing overall certification costs, and providing better customer support.

The cost of using a rating system varies based on project type and size, scope, team experience, and goals. According to a comparative analysis of LEED and Green Globes, while the latter currently has higher up-front fees (due primarily to the cost of the third-party Assessor[13]), LEED documentation takes more time so documentation costs tend to outweigh fees. For most projects, LEED is likely to cost more overall.[14]

The Living Building Challenge (LBC), which, like LEED and Green Globes, is a performance-based assessment program, is possibly the most rigorous and ambitious performance standard in the world.[15] The program was developed and refined during the 1990s and 2000s and the first projects were certified through the International Living Building Institute (now the International Living Future Institute) in 2010. We'll look at Living Building Challenge below.

 **LIVING BUILDING CHALLENGE**

Living Building Challenge℠

http://living-future.org/lbc

The LBC building rating program is based on the belief that current green design is largely one of reducing negative impacts and that what is instead needed is a fundamental change in how we design and build: the only truly sustainable building is one that can give back more than it receives.

Under the Living Building Challenge program, projects can achieve three types of certification: Net Zero Energy Building Certification, Petal Certification, and, the most difficult to attain, Living Building Challenge Certification. In the latter, all requirements are mandatory, including that buildings generate their own energy and process their own waste, that no off-site water is used, and that certain toxic materials and chemicals, including polyvinyl chloride (PVC), formaldehyde, volatile organic compounds (VOCs), and 18 others, are not used. Certification is performance-based and is awarded on actual, rather than modeled or anticipated, performance. Projects must therefore be operational and monitored for at least 12 consecutive months prior to evaluation. The Living Building Challenge Certification is so difficult to get that very few buildings have reached this level. In Chapter 2, we saw the 2,500 square foot Smith College Bechtel Environmental Classroom, which is one. Another is the Bullitt Center, a six-story 50,000 square foot office building (located in downtown Seattle), which, in April 2015, became the first office building to earn Living Challenge Building Certification.

Joe Mabel

As with every building that receives the highest level of certification in the LBC program, 100% of the energy used at the Bullitt Center is generated by renewable energy systems on-site. Rainwater is collected, stored, and treated on-site and, with reclaimed greywater, provides 100% of the building's water needs; all human waste is composted; and, among many other features, all workstations are within

The Bullitt Center under construction

30 feet of large operable windows, offering all workers access to fresh air and natural daylight. According to Denis Hayes, president and CEO of the Bullitt Foundation,

> *"We generate as much electricity as we use from solar panels on our roof, so society doesn't have to build a new power plant. We capture rainwater for all purposes... so society doesn't need to build a new reservoir. We use composting toilets so society doesn't need to build new sewage treatment capacity. We return treated greywater to the soil on site, reducing the need for stormwater drains. These social benefits matter, even if our economy doesn't currently choose to value them."* [16]

In 2014, the Bullitt Center produced 60% more energy from solar panels on its roof than it used, largely due to efficiencies that exceeded expectations, making it the most energy-efficient office building in the United States and possibly in the world, an especially remarkable feat considering the building is located in the cloudiest major city in the contiguous states.[17]

Other rating systems

LEED, Green Globes, and the Living Building Challenge are not the only certification programs. Others include:

- National Green Building Standard (NGBS)
- Energy Star
- PHIUS+
- HERS

ANSI/NAHB/ICC 700 – National Green Building Standard (NGBS)

www.homeinnovation.com

The National Green Building Standard was launched in 2007 and is the first point-based rating system for green residential construction, remodeling, and land development to be approved by ANSI. It is administered by the Home Innovation Research Labs (formerly the NAHB

Research Center), an independent subsidiary of the National Association of Home Builders (NAHB). NGBS certifies that a single-family home, apartment building, or land development (as long as some of the parcels will eventually be developed with residential buildings) is designed and built to achieve high performance in six areas: site, resource efficiency, water efficiency, energy efficiency, indoor air quality, and building operation and maintenance.

The NGBS was developed as a standard by the NAHB and the International Code Council. NGBS uses a mix of mandatory and discretionary practices. Points are awarded and projects may be certified in one of four levels (Bronze, Silver, Gold, or Emerald certification level, depending on the number of green practices). As of 2015, almost 50,000 homes had been certified under this program.[18]

Energy Star Certified
Buildings and (Industrial) Plants
www.energystar.gov/buildings

Many readers will be familiar with the blue energy star label that is awarded to home appliances such as washing machines and dryers that meet a certain energy-efficiency baseline (see Chapter 5.) Energy Star is also an energy-rating program for residential and commercial buildings. Developed by the U.S. Department of Energy and U.S. Environmental Protection Agency, Energy Star focuses on energy performance; it does not evaluate the impact of other factors such as materials, indoor air quality, or recycling. The system compares the energy performance of a particular building to that of a national stock of similar buildings. Many state and municipal governments have adopted Energy Star as a minimum design and construction requirement for energy, and Energy Star homes are typically 20–30% more energy efficient than standard homes.[19] (Energy Star ratings are used as benchmarks for meeting the **2030 Challenge**, a call from the independent, nonprofit organization Architecture 2030 to the design and construction communities to commit that all new and renovated buildings will, on average, produce as much energy as they use— zero net energy—by 2030.)

Phius+ Passive House

www.passivehouse.us

The **PHIUS+** certification program is a leading passive building certification program in North America. The program was developed by the Passive House Institute US (PHIUS), initially affiliated with the International Passive House Institute in Germany. Certification rests on the use of "passive design," which means:

- The building has continuous insulation through its entire envelope without any **thermal bridging**. (Thermal bridging occurs when a poorly insulated area allows a path for heat to transfer. The studs in an insulated wall are an example.)

- The building envelope is extremely airtight, preventing infiltration of outside air and loss of conditioned air.

- High-performance windows (typically triple-paned) and doors are specified.

- The building uses some form of heat- and moisture-recovery ventilation and a minimal space conditioning system.

- The increase in interior temperatures from solar radiation (called solar gain) is managed to maximize it when required for heating and to exclude it in the hotter months.

A structure built or renovated to PHIUS standards is exceptionally energy efficient, comfortable, and quiet, with good indoor air quality. PHIUS+ combines passive design verification with a stringent Quality Assurance and Quality Control (QA/QC) program on-site. Project testing and inspections are conducted by specialized PHIUS+ Raters and the on-site inspections and testing help assure PHIUS and the project teams that a building will perform as designed. As a result of a collaboration with the U.S. Department of Energy, PHIUS+ certification also earns U.S.DOE Zero Energy Ready Home status under a program designed to identify homes that generate as much energy on-site as they use. Certification for larger projects earn Energy Star designation.

The Trolle residence, a 1,650 square foot, three bedroom single-family house in a cold northeast location, is built to PHIUS+ standards and includes a frost-protected foundation with a concrete slab insulated to R-58 and triple-insulated exterior walls (insulated 2x6 studs, taped plywood sheathing to make the structure air tight, with two layers of rigid insulation over the top), which resulted in a wall insulated to an R-value three times greater than code minimums. The attic space, deemed too small for storage, was filled with 24 inches of blown-in cellulose, with an insulating value up to R-86. The majority of the heating load is satisfied by internal and solar radiation, although the house also has a one-ton, air-source heat pump; an energy recovery ventilator augments ventilation. The owner/builder is happy: "...it cost my family only

Michael Trolle

A certified Passive House in Connecticut

$200 worth of electricity to heat the ... house this winter, with the interior temperature at 70°, day and night. A high level of comfort was assured because the interior surface temperature of the floors, walls, and roof was the same as the room air temperature, and air leakage was nonexistent. It's a night and day comparison to conventional code-based construction."[20]

Home Energy Rating System (HERS)

Concerned specifically with the energy-efficiency of homes, HERS was developed by the nonprofit Residential Energy Services Network (RESNET), a standards-making organization for building energy efficiency rating systems. RESNET developed the HERS energy-use index that measures a home's energy efficiency. A certified RESNET Home Energy Rater assesses the energy efficiency of a home, assigning it a relative performance score (the HERS Index Score); the lower the score the more energy efficient it is. To put this in perspective, the U.S. Department of Energy has determined that a typical resale home scores 130 on the HERS Index while a home built to the 2004 International Energy Conservation Code is rated at 100. For more information see *http://www.resnet.us/energy-rating*.

Infrastructure rating systems

There are several rating systems that certify green infrastructure projects; Greenroads is one. This program is designed to measure roadway sustainability practices such as the recycled content of materials, the use of porous pavement, and energy-efficient street lighting. Its first project, in Bellingham WA, was certified in 2012. Among the project components are recycled porcelain aggregates (made from crushed toilets), porous pavement, and LED lights. Several other statewide rating systems have been developed including the Illinois Livability and Sustainable Transportation Tool (I-LAST) and GreenLITES (Green Leadership in Transportation and Environmental Sustainability) in New York, which is a self-certification program.

Although there are isolated rating systems such as the previous, there is currently no rating system comparable to LEED for assessing the sustainability of infrastructure projects. The Institute for Sustainable Infrastructure (ISI) hopes to change this with its Envision Sustainable Infrastructure Rating System developed in conjunction with Harvard University. Envision provides guidance for infrastructure and civil works projects during planning and design and quantifies sustainability for completed projects. Several projects have been awarded Envision certification, including a pipeline project in Texas, a fish hatchery in Alaska, and a stormwater project in Los Angeles.[21]

International rating systems

Although there is currently no global rating system, there are efforts to develop common metrics that will help compare buildings in different cities around the world.[22] Many countries including Japan, Australia, United Arab Emirates, Germany, South Africa, Brazil, China, India and others, however, have introduced their own rating systems over the past few years. Although these systems vary, many of them can be traced back to LEED and its U.K. model BREEAM.

The expansion of assessment tools has followed the development of the World Green Building Council (WGBC), a worldwide network of green building councils, including the U.S. Green Building Council. Since its founding in 1999, the WGBC has become the world's largest international organization influencing green building, and now represents and assists green building councils in more than 90 countries.[23]

Summary

As we've seen, codes and standards are not the same. Codes outline legal requirements that must be met and have mandatory provisions. Standards typically identify industry requirements such as quality, testing, capacity, compatibility, and performance. Some standards, such as the International Energy Conservation Code (IECC) and ASHRAE 90.1 are crafted as model codes that can be adopted by jurisdictions (which may not have the technical and financial resources to develop their own codes). Codes are typically adjusted to meet local needs and concerns.

Neither conventional standards nor codes provide information on how a project is performing or its environmental impact. Green rating systems help fill this need and play an important role in developing a common way to talk about green design and construction. Some green rating systems assess a variety of environmental issues that together measure overall building performance. LEED, Green Globes, and Living Building Challenge are examples. There are also single-attribute green rating systems such as Energy Star and HERS that rate the energy performance of buildings. All of these voluntary standards are strategies for improving building and energy performance. This knowledge is having an impact on codes and on public expectations regarding best practices. It is becoming increasingly necessary for those in the building trades to understand changing code requirements as well as the influence that codes, standards, and green rating systems are having on best practices. Even if an owner does not choose to have their building certified as green through a formal program, the inefficiencies of the past are rarely acceptable today.

The expanding market for green buildings has driven a corresponding market for green materials and products. New products arrive on the market daily, sometimes with confusing and vague claims, which can make it difficult to determine the true characteristics and quality of a product. Standards play an important role in sorting through the confusion and providing metrics to assist the general public and contractors in making informed choices. In the next chapter, we'll look at product characteristics and some of the resources available to contractors and designers to assist them in making sense of this aspect of green buildings.

Glossary

2030 Challenge—a call to the design and construction communities that all new and renovated buildings will be zero net energy by 2030.

ANSI (American National Standards Institute)—certifies standards developed by other organizations.

ASHRAE (American Society of Heating, Refrigerating and Air-Conditioning Engineers)—a source of technical standards for the HVAC industry.

ASTM International (formerly American Society for Testing and Materials)—develops standards for a wide range of products, materials, and systems.

Authority having jurisdiction (AHJ)—an agency such as a city's building department with jurisdiction over a project.

BREEAM (Building Research Establishment Environmental Assessment Method)—developed in 1990 by the Building Research Establishment in Great Britain, a design and assessment method for sustainable buildings; it was the model for LEED.

Building codes—mandatory requirements that promote safe practices in the design and construction of buildings.

Certification—a document used to demonstrate that a product, system, or building has met certain performance criteria.

Energy Star—an energy-rating program for residential and commercial buildings developed by the U.S. Department of Energy and the U.S. Environmental Protection Agency.

Green Globes—building assessment programs for new and existing buildings, distributed and managed by the Green Building Initiative.

Green rating systems—programs designed to measure the environmental and social impact of products, systems, and buildings.

Home Energy Rating System (HERS)—a residential energy-use index developed by Residential Energy Services Network (RESNET).

ICC (International Code Council)—an association that develops coordinated building safety and fire prevention model codes and standards, including the International Green Construction Code (IGCC).

Interior fit-out—the process of making interior space suitable for use (also called build-out).

LEED (Leadership in Energy and Environmental Design)—a voluntary green building certification program developed by the U.S. Green Building Council and administered by the Green Building Certification Institute (GBCI) that recognizes best-in-class building strategies and practices. LEED includes a suite of green building rating systems as well as professional credentials.

Living Building Challenge—building certification programs developed by the International Living Future Institute.

NAHB (National Association of Home Builders)—a trade and membership association that helps promote housing policies.

National Green Building Standard—a point-based rating system for green residential construction, remodeling, and land development developed by the National Association of Home Builders and the International Code Council and ANSI-approved.

PHIUS+—a passive building certification program

Plug-load—the energy drawn by unregulated appliances and products.

Standards—guidelines developed as a way to measure the quality or characteristics of something. Standards may be adopted as mandatory codes.

Thermal bridging—a heat-loss situation that occurs when one area has significantly higher heat transfer capability than the surrounding area.

UL (Underwriters Laboratories)—an organization that writes testing standards and certifies products for safety.

Green Materials and Products

It's not possible to rethink how we build without also considering the materials and products used. In earlier chapters we looked at some of the programs available to measure building performance and energy efficiency. Assessment tools such as LEED define a building's potential impact on the environment, on workers, and on end-users, and assist the construction team in decision-making. Building performance is dependent on several factors including site orientation, design, and construction practices, and, perhaps equally important, the selection of products and materials. This chapter reviews the obstacles faced by contractors and others in choosing building products—from sealants and adhesives to air handling equipment—that meet stringent material and performance requirements. It also considers resources available to help sort through the sometimes confusing and vague claims made about the new (and often untested) products that seem to hit the market weekly.

Materials and products have changed dramatically since the Industrial Revolution. During the 19th and early 20th centuries, we moved away from the use of natural, minimally processed, and locally available materials to a construction industry dependent on processed, engineered, and synthetic materials and products. By the mid-20th century, buildings that soared into the sky and used products such as curtain walls, sheet glass, poured concrete, elevators, and central heating and air conditioning were common all over the world.

Along with new materials and construction practices came an explosion in chemical discoveries, especially following World War II. As noted in earlier chapters, many building components were developed that depend on synthetic chemicals to provide desired characteristics such as durability, strength, adhesion, and flexibility. Their use is now common in everything from coatings to roofing membranes, insulation, piping, vapor barriers, flame retardants, wood preservatives, and more.

Oregon Dept. of Transportation

The construction and manufacturing industries understand the potential risks associated with materials such as asbestos, lead, and formaldehyde, and are responding. There has been a huge increase in the availability of products that incorporate green characteristics. Not only are builders and their clients demanding them, but regulations are also requiring them.[1] Several states have regulations limiting the use of volatile organic compounds in construction, panel and floor covering adhesives, and general purpose adhesives, for example. In addition, some voluntary green building assessment programs, such as LEED and the Living Building Challenge, impose restrictions on the use of materials and products that are toxic. As concerns over the health implications associated with certain materials have grown, so too have liability concerns.[2] This creates an added emphasis on the use of green materials.

The choice of suitable products for high-performance building projects can be confusing and challenging. This chapter explores what is meant by green materials and products, reviews some of the difficulties inherent in product selection, and reviews resources available to clarify the process.

What are green materials and products?

Materials are the substances from which a thing is or can be made. Materials may be used in a stand-alone manner (such as wood, for example) or may be the elements or ingredients of a product. For example, gypsum is a raw material in the product drywall; calcium, iron, and sand are three of the materials from which the product cement is made.

There are no clear definitions nor a consensus on the criteria for determining if a product is green; any material or product can be called "green" if it possesses the right attributes. What are these attributes and what characteristics distinguish a green product from its conventional counterpart? The characteristics are similar to those used to define a high-performance building:

- The product is renewable or from well-managed operations (such as wood grown in a sustainable-managed forest) that aren't disruptive to local social or environmental systems.

- It does not contain synthetic chemicals that are harmful to people and animals.

- It is made from salvaged or recycled materials.

- It reduces or eliminates the use of fossil fuels throughout its life cycle.

- It is locally or regionally available (to reduce lengthy shipping and the associated energy and pollution costs).

- It is durable, low maintenance, and reusable, recyclable, or compostable at the end of its use.

The challenge in product selection

Using a checklist of green characteristics is an imprecise way to determine if a product is truly sustainable because there are multiple issues and complications in the selection of green materials and products. These complications pose challenges for the specifier. For example, is a product that is recyclable better than one which contains no toxic chemicals? Is a manufactured product with superior durability always more desirable than one with a shorter life span? Is a product made from renewable materials better than one that is locally manufactured?

To add to the difficulty, a product that appears green may not necessarily be superior to a conventional product. Low-e windows provide us with an example: low-emissivity windows that reduce the transfer of heat are typically considered superior to traditional windows because of their insulating properties. But their defining characteristic is typically achieved with a metallic additive[3] that renders the glass difficult, if not impossible, to recycle. Does that mean it is less green than a traditionally made window that theoretically *could* be recycled? Or if you are tasked with selecting a sustainable carpet, is it better to choose pure wool carpet made without pesticides and chemical dyes or recycled nylon carpeting, which keeps plastic out of landfills? Some products are made from multiple materials, with variable characteristics, complicating the selection process.

Adding to the challenge is the large number of new products flooding the market and claiming to be green. The good news is there is lots of innovation occurring in the market, but the bad news is that some manufacturer claims regarding products are vague, and the specifier is left to sift through mounds of data to determine which product best meets the application requirements.

Greenwashing

Greenwashing is a term that refers to the practice of misrepresenting or "spinning" the environmental benefits of a product (or structure). Sometimes the misrepresentation is based on unsubstantiated facts ("Buy this green widget—it's biodegradable!") and sometimes the green claim is based on a single green attribute ("Our widget is green—we use biodegradable packaging"). Some claims are obviously false. For example, "This product is LEED and NAHB certified." (Neither USGBC's LEED program or the NAHB certifies products.) Sometimes a claim is irrelevant or too generic, for example, "This product uses the latest eco-friendly technology." Or, perhaps, the claim only addresses one feature of the product when there are other important ones that are ignored. For example, "This product is maintenance free."[4]

The selection process for green products is the same as for conventional products with the additional challenge of sorting through the claims made by manufacturers for new, and perhaps unfamiliar, green products. Briefly, here are the steps required by the contractor or product specifier:

- Define broad material/product categories. (The Construction Specifications Institute's **MasterFormat** is a commonly used tool for organizing projects into such categories, for example: concrete, masonry, metals, wood, thermal protection, doors and windows).

• Identify performance criteria that match the green requirements for the project (for example, products that contribute to good indoor air quality, or products that are durable and recyclable at the end of their use, or products that do not contain certain toxic materials).

• Research available products; greener options are available for most conventional materials.[5] Many green products are listed in conventional product references such as *Sweets' Construction Building Materials Directory*. Several references specifically for green products are also available, including: Green Seal, Green2Green, Green Home Guide, and others.

• Gather and evaluate technical data from product representatives, government codes and sources (including local, state, and federal codes and agencies such as the U.S. Department of Energy, Environmental Protection Agency, and OSHA, the Occupational Safety and Health Administration under the Department of Labor), professional and trade organizations such as USGBC, the Carpet and Rug Institute, and publications such as *Environmental Building News, GreenSource* magazine, BuildingGreen.com, and others. Labeling and product certifications such as environmental product declarations and others, provide important information, too.

• Select (and document as required) the product that most closely meets program criteria.

Many green products and systems are new and untested in real-world applications and, consequently, some don't perform as well as anticipated. As a result, there is a "friction in the system" that requires a certain amount of trial and error. The message is, do your homework when specifying materials, but don't let the friction stop the innovation.[6]

Green labels and product certifications

Statements regarding the characteristics of a product traditionally come from the manufacturer. As noted, with the increased demand for green products has come an increase in the number of products, some with eco-friendly names and unsubstantiated sustainability claims. Contractors and other product specifiers are demanding data beyond manufacturers claims to ensure that products meet increasingly stringent performance requirements. Labels and certifications are tools designed to meet this demand.

There are currently different product labeling and certification programs that issue various types of information, based on various criteria, and representing different levels of reliability, thoroughness, and independence. Some programs provide information on a single green attribute (for example, a product's recycled content or percentage of volatile organic compounds), while others (such as Cradle to Cradle) look at multiple attributes and may use a process called life-cycle assessment to determine product characteristics (discussion to follow). Some labeling programs conform to a green standard from an organization such as ASHRAE or to the requirements of a green building rating program such as LEED (for example, the Forest Stewardship Council that labels wood products). Some are developed by trade organizations (for example, labels issued by the Carpet and Rug Institute). Some programs mix different characteristics. For example, Master Painters Institute (MPI) partners with Green Seal (a nonprofit organization) to provide certification of recycled paint, for which Green Seal verifies the environmental attributes (such as no harmful ingredients) while MPI verifies performance.[7]

Labels can help demystify the green product specification process.

Green labels and certifications are based on standards or on statements of green attributes. As discussed in the last chapter, green standards may be created by trade organizations for products in their area of expertise (for example, the Carpet and Rug Institute that sets product emission standards for carpets, cushions, and adhesives), by nonprofit organizations such as the Forest Stewardship Council (with standards that cover wood resources and the management of associated lands), by government agencies, and by standards writing organizations such as ASTM, the International Code Council, and others. Some retail companies develop their own green standards and associated green labels; Home Depot's Eco Options label is an example. According to the Home Depot website:

> *Every product with the Eco Options label has less of an impact on the environment than competing products. Specifically, Eco Options products offer one or more of the following benefits: Energy Efficient, Water Conservation, Healthy Home, Clean Air and Sustainable Forestry.*

The most trustworthy labels or certifications are those awarded by an independent third-party that has no business or monetary relationship with a product's manufacturer or a building's contractor, designer, or specifier. **Third-party certifiers** review the manufacturing process of a product and independently determine whether the product complies with specific standards for safety, quality, or performance, and generally provide a transparent, open, and clear system that standardizes how certification is awarded. The previous chapter reviewed several third-party certification systems for buildings, including LEED, Green Globes, and Living Building Challenge. There are also third-party certification programs for products such as Green Seal. These and several other well-regarded programs are listed in Table 5.1.

Table 5.1 Examples of Product Labels and Certifications

NAME	CERTIFYING ORGANIZATION	CHARACTERISTICS
ENERGY STAR®	U.S. Environmental Protection Agency (EPA) *www.energystar.gov*	Energy Star is a program of the U.S. Environmental Protection Agency and helps consumers identify energy efficient products. This label means that a product meets higher energy efficient standards than others in its category. The Energy Star label is found on many products such as air conditioners, hot water tanks, and washing machines. Products are tested and reviewed by EPA-recognized third-parties.
FSC®	Forest Stewardship Council® *www.fscus.org*	FSC is a third-party certification program that addresses numerous aspects of sustainable forestry, including ecological functions, old-growth forests, plantations, restoration, native habitat, indigenous people's rights, and sound management for timber production. FSC issues three types of certifications: forest management, chain of custody, and controlled wood. Certification is issued through FSC-recognized third-parties.

(continued on next page)

Table 5.1 Examples of Product Labels and Certifications *(continued)*

NAME	CERTIFYING ORGANIZATION	CHARACTERISTICS
Sustainable Forest Initiative® SUSTAINABLE FORESTRY INITIATIVE SFI-01639	SFI *www.aboutsfi.org*	Originally a program developed by the American Forest & Paper Association (AF&PA), SFI has distanced itself from this organization and has become a third-party certification program to promote responsible forest management. The program is managed by an independent nonprofit, with third-party auditors carrying out certification.
Green Seal® GREEN SEAL	Green Seal *www.greenseal.org*	Green Seal is a third-party certifier of a variety of building products: paints, adhesives, lamps, chillers, windows, cleaners, and more. Certification considers product impacts over the entire life cycle of a product. LEED points can be earned by using certain Green Seal products.
WaterSense® look for WaterSense Meets EPA Criteria	Environmental Protection Agency *www.epa.gov/ watersense*	Modeled after Energy Star, the EPA's WaterSense program labels products that conserve water and seeks to educate consumers about water efficiency. Low-flow toilets and motion-activated faucets are examples of the products labeled. Third-party licensed certifying bodies verify that a product meets EPA performance standards.
SCSglobal SERVICES Setting the standard for sustainability™	SCS Global Systems *www.scsglobalser-vices.com*	Provides third-party environmental and sustainability certification, auditing, testing, and standards development. Programs span a cross-section of industries; the Green Products Guide on its website has a directory of certified products.
GREENGUARD™ GREENGUARD PRODUCT CERTIFIED FOR LOW CHEMICAL EMISSIONS UL.COM/GG UL 2818 GOLD	UL Environment *www.ul.com*	GREENGUARD a program of UL (see chapter 4), provides third party certification for low chemical-emitting products. All certified products are subject to a review of the manufacturing process and routine testing to ensure minimal impact on the indoor environment.

As noted earlier, product data historically consisted of little more than marketing claims by a manufacturer. Green labels such as those in Table 5.1 that involve independent third-party verification or testing can provide consumers with more confidence as well as increased detail. Information contained in a label can range from the impacts on indoor air quality (such as the CRI Plus label) to an assessment of the product's broad impact over its lifetime

Table 5.1 Examples of Product Labels and Certifications *(continued)*

NAME	CERTIFYING ORGANIZATION	CHARACTERISTICS
FloorScore®	Resilient Floor Coverings Institute (RFC) with SCS Global Services *www.rfci.com*	RFCI created FloorScore for hard-surface flooring and flooring adhesives, and contracted with SCS Global Services to serve as a third-party certifier. In addition to reviewing and authenticating test results, SCS visits manufacturing sites to verify product content and manufacturing procedures.
Indoor Advantage™	SCS Indoor Advantage—Indoor Air Quality *www.scsglobalser-vices.com*	Expanding on its work with FloorScore, since 2005 SCS has been certifying indoor air quality performance for a wide variety of building products and furniture under its Indoor Advantage and its more stringent label, Indoor Advantage Gold.
Cradle to Cradle®	Cradle to Cradle Products Innovation Institute *www.c2ccertified.org*	The Cradle to Cradle Certified program for products does not consider itself a label but a quality mark. A product is certified using a set of criteria in five catego-ries—material health, material reutilization, renewable energy and carbon management, water stewardship, and social fairness—and receives an achievement level in each category—Basic, Bronze, Silver, Gold, or Platinum—with the lowest achievement level repre-senting the product's overall mark. The program seeks to encourage products and systems that are efficient and waste-free. To have a product assessed for certifi-cation, a manufacturer must work with an assessment body that has been accredited by the Cradle to Cradle Products Innovation Institute.

(such as in the Cradle to Cradle label). The bewildering number and types of labels can be very off-putting (additional resources to help sort through it fol-low). The reader is also urged to see *Green Building Materials,* by Ross Spiegel and Dru Meadows, for additional information and resources.

Other product assessment tools

There are several additional material assessment tools. An **environmental product declaration (EPD)** is a detailed report, developed by a manufacturer, that lists product ingredients and environmental impacts that occur over the entire life cycle of a product, and outlines the impacts a product has in a range of environmental categories such as scarce resource depletion, energy use, waste generation, and emissions. EPDs provide information that is usually considered confidential by companies, and provide it in a consistent way.

EPDs are difficult to achieve because they're very data intensive and manufacturers have not always been enthusiastic about participating in programs that require full product disclosures. As pressure mounts to incorporate green materials and products into buildings, however, this reluctance is changing.[8]

One of the values of environmental product declarations is that life-cycle assessments are used to develop their data. A **life-cycle assessment (LCA)** is a technique for evaluating a product's environmental impact from a raw material which is harvested in some way, through a supply chain involving transportation and delivery, through processing and manufacturing, which turns the raw material into a product that is then installed and used. Some time later—days or years or decades—the product reaches the end of its life and is recycled, degrades back into a raw material, or is disposed. This process from beginning to end is called the product's life cycle and information on the environmental impact of a product throughout the entire process are included in an environmental product declaration.

Life-cycle costing (LCC)

With conventional buildings, decisions regarding products and systems are typically made based on up-front purchase and installation cost estimates. Life-cycle assessments (LCA) are used to evaluate the environmental impacts of a product over its lifetime; life-cycle costing (LCC) analyzes *costs* over the entire life of a product. In addition to initial purchase and installation expense, LCC analyses look at operating costs such as fuel, anticipated repair and replacement costs, residual value or costs (such as sale or disposal), finance costs, and more. LCC has been used for many years and has formed the basis for product decisions for many project types.[9] Green products or systems that are chosen for durability and efficiency may cost more initially, but an LCC can often show economic advantage over time.

Eric Vance/US EPA

*Burning carpet sample
to measure combustion
product releases*

The interest in and use of EPDs is growing: as of 2011 France has required that all high-volume consumer products include an EPD label. Other countries, including the United States, are likely to follow.[10]

While the primary function of an EPD is to disclose information on the environmental impacts of materials and products, there are also labels that identify health impacts and product ingredients: Health Product Declarations (HPD) and the Declare product database and label.

The HPD, initiated by the Healthy Building Network and the publisher of BuildingGreen, is a standard format for reporting product content and associated health information for building products and materials. The system is overseen by the HPD Collaborative and the goal is to provide transparent disclosure about product content and for this information be freely available for all to use.[11]

The similar Declare product database from the International Living Future Institute (sponsor of the Living Building Challenge building assessment system) is a program that provides a framework for manufacturers to voluntarily publish ingredients, sources, and manufacturing locations for their products. (Although the International Living Future Institute does not independently verify manufacturer's claims, it requires that a company leader personally attest to the accuracy of the information[12] and it assesses whether a product contains any ingredients listed on the Living Building Challenge red list. The **red list** of 13 of the worst-in-class toxic chemicals and materials commonly found in building materials today identifies chemicals not allowed in projects seeking certification under the Living Building Challenge.) The Declare label can be used with any product. Living Building Challenge project teams can also use the Declare label for materials documentation, streamlining the process of project certification.

The market is in the midst of innovation, testing, and improvement, and it is worth noting that many green products and systems are new and untested, and sometimes don't survive in the real world as well as they did in the lab. This "friction in the system" shouldn't cause you to throw up your hands and walk away, however, but is an argument for doing the necessary homework. HPDs, Declare labels, and EPDs are all disclosure forms that assist in determining if a product meets project performance requirements and are helpful tools in this process.

Other resources

There are multiple web-based sources of information that contractors and others can access for product information. Table 5.2 at right lists some of them.

The look of green products

Some green products may be distinctive (such as solar photovoltaic panels) and some may have certain limitations (such as a limited color palette), but many have been harvested, processed, or manufactured in alternative ways and yet look just like their conventional counterparts. Again, wood is an example: planks that are harvested sustainably are indistinguishable in appearance from those that come from clear-cut forests. Other examples include Portland cement, which is partially made from recycled fly-ash, or the low-e windows that look very much like the leaky, single-glazed versions in your parent's home. As the demand for sustainable products increases, so does their variety: extremely efficient lights, plastics derived from agricultural products, and insulation made from shredded cotton are just a few examples of familiar products that have been updated to meet new market demand.

Table 5.2 Examples of Online Resources

Website	Organization	What It Offers
http://greenspec.build-inggreen.com	BuildingGreen	The *GreenSpec Directory* contains more than 2,000 product listings (with manufacturer's information) that the editors have determined to be in the top tier for environmental attributes. The list is continuously updated. Building Green also sponsors *Environmental Building News,* which features articles and information and reviews products.
www.ahridirectory.org	CEE/AHRI Verified Directory	The Consortium for Energy Efficiency (CEE) and Air-Conditioning Heating and Refrigeration Institute (AHRI) developed the *Directory of Certified Product Performance.* The directory lists residential and small commercial mechanical equipment that, in addition to being Energy Star qualified, meets the higher CEE efficiency standard. Stated efficiencies are verified through AHRI testing.
www.astm.org	ASTM International	ASTM's *Sustainability Standards Listing* is a helpful resource that lists more than 500 ASTM standards, and 300 other standards and programs from organizations involved in building and product sustainability.
www.greensourcecon-struction.com	*Green Source* magazine	A McGraw-Hill publication that covers many aspects of green construction, including products.
www.RateItGreen.com	Rate It Green	A community of users shares opinions that form the product's environmental evaluation; there is a product directory with user reviews and product and manufacturer's information.
www.greenhome-guide.org	U.S. Green Building Council	A site that allows the user to ask questions and get opinions from others in the industry.
www.pharosproject.net	Healthy Building Network	Healthy Building Network was founded to provide resources to reduce the chemicals in building products. They sponsor the Pharos Project, which offers in-depth analysis of health and environmental hazards for building products and materials. The website lists products and rates product certifications. The organization also publishes an online news sheet and has an archive of research work on chemicals and building products.

Although the common thinking is that product specification is strictly in the hands of the designers, the general contractor and specialty trades have an impact on the types of materials and products used in construction. Sealants, adhesives, thinners and solvents, insulation, and drywall compounds are all products that can contain harmful synthetic chemicals and require careful specification. Contractors play a vital role in the selection of such products.

Get ready for visible green

As noted previously, it's not easy to tell if a building is "green." For a variety of reasons, most green buildings and the products within them look quite conventional, but this may change. There is intensive research and development currently under way on new resource-conserving materials and products, and builders may soon be required to price, install, and maintain products with unprecedented characteristics. Products under development include thermally adaptive **building envelopes** that use algae to harvest solar energy, climate-responsive materials that automatically adjust based on relative humidity, exterior surfaces that elongate or contract depending on degree of solar shading required, and microbial homes that use building components to manage, filter, and reuse waste.[13] In the near future, many green buildings will look very unconventional indeed.

Summary

Historically, material selection was limited by what was locally available: adobe, wood, timber, sod, stone, and thatch. As discussed in Chapter 1, the imagination, creativity, and engineering skills of the construction industry enabled us to move beyond the limitations of local materials to create products and buildings that would have been unimaginable to our great-great-grandparents. Today, however, we're in the midst of another shift and, once again, the construction industry is taking the lead. A reevaluation of the materials and products we use in our buildings is creating a vibrant and growing demand for sustainable construction products, assemblies, and systems and contractors are expected to understand what makes a product suitable for use in a high-performance building. Products are no longer chosen based solely on how well they adhere, how easily they are applied, the quality of the manufacturer's warranty, or the purchase price, but also on a range of other characteristics: what is it made of and does it contain chemical toxins; how was it made and what resources will it require during operation; does it include recycled content, is it durable, and can it be recycled at the end of its life? Green buildings will require contractors to know the answers to these questions.

Contractors face a rapidly changing market, with new and sometimes unfamiliar products, conflicting claims, and lack of transparency and uniformity. Even when a building does not need to meet specific certification requirements (such as LEED or Green Globes), best practices and client expectations are requiring both efficient and healthy products.

Glossary

Building envelope—the physical separators between the parts of a building that are heated and cooled (conditioned) and those parts that are not.

Environmental product declaration (EPD)—a detailed report developed by a manufacturer that lists product ingredients and environmental impacts that occur over the entire life cycle of a product.

Green building materials and products—an imprecise term that describes materials and products that have certain efficiency and other attributes.

Greenwashing—the practice of misrepresenting or "spinning" the environmental benefits of a product (or structure).

Health Product Declaration (HPD)—a standard format for reporting product content and associated health information for building products and materials.

Life-cycle assessment (LCA)—an analysis of the environmental impacts of a product over its entire lifetime.

Life-cycle costing (LCC)—an analysis of costs over the entire life of a product.

MasterFormat—an organizational tool developed by the Construction Specifications Institute.

Material—a substance that serves as the raw matter from which a product is made (e.g., silicon is a raw material of PV cells).

Red list—a list of 13 toxic chemicals and materials commonly found in building materials today, which are not allowed in projects seeking certification under the Living Building Challenge.

Third-party certifiers—independent product evaluators.

Testing solar technologies at the National Renewable Energy Laboratory (NREL) Solar Technology Acceleration Center (SolarTAC)

Dennis Schroeder (NREL)

6

The Economic Benefits of Green Buildings

Some readers may be skeptical about the arguments made in this book and elsewhere for changes in the way we design and build our structures and that "green" is the right approach. Others might argue that massive change is inevitable and imminent, and that "green" building is merely the first evidence of coming transformation.

Regardless of personal inclinations, there is a strong case to be made for the economic links between the construction industry and sustainability. Look at the data: in 2005, green building was valued at $10 billion; in just six years, this number had grown to $78 billion. By the time you're reading this, green building will likely be valued at more than $200 billion.[1] This represents a lot of employment throughout the construction industry. Although the vast majority of our built environment isn't built to sustainable standards, green buildings represent an ever-larger portion of construction work. In addition, continued growth in the volume of green building is reported in all sectors of the industry.[2]

As already noted in previous chapters, there are various issues that drive the development of high-performance buildings. As recently as 2008, "doing the right thing" and an idealistic impulse to have a positive impact[3] were primary. This has changed and, although idealism is still a motivator, building green is increasingly a bottom-line business decision. The economic benefits may be straightforward such as saving money on a utility bill or more complex and hidden such as the dollars saved when worker productivity goes up or health care costs go down.

Economic benefits occur both during the construction process and once a building is occupied. Immediate benefits include the creation of jobs, improved worker health, reduced material and waste disposal costs, tax credits, density bonuses, and other incentives for developers. Reduced operating costs, improved worker productivity, and increased property values and rental incomes all contribute to a positive bottom line.

The creation of construction industry jobs

The demand for green buildings creates employment opportunities: between 2000 and 2008, green construction equaled more than $100 billion in wages; in the following five years, that number tripled.[4] Of more than 3.4 million people in the United States working on green jobs as of March 2013, many of them were in construction.[5] Dozens of professions affected both directly and indirectly by construction—from plumbers and electricians to truckers to product manufacturers and suppliers—can benefit from the growth in green construction. The manufacture and installation of energy-efficient products and assemblies; the production, transmission, and distribution of renewable power; sewage and water treatment systems; pollution prevention; and environmental cleanup are some of the areas that are being impacted. Jobs in the green economy are linked to both new and renovated work in all sectors of the industry and require varying levels of education, from high school and technical training, through college and beyond.[6]

Jobs and green—not everyone agrees

Some argue that instead of adding jobs, switching from fossil fuels to subsidized renewable energy will reduce economic growth and, despite adding work in the construction industry, will result in fewer jobs overall.[7] For information on this perspective, see papers from the libertarian-leaning Cato Institute, including the writings of Jonathan A. Lesser and Patrick J. Michaels.

In addition to direct employment benefits, we know that lots of these jobs are here at home: 50% of parts for wind turbines are American-made, for example, along with 90% of energy-efficient materials such as HVAC systems, siding, and refrigerators.[8] Improved energy-efficiency measures, the installation of renewable energy systems, and increased waste recycling all translate into increased stateside employment. Multiple studies have confirmed the job advantages of green construction. For every million dollars invested in energy efficiency and renewable energy programs, between 1 and 69 people are employed for a year.[9]

Turner Construction's Green Market Barometer

There are lots of indicators pointing to the growing strength of the green construction economy. For example, Turner Construction Company, one of the world's largest and the top green contractor in the United States, generated 53% of its sales revenue from green projects in 2012, up from just 24% in 2006.[10] It regularly surveys real estate owners, developers, and corporate owner-occupants regarding their attitudes about green buildings, and releases the findings in its *Green Market Barometer*. In the latest survey (2012), over half of the 700 companies surveyed said they were very or extremely committed to following sustainable practices in their operations. Their reasons? Anticipated cost savings and impact on their brand/reputation were among the top four. These and other considerations, including customer and employee expectations, indicate a growing belief among businesses that sustainability can provide a competitive edge.[11]

Improved worker health

As discussed in Chapter 3, many of the materials routinely used in construction—sealants, adhesives, plywood, carpets—as well as airborne dust and particle pollution can be hazardous to both workers and end users. Minimizing construction-related pollution and the use of toxic materials can protect workers from a variety of health problems that may reduce productivity and require medical attention. Green projects with superior ventilation systems and materials with reduced or zero toxic synthetic chemicals are healthier for construction workers as well as for future building occupants, reduce health care costs, and improve productivity.

Reduced material and waste disposal costs

Generating less waste can reduce disposal costs. We know from Chapter 1 that construction—from the demolition and renovation of existing buildings and the construction of new facilities—generates millions of tons of waste every year.[12] Green buildings divert—that is recycle or reuse—far more construction waste than do conventional buildings. They do this by eliminating waste where possible, minimizing waste where feasible, and reusing materials that might otherwise become waste.

One way to reduce waste is to create smaller, more compact spaces. Because the use of materials is typically proportional to a structure's square footage and volume, smaller spaces require fewer materials. This translates into lower transportation costs, less packaging, and less waste. The installation of very efficient systems is similarly effective: for example, when a building's exterior is carefully designed to be energy efficient, then heating and air conditioning equipment can sometimes be downsized.[13]

Marisol Dykstra

Waste reduction has significant cost implications: a Booz Allen Hamilton report for example, estimates that, based on projections of the quantity of green building square footage, U.S. building owners see an annual waste disposal savings of almost $80 million.[14]

Do green buildings cost more?

A common view is that green buildings are more expensive to build than conventional buildings and don't save enough to be worth the cost. Many professionals say, "Not necessarily."

An analysis conducted between 2007 and 2009 of 170 green buildings—commercial, institutional, and multi-family residential—compared green buildings around the United States to similar conventional buildings. This study showed, on average, a 2% cost premium. But the benefits, especially when extended beyond up-front costs, exceeded this small first cost increase.[15] A later study prepared for the **World Green Building Council** (WGBC) in 2013 argues that other than a premium for green buildings seeking certification through an assessment program such as LEED, building green does not have to cost more, especially, as noted, when cost strategies are incorporated early into the design and development process.

The **U.S. Environmental Protection Agency** (EPA) and others point out that many green products and materials cost the same or even less to purchase than conventional ones.[16] One of the trends driving down these costs is the number of green products on the market; as the construction industry and others in the supply chain such as manufacturers become more experienced with green products and standards, costs will continue to fall.[17] Still the notion persists that green equals more expensive and often appears as an impediment to better building.[18]

Some argue for a radical approach to assessing costs that extends beyond a specific system or building. An example used by the Rocky Mountain Institute is illustrative: "A standard black-asphalt parking lot bakes in the sun. This shortens its life ... (and) greets users with an unwelcome blast of radiant heat, cooks their cars (which become less efficient ... and more polluting when restarted while running an air conditioner ...), bathes nearby buildings in superheated air (raising their costly air-conditioning loads), and soaks up light ... which requires increased artificial lighting. Switching to light-colored pavement can make the paving material last indefinitely, create comfort for users, keep cars and buildings cool ... improve visibility" and enable more efficient lighting.[19]

Tax credits, density bonuses, and other incentives

To encourage the conversion to a sustainable built environment, there are multiple types of tax and fee incentives for green projects. Incentives include: property tax relief; tax credits and rebates for using renewable energy sources; corporate, sales, and local tax credits and abatements; and relief from permitting and other fees. Financial incentives can be offered for specific levels of green certification and for both short- and long-term goals. Multiple agencies and organizations including federal and state agencies, utilities, local jurisdiction, and nonprofit organizations offer incentive programs.

Examples:

New Mexico offers sustainable building tax credits for commercial projects; sales tax credits for energy equipment and systems can be utilized in Florida; and Cincinnati OH, provides property tax relief for newly constructed or rehabilitated commercial or residential properties that are certifiably green. Along with several other jurisdictions around the country, Mecklenburg County NC, gives permit-fee rebates to projects with green certification.

Many municipalities allow for percentage increases in Floor Area Ratio (FAR) or other measures of density, contingent upon certification or proof of building green. In other words, if you build to certain green standards, you can build more. Many of these programs are designed to encourage urban infill projects and can be particularly attractive to developers and owners in cities and counties that have capacity shortfalls.

Examples:

Bar Harbor ME; Cranford NJ; and Nashville TN, all award a residential unit density bonus on projects in which all dwelling units meet specific, verifiable standards.

Some jurisdictions allow for faster document approval and permitting if a project meets a designated green threshold. Streamlining the permitting process for building, plan, and site permits can save green developers substantial time and money.

Examples:

Chandler AZ; Chicago; Miami-Dade County FL; Catawba County
NC; San Diego; and Dallas, are among those municipalities and
counties that provide faster permitting for green buildings. Each
has different requirements for what constitutes green and how
verification is made.

A source of information on incentives

An excellent source for information on state, local, federal, and utility
financial and other incentives that promote renewable energy and
energy efficiency is DSIRE (Database of State Incentives for Renewables
& Efficiency, *www.dsireusa.org*). A map enables the user to click on a
state for comprehensive, specific information.

Lower energy and water costs

The United States spends over a $1 trillion a year on energy.[20] About 40% of our
total energy is consumed in residential and commercial buildings and increasing equipment and system efficiencies to reduce the energy consumed translates into lower costs.

There are multiple ways that green buildings reduce direct energy use over
the long-term.

- High-performance buildings have outer shells (**building envelopes**)
  that are designed to be "tight" so that air, moisture, and heat infiltration are low, and that are insulated to levels beyond what is required
  by codes. A well-insulated building with good air and water barriers
  and efficient HVAC systems typically requires less (and sometimes
  no) additional heating and cooling other than what is provided
  by natural systems. Smaller mechanical systems typically result in
  lower costs.

It is worth noting that a **tight building** may be prone to mold and other damage if moisture, such as from a plumbing leak, gets trapped inside the building. When moisture accumulates, this can lead to the growth of microorganisms, such as mold and bacteria, which can cause a variety of health problems. As with any structure, green buildings require proper ventilation, high efficiency air filters and measures to reduce mold and mildew, and operating and maintenance practices that carefully adhere to the design guidelines and manufacturer's specifications.[21]

- Green buildings incorporate durable equipment that can last longer and require less frequent replacement. For example, an **LED light** can last 25 times longer than a comparable traditional incandescent bulb.[22] New York's Metropolitan Museum of Art is an example of the cost savings possible with energy efficient components. In one of the museum's galleries, 55-watt halogen bulbs were replaced with 12-watt LEDs. This change resulted in comparable light levels but a 75% reduction in energy use and $100,000 in savings.[23] (For more on this project, see Chapter 8.)

An economic argument often made for the reduction or elimination of imported fossil-fuel-based energy is the exposure to fuel cost variability. Although buildings that rely on renewable energy sources provide multiple benefits, including protection from fuel price spikes and unstable supply, the increase in natural gas production in the United States has reduced the amount of fuels we import. Less imported petroleum has reduced some of the concerns associated with dependence on foreign supplies.

- In addition to energy cost savings, a combination of indoor and outdoor water conservation strategies can result in lower water costs, too. Over the past 10 years, the dollars spent for water and sewage services have increased well beyond the consumer price index.[24] As noted in Chapter 1, in just four years, between 2010 and 2014, average water costs rose 33%.[25] As utilities are forced to pour money into aging pipes, treatment, and distribution systems, and as the population and drought conditions across parts of the United States both increase, this trend is likely to continue. Although codes and best practices have resulted in improved efficiencies (for example, before 1992 standard toilets used 3.5 gallons of water per flush; now a typical toilet uses 1.6 gallons[26]), green buildings strive for even greater efficiencies.

Buildings aren't designed with just more water-efficient plumbing and irrigation, however; some are designed to use no off-site water at all. As discussed in Chapter 4, the Bullitt Center in Seattle, a six-story office building, is an example of a building with on-site collection, storage, and filtration systems.

An increase in water efficiency and conservation saves money in two additional ways: using less water reduces the costs paid for heating the water and for treating wastewater.

Technology also plays a role in reducing energy use and saving money. Building Information Modeling systems (BIM) and integrated design approaches improve product choices and assembly designs, and once a building is occupied, the use of **smart technology** such as occupancy lighting controls can mean ongoing energy savings.

Reduced operation and maintenance costs

Although up-front costs for high-performance systems may, in some cases, be somewhat greater than for conventional systems, the durability of green products, assemblies, and buildings often results in lower repair and maintenance costs and longer life. Durable buildings cost less to operate because repairs and replacement of worn or failed components are less frequent than with conventional systems or buildings. A report from Booz Allen Hamilton states that, as of 2012, the annual operations and maintenance (O&M) savings for green buildings was $0.32/sq ft. This translates into more than $1 billion.[27] In addition to lower O&M costs, durability has another economic benefit: with a product of superior durability, the embodied energy (the energy used to extract raw materials, process, manufacture, and install a product) can be amortized over a longer period.

Increased property values and higher rental income

Evidence from McGraw-Hill, CoStar, and other organizations indicate that green buildings have higher dollar value, higher average occupancy levels, and lower turnover costs than equivalent conventional buildings. Studies have shown that U.S. buildings that are LEED or Energy Star certified get 3% higher rents, and sell for 13% more than comparable properties. The CoStar Group puts rent premiums even higher, between 5% and 8% nationally.[28]

Higher income, higher rents, and higher occupancy are some of the criteria used to assess property value. According to the Center for Insurance Policy and Research, for commercial properties, increases in these three translate into a 5% premium for owners.

Insurance and green buildings

One of the ways that owners reduce their risk is through insurance coverage. This has become a central issue across the United States because of extreme weather events. Building owners are not the only ones who worry about fires, floods, and other natural disasters; between 1980 and 2014, the insurance industry's weather-related losses increased nearly fourfold in the United States.[29] As severe weather events—droughts, floods, hurricanes, extreme rainfall—become more frequent, it is increasingly important that building systems be designed, as green buildings are, to be more resilient. Insurers are noting the ability of some green systems to better withstand extreme events. For example, in some states, particularly those at risk for wind damage, insurance providers offer discounts to policyholders who install living roofs. Another way insurers are acknowledging the benefits of green systems is by offering coverage that, in the event of a loss, will pay for repairing or rebuilding a home with green materials and practices.[30]

Healthier, more productive building occupants

As discussed in Chapter 2, the health benefits of green buildings extend beyond workers to building occupants. Indoor environmental conditions can have a measurable relationship to office worker performance. Because green buildings put a premium on indoor air quality, gas-emitting toxic materials are minimized or eliminated and accommodation is made for natural daylighting and ventilation. Green buildings are healthier, more comfortable, and more pleasant to work in than conventional buildings, resulting in greater user satisfaction, which, in turn, leads to increased productivity, and lower rates of employee turnover and absenteeism. It's also easier to recruit and retain workers who like and are comfortable in their workplace.[31]

The effects of physical surroundings were even shown to have a measurable impact on shopping behavior. A study from the early 2000s presents evidence that a major retailer experienced different level of sales in their stores that had natural daylighting than in those with artificial light. Their stores with skylights experienced 40% higher sales than those without skylights.[32]

Environmental and community cost benefits

We know that sustainable buildings provide multiple environmental benefits: the preservation of natural habitats and open space, increased biodiversity, reduced air pollution and greenhouse gas emissions, and responsible water management all contribute to the health of our local communities and beyond. The installation of green infrastructure can also save communities money. For example, stormwater systems that mimic natural filtration systems to manage runoff can result in reduced stress on conventional storm drains and cost savings.

Summary

Construction is how we shape our physical experiences and, as discussed in Chapter 1, recent building practices have often been both breathtaking and problematic. Gradual realization of the problematic aspects has led to what is really a revolution in the construction industry: significant changes in how buildings, neighborhoods, and infrastructures are conceived and designed; significant changes in construction methods and approaches; and adjustments in the operation and use of buildings. Green approaches—emphasizing efficiency and conservation, the reduction or elimination of waste, increased use of renewable energy, the importance placed on human and environmental health—are no longer seen as mere fads. Green has become an economic imperative. It is not just that regulatory agencies are mandating these changes; the public is increasingly insisting on them.

This chapter looked at some of the immediate benefits resulting from green construction: the creation of jobs, financial and development incentives for building owners, reduced material and waste disposal costs, and health benefits to workers. The chapter then explored the longer-term benefits such as reduced operation costs, increased property values and incomes, improved durability and resilience, as well as health and productivity benefits.

This and the previous chapters provide the context for understanding the upcoming chapters on how green is affecting the construction industry and its workers. The next part of this book explores the specific ways the construction industry has changed, and how today's workers can get maximum speed in, and take advantage of, these industry changes.

Glossary

Built environment—human-made buildings and parks, transportation systems, energy and water infrastructure and other constructed physical components that form our surroundings.

LED light—LEDs, or light-emitting diodes, are semiconductor devices that produce visible light very efficiently when an electrical current passes through them.

Smart technology—systems equipped with or using electronic controls.

Tight building—a building with an envelope designed to greatly restrict air, heat, and moisture flow from conditioned to unconditioned spaces.

U.S. Environmental Protection Agency (EPA)—an agency of the federal government whose mission is to protect human health and the environment.

World Green Building Council (WGBC)—a worldwide network of green building councils, including the U.S. Green Building Council.

Part 2

Workers and Green Construction: Challenges and Opportunities

Green Construction and the General Contractor

The reader learned in previous chapters that changes are occurring in the construction industry. Some of these changes have to do with technology, workforce demographics, and cost. But many are driven by the increased emphasis on building performance, in other words, green or sustainable construction. Efficiency standards and codes are tightening, design and construction practices are incorporating new best practices, and unfamiliar materials and products are coming on the market almost daily. Designers, engineers, and builders who want to stay current are facing a new reality, too: the old ways of doing business are changing and, in order to maintain a competitive edge, contractors must adapt.

Due to the new emphasis on performance and the incorporation of green principles, these changes impact workers across the entire industry but in different ways. Given the central role of general contractors (along with designers and engineers), they are on the front lines. This chapter explores some of the new or enhanced skills required of the **general contractor** (GC) and his or her job superintendent. Before we look at how the GC's job has changed, it would be helpful to put the role of the general contractor in some context, review the different ways that **projects** can be organized (delivered), and define the typical players.

Industry sectors

Although the construction industry is complex and employs people across a wide spectrum of the economy, not all construction work is equally complex, requires the same skills, or has an equal impact on the economy. The construction industry includes everything from small projects easily handled by a single worker to huge power plants or skyscrapers that require decades of planning and construction and hundreds of people to complete. Some projects require extensive community and regulatory review, whereas others (especially in more rural areas) might be constructed with very little.

Construction is generally grouped into one of four broad sectors: **commercial**, **residential**, **industrial**, and **infrastructure**. These four sectors typically differ in complexity, size, and type of project; the technology and equipment required; and how the project is funded. There are green buildings and projects in all the industry sectors, led by the commercial market.

The commercial sector includes offices, large apartment complexes, theaters, schools, hospitals, and other such facilities, which are usually designed by architects with engineers' support. Often commercial buildings use complicated materials and systems and require specialized construction. Hospitals and laboratories are examples. This sector has historically been the strongest in the green market and this trend continues; according to a February 2015 release from the USGBC, more than 40% of new commercial buildings are now green.[1] The David and Lucile Packard Foundation reviewed in Chapter 2 is one example. The green renovation of commercial buildings is also gaining market share (for example, the Empire State Building; see Chapters 4 and 9).

The residential sector includes both new construction and renovation of single- and multi-family residential properties. Buildings in this sector,

Ryan Browne/Cook+Fox Architects

especially single-family residences, are often wood frame and fairly low-tech, and much of the sector is built by small general and specialty trade contractors. While the commercial sector has shown the most recent growth in green construction, single-family residential is also becoming greener and many single-family remodelers and home builders report increasing amounts of work in the field. As green becomes the standard way to build in the commercial sector, this wider adoption of green may help push the single-family home market to become even greener in the future, with consumers increasingly demanding green homes.[2]

The third construction sector—industrial projects—include refineries, electrical stations, manufacturing plants, and similar facilities. These projects are typically highly technical and specialized and, because of complicated systems and machinery, are typically designed by engineers and require specialized construction expertise and licensing to build. Although not as predominantly green as commercial facilities, the industrial sector is also increasing its share of green construction.

Construction also includes the infrastructure sector, which comprises transportation and service projects such as roads, tunnels, bridges, water collection and distribution, waste management systems, and more that are required to keep our communities functioning. Communities across the United States are installing green alternatives to traditional infrastructure, typically as part of stormwater management systems: vegetation, soils, permeable paving, and other landscaping techniques that mimic natural processes relieve stress on municipal storm systems.

Getting off the ground: project organization and the delivery method

Projects are developed and built by individuals, agencies, organizations, and companies that, in most cases, come together for a specific project and move on at its completion. That this group of people typically changes from project to project is a defining feature of construction. On large projects, there may be hundreds of individuals involved in planning, designing, approving, and constructing a building or facility. On conventional projects, some of these people, such as the architect and the bankers, for example, may be involved from the very beginning of a project; others, such as building inspectors and the fire department, aren't involved until the project is under construction; and still others, such as real estate agents, may play a role only at or just before completion.

At an early stage in a project, the owner makes a determination regarding how the project will be organized and administered to best meet his or her situation and goals. For example: will the building performance goals require that team members be brought on board early in the process; how can the organizational structure help minimize risks; what are the project's cost and time constraints; how much of a role will the owner want to assume? The answers to these and other questions will determine the **project delivery** method, the organizational structure for completing the project. The delivery method determines the point at which the contractor gets hired and the level of potential collaboration between the parties, how the project is administered, the number of contracts the owner executes, the roles of the team members, the speed with which the project can be completed, and more.

There are multiple types of project delivery methods and some are more appropriate than others on high-performance, or green, buildings. The most common types are: the **Lump-Sum/Design-Bid-Build delivery method**, the **Design-Build delivery method**, and the **Construction Management delivery method**. A newer type of delivery method is **Integrated Project Delivery** (IPD), which was discussed in Chapter 3. Each of these delivery methods has variations, and each has advantages and disadvantages. As it is helpful to understand how projects are managed, let's look briefly at each.

- The Traditional/Lump-Sum/Design-Bid-Build project delivery is the most familiar to the industry and assumes a linear and straightforward process: the owner hires a designer, who, with the assistance of engineers, completes the design and the construction documents; estimates (competitive bids) are offered by various contractors; and the qualified contractor with the lowest bid is typically awarded a contract. This delivery method is often characterized as the lowest-cost approach and neither the general contractor nor subcontractors have any significant input into the design. Because of its lack of collaboration, this delivery method is perhaps the least desirable for a high-performance building.

- Design-Build is a delivery method marked by the owner hiring a single firm to provide both design and construction services. Although there tends to be improved communication between the architect and contractor and both are involved throughout the process, there is no firm price up front and few checks and balances between the major players. But due to the high degree of collaboration possible between the designers and builders, this delivery method is compatible with green projects.

- Construction Management (CM) is a delivery method in which management services are provided to the owner before construction has begun, or before a contractor has been hired, and the CM acts as the owner's representative throughout the entire process. The CM provides a range of preconstruction services such as constructability reviews, cost analyses, scheduling, and value engineering. Working with the designer, the CM assists in producing construction documents that best meet the owner's requirements. During construction, the CM either oversees the work and hires the appropriate contractors but does not use his own workforce, or operates as a general contractor. A construction management delivery is suitable for use on green projects.

- Integrated Project Delivery (IPD) is a relatively new project delivery method[3] marked, in part, by an incentivized collaborative process in which the parties share in cost savings. IPD utilizes software such as **Building Information Modeling** (BIM), which is designed to smooth and speed the flow of information to the parties, reduce costs, and minimize errors. On IPD, the general contractor and major subcontractors provide input and guidance during the design process. IPD incorporates many of the traits that are compatible with the development of high-performance buildings and, due to technology, transparency, and collaboration, has the potential to deliver green buildings at the same or lower cost as conventional buildings.[4]

> Integrated Project Delivery is especially well-suited to green projects.

(For a further discussion on project delivery see the author's book *Construction Project Management: An Introduction*, Chapter 6.)

The players

All projects require a team. With any project—conventional or green—the individuals and agencies involved can be grouped into three primary groups or teams, each with distinct responsibilities and obligations:

- **The owner's team**—establishes the project goals, determines the budget and finances the cost, identifies key dates, provides the site, and selects the other major players.

- **The designer's team**—provides planning and design services, and administers the construction contract between the owner and the contractor.

- **The contractor's team**—coordinates and is responsible for the physical work as well as the performance of subcontractors and product suppliers.

Although the roles of the owner, designer, and contractor have been established over time and are fairly standard, projects with high-performance goals put added layers of responsibilities on all the parties. Let's look briefly at each of these three teams.

The owner's team

The **owner** comes up with the project concept or idea, establishes the time and budget constraints, provides the site, figures out how to pay for the project, and hires many of the people who will help make it happen. Owners may be private individuals, organizations, corporations, or businesses, or may be public agencies such as school districts, transportation departments, and the like. There are two basic types of owners: public owners and private owners. They are distinguished primarily by the type of financing used on a project.

Public owners include all public entities such as local, state, and federal governments, as well as some educational institutions, public hospitals, and other institutions. Publicly owned projects are paid for with public funds (typically, bonds or general tax revenues). A new library built at a community college is an example of a project owned and built by the public and paid for with

Marisol Dykstra

public funds. A new highway through town, the replacement of old sewer and water lines, and the construction of a local park are other examples.

As public projects are paid for with taxpayer money, they have layers of oversight that private projects typically do not. One primary example is that public jobs must follow applicable procurement policies and regulations. In some case, projects must be publically bid and, on a lump-sum job, the qualified general contractor who promises to complete the work for the best price generally gets to do the work.

Private owners have more latitude than public owners; there are fewer regulations governing what they can do. This is because they are paying for the project themselves (typically, through short-term construction loans) and typically do not use public dollars. Private owners have no rules regarding how they hire contractors and they are free (apart from outright discrimination) to hire pretty much whomever they choose. Funding for privately owned projects is by the owners themselves or through lending institutions such as banks. Private owners include ordinary citizens, organizations, agencies, institutions, companies, and businesses.

Most commonly, the owner has separate contracts with the designer and with a general contractor. Owners may or may not have other people or companies working with them. On small private jobs such as a renovation project or a simple house, the owner may work directly with the general contractor. On larger projects, the owner will have the assistance of both employees and consultants, including a project manager to manage the owner's interests and coordinate the construction contract, accountants, attorneys, marketing people, and, in most cases, financiers to help fund the work. Construction projects are expensive and owners need funds for many things: to secure the building site, pay designers and contractors (who, in turn, buy materials and products), and deal with unexpected situations and conditions. Private owners rarely have the money to fund these costs themselves and must therefore obtain loans. The individuals or agencies financing a project are typically important (and sometimes active) members of the team.

The owner's team makes the decision whether to develop a high-performance building and sets priorities. For example, perhaps the owner and her team determine that they will pursue building certification through LEED or another program. Even if they decide against pursuing formal certification, what are project performance goals and objectives? Maybe the project is located in a very arid region and priorities will include maximizing rainwater collection; perhaps the owner wants to emphasize natural cooling techniques, or reach zero net energy use. The owner hires the necessary expertise, including perhaps a green professional, to help the team realize the project goals and objectives. (See Chapter 11 on green professional credentials.)

The designer's team

Tashi-Delek

Designers provide planning, design, and construction administration services to a project. The designer is sometimes referred to as the A/E, an acknowledgment that both architects and engineers can be the primary designer on a project. Architects typically design buildings; engineers design infrastructure and complex commercial and industrial projects such as roads and power plants. Both are licensed professionals whose accreditation is typically administered through the state. (State regulations vary regarding when a licensed professional is required.) For our purposes, we will assume that the designer is an architect.

The designer (sometimes an individual but more often a company) is hired by and is responsible to the owner. The job of the designer is not just that of sitting at a computer monitor and "drawing." Architects (and engineers) have the training to help create solutions that meet an owner's goals within the framework of budget, schedule, regulatory requirements such as building codes, and performance priorities. The architect can provide the owner with a range of services, including assistance in getting the project bid and hiring a contractor, and is typically the owner's representative during construction. On a high-performance building, the designer will work closely with a green professional to ensure that goals are met. (Large construction and design firms typically have in-house LEED-certified professionals.[5]) If certification through a program such as LEED or Green Globes is an objective, documentation will be required.

Like the owner's team, the designer's team varies depending on the complexity of the project and the size and organization of the designer's company. Sometimes the architectural firm is small and one person serves several roles; other firms are large and have many in-house personnel. On large projects, members of the designer's team typically include a principal-in-charge, a project manager, job captains, and others. The designer's team also includes consultants (hired by the architect) to assist in the completion of planning and design. These consultants typically include: engineers (such as structural, civil, and mechanical) to provide the design, drawings, and written specifications for specific technical aspects of the project; estimators who develop cost projections at various points in the design process; and specification writers to assist in the development of the material and workmanship requirements for the project. The designers also work with suppliers and product representatives to assist in the selection of specific products, materials, and systems.

> The designer's team hires the engineers and other consultants

The design approach used on many conventional buildings (typically procured under a traditional delivery method) results in the players—from the designers to the guys in the field—working primarily in isolation. As each piece of the design puzzle is completed, drawings are handed off for inclusion in a set of drawings that will be priced by contractors competing for the work. As a consequence, the owner, the designers and engineers, and the general contractor and the major subcontractors may never sit down and discuss in detail project and performance goals and may, in fact, work at cross-purposes.

As has been noted, the design and construction processes are unusually collaborative on buildings with high-performance goals that use construction management or Integrated Project Delivery methods. Everyone is brought into the design process early so that their input and expertise can inform the design. There are opportunities for interaction and collaboration not normally afforded by the traditional process. For example, the plumbing contractor might design a very efficient piping layout that, in turn, allows the HVAC engineer to reduce equipment size; the design team may site the structure to take advantage of natural breezes that will reduce the cooling loads calculated by the mechanical engineer; and the interior designer may specify a highly reflective paint that will result in reduced lighting loads. Team members are more likely to see the whole picture. The designer will typically facilitate this collaborative process.

The contractor's team

Contractors (also called constructors or builders) are individuals or firms that agree to construct a project in accordance with contract documents (the drawings and other written, printed, or electronic matter that make up the contractor's legal agreement with the owner). General contractors and specialty tradespeople are all constructors. Although some green buildings, particularly large ones, use the construction management (CM) delivery method with a **contract manager** who may or may not function as a general contractor, for this text, we will focus specifically on the role of the traditional general contractor.

In addition to ensuring that all the physical work (no matter who performs it) meets the requirements of the contract, the contractor is responsible for managing and controlling cost and schedule requirements, administering payment and contract modification procedures, securing necessary permits, coordinating testing and inspections, and much more.

On most (but not all) projects, the owner has a contract with a single contractor who assumes responsibility for the work. This is typically a general contractor (also called a GC). On a conventional construction project, the owner normally provides the general contractor with a fixed set of plans and specifications for the entire project. General contractors may be hired to perform a range of services including: constructability analyses, cost estimating,

Alex Snyder

scheduling, comprehensive management, as well as the physical work. Construction services are either bid or negotiated with the owner.

The **prime contractor** (anyone with a direct contract with the owner, most commonly the general contractor) typically enters into subcontracts with various specialty contractors, each of whom agrees to perform a designated trade portion of the prime contract work.

Specialty trade contractors are experts in specific areas of construction: electrical, plumbing, concrete, framing, and so on. As the work of specialty contractors is more narrowly focused than that of the general contractor, they are typically very efficient and, for this and other reasons, it is not unusual for the majority of a job to be carried out with subcontracted crews. Sometimes the general contractor subcontracts *all* the work and acts only as project coordinator. (On some jobs, there may be multiple layers of subcontractors, too, and the GC will be responsible to the owner for their work as well.) A specialty **subcontractor** (often called a *sub*) is responsible to a prime contractor and has no contractual relationship with the owner. (It is possible for a specialty contractor to have a contract directly with an owner and, in that case, would therefore be a prime contractor.)

Everything that happens on a jobsite is under the control of the general contractor and, as noted, is his or her responsibility. This is an important point on any project but can be complicated by the requirements of a green project. As much of the work on most projects is done by subcontractors, it is crucial to the success of the project that all subs understand the special requirements imposed by a green building project. These might include restrictions on materials, the interrelationship of the sub's work to overall building performance, and material handling and waste recycling.

The GC's management team

As with the owner and the designer, the GC's team for a project depends on the size and complexity of the project and on the size and organization of the contractor's firm. Larger jobs require a greater number of individuals, some in the contractor's employ, others hired only for a specific project.

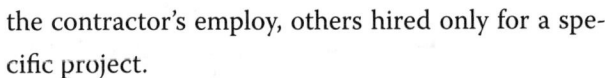

In addition to subcontractors, the general contractor's team, typically led by an executive of the construction company, includes a project manager, a job superintendent, and multiple foremen. Responsibilities associated with these positions vary from company to company but typically:

- A **project manager** (PM) is responsible for the business end of a project: ensuring that the team is in place, contracts are executed, and everything is in **compliance** with required codes and regulations. The PM is typically the person who qualifies and hires the subcontractors, prepares and manages the submittal process for materials and products, and administers the contracts, quality control, and communication and collaboration. Working with the superintendent, the PM is responsible for keeping budgets and schedules on track and monitoring and managing schedule, cost, safety, green certification, and documentation control. PMs are often highly educated, with advanced degrees in construction management or business, and typically work out of the contractor's home office. On high-performance projects, the PM will likely have training and some kind of green credential such as those offered through LEED and others. (Later chapters detail green credentials.)

- A **job superintendent** (also called a construction superintendent) is responsible for coordinating and managing the work and working with the Project Manager to institute management strategies to ensure that work progresses as intended. On green buildings, the superintendent will have additional duties to ensure compliance with certification and documentation requirements, and will be responsible for making certain that everyone on the job understands performance goals and special operational procedures associated with green buildings. These procedures may include everything from how vehicles and pedestrians access the site to stormwater management practices to material and waste handling procedures. Given the requirements of green jobs, many superintendents also have specialized green training or a green credential.

- A **foreman** is responsible for direct supervision of the contractor's workers. Foremen lay out the work, verify that the correct tools and equipment are at the site, ensure that work conforms to contract requirements, and prepare daily time sheets. Each major trade on a large project typically has a foreman. Because superior construction practices are required for green buildings to meet performance goals, the foreman must understand the restrictions placed on these projects and must direct his workers accordingly.

Other skilled workers on the GC's team may include assistants such as field or project engineers or assistant superintendents who are typically responsible for documents and making sure that information gets communicated. They prepare field questions, maintain submittal and tracking logs, and review invoices and other documents. The GC's team may also include software (BIM) operators, accountants, safety professionals, and legal and insurance support.

The general contractor's role on a green project

As noted earlier, on conventional projects the general contractor is typically hired through a competitive bidding process at the end of the design phase. The assumption is that any qualified contractor is capable of completing the work and contracts are typically awarded based on price. (It is beyond the scope of this text to detail the contractor's team and their role on a conventional project; for additional information, see the author's book *Construction Project Management: An Introduction*.)

On a high-performance project, the general contractor or contract manager (as well as the major subcontractors) is ideally hired early in the design process, often through a negotiated as opposed to a standard competitive bid process.

On a project with ambitious performance goals, the general contractor plays a crucial role that extends from the design phase through construction. Let's look at his or her role during design, preconstruction, construction, and close-out.

Design phase

A project team with expertise in the development of sustainable buildings understands that to create a high-performance structure, every system—from the foundation to the roof and the entire envelope, to the HVAC system and the lighting—must be carefully considered as part of the whole. As noted in Chapters 2 and 3, integrative design and construction approaches that regard building systems as interrelated are important for maximizing efficiencies and other benefits. This collaborative process, often referred to as whole building design and construction, begins during design.

> If decisions are made early, the costs for using green principles are typically reduced.

If decisions regarding green components, assemblies, and systems are integrated into a project during the design phase, they do not have to add to overall project cost and can also be selected to best meet the owner's performance goals for the building. The general contractor on a green project understands how to specify, install, test, operate, and repair new types of high-performance systems and provide product, material, and budget advice so that design options can be analyzed and considered. He or she can provide input on material selection, system performance, techniques for decreasing construction waste and improving indoor air quality, and more, and can help the team develop "what-if" scenarios for the cost and construction implications of pursuing specific green goals.

This type of input from the GC early in the process can greatly enhance the development of creative and economical design solutions and can contribute to developing a project's optimum solution based on the owner's requirements. As part of a collaborative and iterative process, the experienced and skilled GC plays a key role in meeting green performance goals.

Preconstruction phase

On any project—green or conventional—the general contractor has multiple responsibilities before the physical work begins. These activities include assembling the construction team, hiring the subcontractors not yet on board, identifying the means and methods of construction, developing a jobsite logistics plan to identify temporary office facilities, pedestrian and traffic access and parking, material storage, staging, and waste management areas. The complexity of this stage is in direct proportion to the complexity of the project. On a green project, preconstruction responsibilities are expanded to include the development of a sustainability action plan and communicating project expectations to subcontractors.

When project goals include pursuing building certification through a point-based system such as LEED or Living Building Challenge, the team will analyze the system's requirements to develop a sustainability action plan. The contractors will need a thorough understanding of the certification program requirements and will need to adhere strictly to a plan that addresses compliance procedures. A green professional hired by the project team may facilitate this process. Even if formal certification is not being pursued, the contractor may be required to meet standards that are not typical on conventional projects such as strict nontoxic material standards, superior interior air quality, and water and energy conservation during construction. A sustainability action plan might include:

- Procurement requirements such as nontoxic material standards, restrictions on sources, and the use of recycled materials

- Protection procedures for the site's natural resources

- Design for minimizing waste

- Targets for energy and water use during construction

- Standards and procedures for pollution control (particulate and noise pollution for example) as well as indoor air quality during construction

Targets are set for items included in the plan, with specific actions and timelines and the processes for meeting them. If the project is pursuing certification, documentation requirements are included in the plan.

The general contractor is responsible for communicating sustainability plans and procedures to subcontractors, before their work begins, to ensure an understanding of how the sustainability plan will impact their work.

Construction phase

In addition to the general contractor's traditional responsibilities during construction (such as hiring and working with subcontractors, managing and coordinating all the physical work, budgeting, and scheduling) there are additional obligations typically required on a green project:

- Rigorous quality control and worker education

- Review of materials and products

- Documentation

Let's expand on what each of these responsibilities includes:

Quality control and worker education

Once a project is under construction, the general contractor and job superintendent are on the front line to ensure that procedures, processes, and products meet the owner's goals and standards. This is a central responsibility on any job but is magnified on a green project with standards that exceed those of conventional buildings. The link between construction practices and building performance means that the quality of workmanship assumes an especially important role.

Although builders strive to do good work, corners sometimes get cut. As noted, less than careful fieldwork on buildings that are designed to meet high-performance goals can mean failure to meet those goals. For example, insulation that is not meticulously installed, has gaps, or is stuffed too tightly into walls will not provide the proper insulating value and may compromise the energy efficiency of the entire building. Quality control during construction includes careful monitoring of work standards and practices and of the items identified in the sustainability action plan, such as the recycling of waste and site protection requirements. Part of the GC's responsibility is to promote

Kelly Ogden

job-wide understanding of the special characteristics and requirements of the project and how the work of each trade can impact—positively or negatively—the eventual success of the building.

Good indoor air quality is a tenet of green design, not just for building occupants, but also for workers during construction. The general contractor on a green project will budget time (and therefore cost) to take actions to reduce worker exposure to potential contaminants. As part of quality control, the GC will work with specialty contractors to ensure that systems, such as HVAC ducting, for example, are free from pollution and excess moisture and that potential health risks to workers are reduced or eliminated.

The GC looks beyond the specifications for ways to establish a "culture" that includes the goals of the sustainability action plan developed during pre-construction. Promoting a "green culture" and an understanding of overall project performance goals increases the likelihood of the project's success. When individual workers understand overall performance goals, they are more likely to be advocates for the plan.

Material and product review

As part of any job, the general contractor is responsible for reviewing product information typically submitted by the subcontractors. On green buildings, the GC's review is broadened to include verification of conformance to sustainability requirements. On all green projects, there are certain material and product restraints or standards such as minimum efficiency ratings, requirements regarding the presence of certain synthetic chemicals and the percentage of recycled content in products, and product recyclability at the end of use.

Sometimes the constraints are substantial; buildings certified under the Living Building Challenge, for example, have strict requirements against the use of certain chemicals common to the construction industry including asbestos, PVC, creosote, and several others. Buildings that use any of the listed chemicals are not certified. Typically the GC will need to submit paperwork to prove that materials and products meet design specifications for an FSC label from the Forest Stewardship Council, for example, or an Environmental Product Declaration or an Energy Star label.

It is a common perception that contractors do not have a role in the selection of materials and products. In many instances, however, contractors are vital to the material selection process. Sealants, drywall compounds, fireproofing materials, adhesives, duct cement, and insulation are all items that should be held in the same care as **finish materials** that are used to form decorative and protective coatings such as drywall, paints, coatings, and such.[6] On a green project, the GC may be required to verify material compliance with even commonly used, off-the-shelf products.

Documentation

All projects require certain levels of documentation to verify that materials, products, and more meet program requirements. Projects that seek certification under a green building program such as LEED may require a great deal of documentation. Often this documentation is compiled on a continuing basis, thus allowing the construction team to make informed decisions when faced with changing conditions. For example, if the data show that the recycled percentages of the materials installed exceed requirements, the construction team might be able to choose a product with less recycled content but one that is locally manufactured.[7] Documentation is eventually reviewed as part of the certification process.

Prior to the start of construction, the team will carefully review documentation requirements and, as noted, catalog these in the sustainability action plan. Most documentation is now electronic and automated. Some may be required at the completion of the design phase; other documentation is submitted during construction. In addition to verification of materials and products, the general contractor may need to submit documentation supporting the team's compliance approaches: data showing compliance with energy performance requirements, a drawing showing the area set aside for recycling during construction, verification regarding pollution control procedures, stormwater management plans, and so on.

Typically, the general contractor, in some cases working with a green professional, is responsible for compiling and submitting all necessary documentation and submitting it as required by the owner or certification program.

Smart buildings

Many of today's green (and some conventional) buildings incorporate cutting edge "smart" technology to optimize performance. Computers can now program systems to respond to current conditions and can connect a variety of independent building systems (such as lighting and HVAC, for example) that share information to optimize total building performance.[8] Smart building technology can monitor and automatically adjust HVAC outputs, according to conditions such as occupancy and temperature; can direct shading devices on the exterior of the building to automatically respond to changes in sun angles; can be programmed to open or close windows as more or less ventilation is required; and can turn interior lighting on and off in response to changes in the amount of daylight in the building. Sensors can even rotate solar panels to track the sun. Technology can enable systems to be networked so that, for example, a motion sensor might activate a security system as well as lighting levels. These systems can be programmed to meet the various needs of the building with the goal of occupant comfort, control, and, ultimately, energy efficiency. The increasingly common application of smart technology is one example of why builders increasingly need to be computer literate.

Close-out phase

The general contractor always has multiple responsibilities during the end of construction (close-out), including completion of the physical work, securing documentation from the authority having jurisdiction (such as the local building department) that the project can be used as intended, demobilizing the site office, transferring power and other services, and cleaning. On a green project, GC responsibilities also include:

Alex Snyder

- Flushing out systems to remove any contaminants and to maximize air quality before the building is occupied

- Conducting the intense quality assurance process, called **commissioning**, to ensure that all HVAC, electrical, plumbing, and safety systems are operating as intended

Contractors and subcontractors perform final close-out reviews

- Finalizing green documentation as required by the owner or certification program; this is the last opportunity to make certain that the subcontractors comply with the green action plan developed during design and preconstruction

- Providing special operation and maintenance training on systems and assemblies for facility managers and others who will be responsible after occupancy

Because administrative and management personnel in the general contractor's firm need to evaluate materials, products, systems, and construction strategies, these individuals need a solid understanding of green construction costs, products, installation, and use. Growing numbers of firms have a licensed green professional on staff. (See Chapter 9 for information on green professional credentials.)

Resources for general contractors

There are many organizations and trade groups that are helpful to general contractors and others who wish to better understand green practices. Many of them have local chapters that offer classes, workshops, and opportunities for networking with men and women who work in green construction. USGBC is probably the place to start. It's a membership organization with chapters around the country and anyone working in green construction is likely to

Energy retrofits and construction jobs

As discussed in Chapter 2, there is green construction work waiting to be done on existing buildings. The U.S. building stock includes millions of buildings, the majority of which are energy wasteful and inefficient. Many homeowners, businesses, and public agencies understand that retrofitting their home or office can save money, and there are a variety of incentives in place to encourage this. One such effort is the City Energy Project. With several million dollars in seed funding, two leading advocacy organizations have set up a multi-year effort to boost energy efficiency in existing buildings across 10 cities. The City Energy Project is designed to help mayors develop aggressive plans for tackling energy waste in large, existing buildings and to develop strategies that are, in part, tailored to their local building sector. The eventual goal is to save $1 billion in energy costs annually across the 10 participating cities: Atlanta, Boston, Chicago, Denver, Houston, Kansas City, Los Angeles, Orlando, Philadelphia, and Salt Lake City.

This project is designed to aid mayors in learning from other cities, to assist mayors in setting targets for building efficiencies, and to monitor progress and track cost savings and other impacts over multiple years.[9] Energy retrofits are not just happening in specially designated cities: building owners in both the private and public sectors are seeing economic benefits by upgrading equipment, adding controls and monitors, replacing inefficient windows, and more. Energy retrofitting includes small inexpensive projects and very large costly ones. (The energy retrofit for the Empire State Building, for example, cost more than $550 million.) Energy retrofits translate into direct work for general and specialty contractors as well as indirect jobs in the many industries that support construction, such as manufacturing and transportation.

be associated with USGBC. All chapters sponsor meetings and educational workshops (to locate a chapter, see *www.usgbc.org/chapters*). There are other resources, and Table 7.1 lists a few of general interest to the industry. Builders Exchanges, the National Association of Home Builders (NAHB), and the Construction Specifications Institute (CSI) have local chapters or affiliates; the rest are good sources of information. (See Chapters 8, 9, and 10 for additional resources, including specialty trade organizations.)

Table 7.1 Resources of General Interest to the Construction Industry

ORGANIZATION	DESCRIPTION
U.S. Green Building Council (USGBC) *www.usgbc.org/chapters*	A member of the International Green Building Council and the primary green organization in the U.S. USGBC developed the LEED green building rating systems. There are chapters around the country.
Builders Exchanges (See local chapter websites)	In addition to plan rooms where contractors can access information about projects, most builders exchanges offer industry news and information, and are great for networking. Many exchanges provide information on green topics and other items of interest to the green construction industry. Two examples of exchanges that are active in promoting green skills are the Arizona Builders Exchange in Phoenix, which publishes a Green/Renewable Energy compilation of green news articles relevant to their members (See *http://azbex.com/ category/green-renewable-energy*), and the North Coast Builders Exchange in Santa Rosa CA, which has seminars and workshops on various topics related to green building. (*www.ncbeonline.com*).
Construction Specifications Institute (CSI) *www.csinet.org*	This organization encourages best practices through standards/ formats/professional education and certification. CSI has chapters nationwide and, in addition to specification writers, its membership includes builders, engineers, architects, attorneys, real estate professionals, and students. A great organization for networking and training.
National Association of Home Builders (NAHB) *www.nahb.org*	NAHB is a trade and membership association that helps promote housing policies, with more than 100,000 members, and provides green training through some of its local Builders Associations (to find a local chapter, see *www.nahb.org/local_association_search_form. aspx*). In 2007, they partnered with the International Code Council (ICC) to establish the ANSI ICC 700 National Green Building Standard for residential projects.
U.S. Department of Energy *www.doe.gov*	DOE has lots of information on green construction. For information on energy Incentive programs in each state, see *www.energy.gov*.
U.S. Environmental Protection Agency (EPA) *www.epa.gov*	The EPA has information on science and health as well as the environment. Its website has a map with links to local EPA activities. They sponsor the Energy Star and WaterSense programs.
National Resources Defense Council (NRDC) *www.nrdc.org*	NRDC is an environmental action group that, among other services, provides useful information on renewable energy systems.
National Renewable Energy Laboratory (NREL) *www.nrel.gov*	The primary research laboratory for DOE's Office of Energy Efficiency and Renewable Energy, and a good source of technical information and data on renewable energy.

Summary

A contractor is an individual or firm that agrees to construct a project in accordance with drawings and other contract documents. The two primary types of contractors are General Contractors (GC) and Specialty Contractors. The GC is the contractor with primary responsibility for the construction, improvement, or renovation project under contract, and is the party signing the prime construction contract for the project. On "traditional" projects, the GC is hired at the completion of design. The GC is responsible for all the work (and safety) on the job and typically hires and manages all the subcontractors and suppliers for a project; she may or may not perform work with her own crews. Specialty Contractors are experts in and hired to complete specific areas of construction such as mechanical, electrical, and plumbing tasks; they are typically hired by the GC as subcontractors.

Although the roles of the owner, designer, and contractor differ depending upon the delivery method, the General Contractor (or in the case of a project that uses the Construction Management delivery system, the Contract Manager) is responsible for the successful completion of the work, and the key person or organization once construction begins. Determining the means and methods of construction, coordinating and managing the work, hiring and managing subcontractors and suppliers, ensuring the work proceeds on time and within budget, obtaining permits, and more are responsibilities of every General Contractor. On a green project these responsibilities are expanded and typically begin earlier in the process. The contractor on a green project must understand the project's sustainability goals, have experience in the type of green construction required, and ensure that construction methods and techniques, purchasing of products, and management of construction waste meet the owner's sustainability requirements.

On most high-performance building projects, the GC is hired during the design process so that their expertise and experience can be tapped to improve the final design. The process of designing buildings that meet the high-performance goals of minimizing (or eliminating) exterior energy and water sources, protecting natural environments and ecosystems, minimizing waste, and maximizing durability requires creativity, analysis, and, often, unorthodox thinking. This process benefits from the experience of skilled contractors with expertise in materials and products, costs, installation, and operations. A successful green building relies on the collaboration of the contractor's team during design and beyond.

During preconstruction, the GC develops a sustainability action plan to identify specific program requirements. Sometimes the requirements are based on a green building certification program such as LEED; sometimes they are owner requirements. The GC will identify special requirements and determine how compliance will be met and will make note of any documentation required and ensure timely completion and submission to the owner or certifying program such as LEED.

Quality control during construction is more rigorous than on most conventional buildings. In addition to verifying that products meet the quality and specifications of the project, green buildings are likely to include constraints on the types of materials and products that can be used. The GC will be responsible for making sure that material and product standards are met and that documentation is compiled as required. At close-out (and, ideally, throughout construction), commissioning will occur to verify that major systems are working as intended. Prior to turning over the facility to the owner, the GC will coordinate flushing out systems to eliminate any contaminants.

Ensuring that workers understand their roles on a green project falls to the GC, as does making sure at close-out that facility managers understand special operating and maintenance requirements for systems that may be unfamiliar.

The GC is the key contractor on a green project, but, given the importance of subcontractors on most jobs, they, too, have increasing responsibilities. The next chapter examines how green construction is impacting mechanical, electrical, and plumbing contractors.

Glossary

Commercial sector—a sector of the construction industry that includes offices, large apartment complexes, theaters, schools, hospitals, and other such facilities.

Compliance—conformity in fulfilling official requirements.

Construction Management project delivery—a system of organizing projects in which a contract manager (CM) is hired early in the process and acts as the owner's representative. During construction, the contract manager typically coordinates the physical work but may or may not do it him or herself.

Contract documents—the drawings and other written, printed, or electronic matter that make up the contractor's legal agreement with the owner.

Contractor (also called constructor or builder)—an individual or firm that agrees to construct a project in accordance with contract documents (the drawings and other written, printed, or electronic matter that make up the contractor's legal agreement with the owner).

Design-Build delivery method—a system of organizing projects marked by the owner hiring a single firm to provide both design and construction services.

Designer—an individual or firm that provides planning, design, and construction administration services to a project; they are typically licensed architects or engineers.

Finish materials—materials such as drywall, wallpaper, paints, and so on that are used to form decorative and protective coatings.

Foreman—an individual who is responsible for direct supervision of the contractor's workers.

General contractor (GC)—an individual or firm hired by and responsible to an owner for coordinating the completion of a project; the GC hires subcontractors and suppliers.

Industrial sector—a sector of the construction industry that includes refineries, electrical stations, chemical processing plants, factories, and similar facilities.

Infrastructure—a sector of the construction industry that includes transportation and service projects such as roads, tunnels, ferries, water collection and distribution, and waste management systems that are required to keep our communities functioning.

Integrated Project Delivery (IPD)—a system of organizing projects that is based on a highly collaborative approach to project design and construction.

Job superintendent—the person on the contractor's team responsible for coordinating and managing the work. Also called construction superintendent.

Owner—an individual or entity that comes up with a project concept or idea, establishes the time and budget constraints, provides the site, figures out how to pay for the project, and hires many of the people who will help make it happen; owners may be private or public entities.

Prime contractor—anyone with a direct contract with the owner, typically the general contractor.

Project—a unique activity that has a beginning and an end, uses resources, is not routinely done, and requires managing.

Project delivery—the organizational structure for completing a project. Also called delivery method.

Project manager (PM)—an individual who is typically responsible for the business end of a construction project, in contrast to the job superintendent who is responsible for production.

Residential sector—a sector of the construction industry that includes both new construction and renovation of single- and multi-family properties such as houses, condominiums, and apartments.

Specialty trade contractors—contractors who are experts in specific areas of construction.

Subcontractor—an individual or firm that has a contract with another contractor; in construction, subcontractors are typically in specialty trades.

Traditional delivery method—a general contractor is hired on a lump-sum-bid basis after design is complete. Also called Lump-Sum and Design-Bid-Build delivery methods

Green Construction and the Mechanical, Electrical, and Plumbing Trades

Specialty trade contractors perform specific crafts or trades on a project and are involved in everything from heating and lighting systems to site work, roofing, masonry, carpet installation, painting and more. Over six million people work in the construction industry[1] and the majority are employed by specialty contractors.[2] As with general contractors, these subcontractors may require a license. Licensing requirements are determined by individual states; *who* needs to be licensed, *when* a license is required, and *how* one gets licensed vary greatly.

The type and number of specialty contractors on a job depends on the type, size, and complexity of the project. On a small job such as a residential addition or remodel, there may be no specialty contractors and the general contractor may perform all the work himself. On large and complex projects, there could be dozens of individual specialty contractors. Specialty contractors are typically (but not always) hired by and are responsible to the general contractor (who, in turn, is responsible to the owner). Due to their contractual obligations with the GC (or contract manager), trade contractors are called subcontractors or subs, for short. If they have a contract directly with the owner, they would be *prime* contractors.

Alex Snyder

Because of their importance to the proper functioning of a building—especially one that has high-performance goals—the mechanical, electrical, and plumbing sub-contractors (sometimes referred to by the acronym **MEP**) are key trade contractors on a project. The work of the MEP contractors includes all the equipment, assemblies, and systems that perform a central role in the proper functioning of a building. MEP engineers and contractors design and install the systems that heat and cool a building, provide ventilation, supply water and dispose of wastes, and provide power, wiring, artificial lighting, and more. Because of the emphasis on energy and water efficiency, these professionals play a crucial role in the development of high-performance systems and buildings.

How MEP work is contracted varies from project to project. On some projects, there are separate contractors for each of the three trades; on others, there might be a single contractor (typically referred to as a mechanical contractor) doing HVAC and plumbing (and), with a second contractor for the electrical work; in some cases, a single contractor does all three. This chapter examines each of the three primary trades and how they are affected by the new and increasing emphasis on green design and construction.

Mechanical: HVAC (heating, ventilating, and air conditioning)

Mechanical contracting identifies a category of contractors that includes HVAC and plumbing; as noted, some contractors do one or the other and some do both. Some HVAC contractors offer refrigeration services that make it possible to store (and transport) perishable items. These contractors are referred to as **HVACR** contractors. For our purposes, we'll assume that mechanical does not include plumbing, which is discussed in a separate section later in this chapter.

An HVAC system (typically designed by a mechanical engineer or by the HVAC contractor) includes the pumps, pipes, valves, furnaces, fans, chillers, and other equipment that maintain thermal and air quality by heating, cooling, and ventilating spaces. The HVAC contractor is responsible for buying (**procuring**), installing, and testing the components of these systems and, as noted, is typically considered a major subcontractor on a job.

Heating, ventilating, and air-conditioning systems account for nearly 40% of the energy used in commercial buildings in the United States. This opens up considerable incentives for building owners, and opportunities for HVAC contractors (and manufacturers) to provide money-saving systems for both new construction and retrofits.[3] As their work is directly related to energy and water costs, on a green building project the HVAC contractor, along with the GC and the other major subcontractors, is ideally brought on board early during the design process.

Historically, manufacturers determined what products were available to the HVAC industry. This changed as regulating and standards-writing organizations such as ASHRAE were organized and model codes such as the Uniform Mechanical Code, the International Mechanical Code, and others were developed to support the industry and respond to tightening regulations. The growing interest in and requirements to improve energy and water efficiency, the technical research provided by organizations such as ASHRAE, and the increasing market demands for sustainable buildings have driven the development and use of systems that are often healthier and more comfortable for occupants than many conventional systems as well as more resource-conserving and efficient.

Highly efficient HVAC systems and components require new design approaches.

Solar and "passive" heating systems, geothermal and radiant heating, smart buildings, and sophisticated equipment and controls capable of multiple functions are just a few of the complex equipment and assemblies being designed, installed, operated, and maintained by HVAC contractors and technicians. These systems require new approaches to calculating heating and cooling loads, sizing equipment and assemblies, installation practices, commissioning services, and operation and maintenance knowledge.

The HVAC contractor working on a green project will pay particular attention to several areas:

Heating and cooling load calculations

Sometimes the HVAC contractor needs to calculate **heating and cooling loads (demand)**. On a green building, load calculations take into account a broad set of variables not always considered when designing systems for conventional buildings. Among the factors taken into account are: how the building is oriented on its site relative to solar and wind resources; the size, efficiency, and placement of windows; the presence of solar mass in the structure; the amount of insulation; overhangs; and the presence of shading devices and vegetation on the building site.

Right-sizing

Many heating, ventilating and air-conditioning systems, particularly in commercial buildings, have more **capacity** than is required to keep the occupants comfortable.[4] Oversized HVAC systems can have negative effects on energy and water use, on occupant comfort, and the economic outcomes for the building. A green mechanical system is based on precise demand; systems that are

An August 2015 study published in *Nature Climate Change* reported that most office buildings set temperatures based on a decades-old formula that uses the metabolic rates of men to determine heating and cooling requirements. But conditions have changed: half the work force is women, with lower metabolic rates and often wearing thinner clothing. "In a lot of buildings, you see energy consumption is a lot higher because the standard is calibrated for men's body heat production," said Boris Kingma, a coauthor of the study and a biophysicist at Maastricht University Medical Center in the Netherlands. "If you have a more accurate view of the thermal demand of the people inside, then you can design the building so that you are wasting a lot less energy ..."[5]

sized to meet actual occupant needs can use smaller equipment, cost less to operate, and can free up mechanical space for other uses. Right-sizing extends to small equipment such as fans in kitchens and bathrooms.

Using low-impact products and systems

The growing emphasis on using efficient systems that reduce or eliminate the use of fossil fuels is resulting in the development and installation of a variety of innovative systems. The newly renovated 300,000 square foot Exploratorium, San Francisco's legendary science museum, has such a system. With the goal of becoming one of the world's first **zero net energy** (ZNE) museums, their new home, located in a completely renovated 800 foot long historic pier that juts into the San Francisco Bay, is heated and cooled by water that circulates directly from the bay, through a series of tubes embedded in concrete floor slabs. The system is divided into 82 separate heating zones to more effectively target demand, and the heat that radiates through the floor is comfortable, healthy, and quiet. The use of heat exchangers enables the bay to act as a heat

THE TRADES AT WORK

Installing a radiant floor system

Ingrid Mattson/Uponor

Workers install tubing for the Exploratorium's radiant floor system. An integral part of the system's heating and cooling capabilities comes from water that is circulated from the San Francisco Bay through the piping.

source in the winter and a heat sink in the summer, saving the facility the need for evaporative cooling towers and an estimated two million gallons of water.[6] (The Exploratorium has the advantage of sitting directly over a large body of water. If such a site is not available, a different solution would, of course, be required.)

An emphasis on indoor air quality

As noted in Chapter 1, many of our buildings have significant levels of indoor air pollution that can cause a variety of health problems for both construction workers and, later, building occupants. In addition to considerations of thermal comfort, the green HVAC contractor will be concerned with ensuring clean and fresh air by reducing or eliminating materials that contain chemical pollutants, venting out any particulates and other unwanted substances in the air during construction and through the life of the building, and by ensuring sufficient natural **air changes** (how much air moves in and out of a room).

Construction best practices

Meeting green building performance goals requires increased attention to installation practices such as the sealing and insulating of ducts and all envelope penetrations to reduce air infiltration and eliminate water leaks, avoiding condensation (a cause of mold and mildew growth) and controlling humidity from indoor and outdoor sources. Often the HVAC contractor will need to work closely with others to design and install creative solutions. The selection of nontoxic materials, the reduction of waste, and product durability will be concerns for the HVAC contractor.

The careful selection of equipment and the creative design of assemblies to produce the best outcomes mean almost nothing if everything isn't properly installed and operated. As noted earlier in this text, how a building performs post-occupancy can be very different from its design goals. Performance efficiencies drop, sometimes dramatically, without careful operation and maintenance plans. A study by the New Building Institute, for example, found that poor maintenance and operational practices can increase a building's energy use by 30–60%.[7] One of the roles of the HVAC (and other) subcontractors is to provide the owner and/or facilities manager with detailed information and training, as required, on equipment operation and maintenance procedures.

As noted in the previous chapter and others, there are a variety of resources available to help those in the trades. These include nonprofit organizations, trade associations, blogs and publications, and websites. Table 8.1 lists several specific to HVAC and the MEP trades generally.

Not all of these resources have vigorous green construction programs, but the reader is urged to check local chapters. For example, the Mechanical Contractors Association of America/Mechanical Service Contractors of America offers hour-long webinars on topics of interest to their member contractors working in green and sustainable mechanical construction, service and plumbing (*www. mcaa.org/green*), and, as noted, ASHRAE provides a wide variety of professional development training including a professional certification program.

Table 8.1 Resources of Special Interest to HVAC Contractors

American Society of Heating, Refrigerating, and Air-Conditioning Engineers (ASHRAE) *www.ashrae.org*	ASHRAE's focus is on building systems, energy efficiency, indoor air quality and sustainability within the industry. The organization does research, writes standards, provides continuing education, and offers a High-Performance Building Design Professional Certification for those in the HVAC sector of the industry. ASHRAE 90.1 and ASHRAE 189.1 are widely followed energy standards (90.1) and green building standards (189.1) that are the basis for many codes.
Air-Conditioning Contractors of America (ACCA) *www.acca.org*	A trade association for individuals and businesses in the HVAC sector, it provides technical, legal, and marketing data plus directories, a magazine, a blog, consumer info, a career center, classes in various aspects of the industry, apprenticeship programs, and general certification programs in HVAC.
Sheet Metal and Air Conditioning Contractors' National Association (SMACNA) *www.smacna.org*	SMACNA is an international association of union contractors in heating, ventilating, and air conditioning; sheet metal; kitchen equipment; specialty stainless steel work; manufacturing; siding and decking; testing and balancing; service; and energy management and maintenance.
Mechanical Contractors Association of America/ Mechanical Service Contractors of America (MCAA) *www.mcaa.org*	Founded in 1889, MVAA is a member-based organization for firms involved in heating, air conditioning, refrigeration, plumbing, piping, and mechanical service; they provide educational programs and materials to their members.

Electrical

Electricians install, maintain, and repair electrical wiring, products, and systems, including lighting, security, circuit breakers, switches, and fuses, as well as low-voltage wiring used for voice, data, and video transmission. The majority of electricians work directly in construction; others are employed in the manufacturing and power generation sectors. Electricians are among the highest-paid specialty trade workers, and the U.S. Bureau of Labor Statistics projects that, by 2018, the career is expected to grow substantially, driven in large part by remodeling residential and commercial buildings.[8]

Electrical contractors are well positioned to capitalize on the rapidly increasing green construction market. Due to their important role, in not too many years, according to some predictions, the "electrical contractor" will transition into the "energy contractor."[9]

THE TRADES AT WORK

Electrician hooking up a control module

Alex Snyder

An electrician hooks up an electronic control module as part of a 250-panel solar project in Ohio.

As with the HVAC contractor, today's electrical contractor ideally joins the other major subcontractors in providing input during design. For example, when brought on board early, electricians can ensure that artificial lighting requirements are closely linked to design choices such as the size and placement of windows and the penetration of daylight into a building. In addition, lighting plans can be developed that match the light source with anticipated use—task lighting or lights that can be adjusted according to occupant need. Alternative lighting sources such as light-emitting diodes (**LEDs**), dimmer and motion-sensing switches, and other controls are standard practice in green buildings.

Alternative energy systems, whether residential- or commercial-scale, require the services of electricians. The contractor working with solar photovoltaic (PV) systems needs knowledge of PV materials, equipment, and codes as well as wiring and distribution. Working on a wind system requires knowledge of hydraulics, torqueing, and gearing for proper setup of the turbines to capture the maximum amount of energy. In addition to on-site wind and solar photovoltaic systems, there are community-scale systems that require the skills of electricians, including geothermal and hydroelectric systems, smart building controls, electrical transmission grids, and alternative-fuel fueling stations.

Lighting retrofits

At the end of 2014, the Department of Energy issued new energy standards for linear fluorescent lights. These lights are everywhere: in offices, schools, grocery stores, and shops. In fact, there are more than two billion of them in place and, on average, each one is on for 12 hours. Substituting higher-efficiency lights to meet the new standards is projected to save many billions of dollars in energy costs.[10]

Although DOE's new lighting regulations don't address incandescent bulbs, there are interesting possibilities for savings with these bulbs as well. New York's Metropolitan Museum of Art's recent lighting retrofit, noted in Chapter 6, is an example. The Metropolitan is the world's largest museum, with over 400 galleries, 2.2 million square feet of floor area, over 65,000 light bulbs, and annual heating and cooling costs in excess of $15 million. To reduce costs, it has implemented sustainability initiatives throughout the museum, for example, replacing many of the incandescent bulbs with energy-efficient LEDs. In the museum's European Paintings galleries, each of the 3,800 55-watt incandescent halogen bulbs was replaced with a 12-watt **LED**. This retrofit has had multiple benefits. Not only has the quality of lighting been improved; the more efficient lights have resulted in a 78% reduction in energy use and over $100,000 in annual savings. The LEDs produce less heat than the old halogen bulbs so the gallery also has a reduced, and less costly, cooling load and, because the LEDs last approximately 10 times longer than the halogen bulbs (5 years vs. 6 months), there is less waste and the maintenance staff don't have to spend as much time changing light bulbs.[11]

Electricians are also involved in energy management, including performing energy audits; examining where, how, and to what extent energy is being consumed by a building; and providing customers with options for controlling and reducing energy use.

As with other careers in construction, electricians may be called on to provide material and product recommendations and cost figures for energy-efficient and high-performance products. Electricians on green projects must coordinate their work with other trades and manage construction waste to integrate into the project's recycling and waste management system. Some building rating systems, for example, the Living Building Challenge, require post-occupancy data; such requirements impact electrical trade workers and others involved in metering.

As with other trades, there are multiple resources that provide information; some emphasize green training and skills.

Table 8.2 Resources of Special Interest to Electricians

Independent Electrical Contractors Association (IEC) *www.ieci.org*	A national trade association for **merit shop** (non-union, also called open shop) electrical and systems contractors, IEC has almost 3,000 member companies in 60 chapters throughout the U.S. It provides training, apprenticeships, and credentialing.
National Electrical Contractors Association (NECA) *www.necanet.org*	NECA is a trade association that provides advocacy, education, research, and standards development. NECA members are primarily small businesses, but many large, multinational companies are also members. With 119 chapters, NECA offers a variety of training and apprentice opportunities.
International Brotherhood of Electrical Workers (IBEW) *www.ibew.org*	A trade union that represents several hundred thousand workers, IBEW provides training, credentialing and a jobs board; a website includes a local union directory and links to other labor organization sites.
Illuminating Engineering Society of North America (IES) *www.ies.org*	A trade organization of manufacturers of lighting products, lighting designers, electricians, building contractors, and individuals working in affiliated lighting fields, IES sponsors conferences and seminars and has a scholarship program.
Association of Energy Engineers (AEE) *www.aeecenter.org*	An international membership organization with 95 chapters in the U.S., AEE sponsors multiple training programs and certificates in various aspects of green construction, including the Energy Manager in Training program and Green Building Engineer Certificate.

As we have seen, electricians have multiple, and major, roles on green building projects. As a consequence, there are a variety of training and certification programs for these workers. The Association of Energy Engineers is an example; it offers an Energy Manager in Training program and a Green Building Engineer Certificate, plus programs in commissioning, auditing, water efficiency, lighting efficiency, renewable energy, and more. AEE certifications require mandatory training followed by a written exam, which, in some cases, may be taken at remote locations.

Plumbing

Plumbers install and repair the water and gas supply to and from a building and its components: the pipes, fittings, and fixtures used to carry potable water, gas, sewage, and wastewater. They are responsible for hot water services, gas services, the installation of septic systems, fire protection services, and stormwater and sewage drainage systems. The Bureau of Labor Statistics groups plumbers with pipefitters and steamfitters, and projects that this sector of construction is likely to show vigorous growth in jobs in the coming years.[12]

Plumbers play a key role in developing high-performance systems.

There is growing pressure from multiple sectors—private building owners, municipalities, states, and the federal government—to manage water resources as carefully as possible. As noted in Chapters 1 and 2, this need is highlighted due to the severe drought conditions across the United States. For this and other reasons, codes are tightening and water districts are stepping up pressure to reduce consumption. For example, many local water districts and municipalities are using their buying power to purchase water-saving devices such as faucet aerators, high-efficiency shower heads, and high-efficiency toilets from manufacturers, and then offering them to consumers at heavily discounted prices, thus providing retrofit incentives to the public.

In addition to efficient products such as extremely low-flow toilets, composting, and waterless toilets, there are other systems that require plumbing expertise. Waterless urinals, dual piping to enable **greywater** use, and rainwater

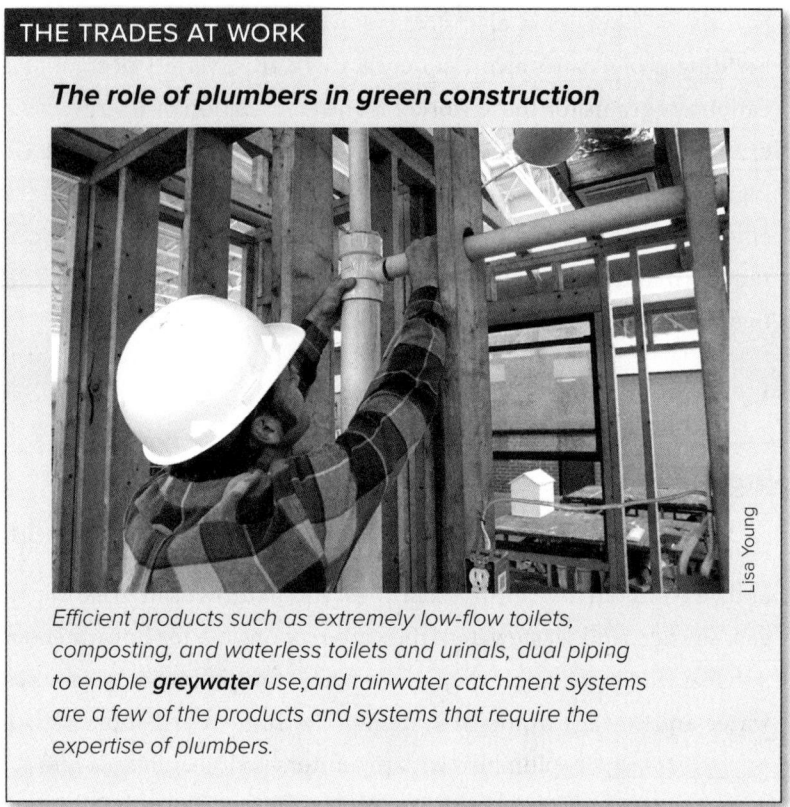

THE TRADES AT WORK

The role of plumbers in green construction

*Efficient products such as extremely low-flow toilets, composting, and waterless toilets and urinals, dual piping to enable **greywater** use,and rainwater catchment systems are a few of the products and systems that require the expertise of plumbers.*

catchment systems are products and systems that are increasingly requested. Codes, customer demand, and new products are creating increased need for plumbers with expertise in sourcing, installing, and maintain high-performance assemblies and systems.

Owners, whether or not they opt for green building certification, will need guidance from a plumbing contractor to look carefully at how water supply, use and drainage, fixture and equipment selection, and piping layout can contribute to substantial improvement over code requirements. (As noted elsewhere in this text, codes represent a minimum standard to which all projects must comply. Green buildings *exceed* these minimum standards.) Plumbers working on high-performance projects require expertise on green products and fixtures, and are likely to need to understand greywater and rainwater collection and distribution systems, and green/living vegetative roofs.

In addition to specifying efficient fixtures and appliances, there are other approaches that plumbers (and designers) can explore on green buildings, some of which we looked at in Chapter 2:

- **Rainwater harvesting:** Systems to collect rain may be as simple as a rain barrel filled by a downspout or a highly sophisticated collection, storage, filtration, and distribution systems capable of satisfying a building's total water need (see the Bullitt Center in Chapter 4).

- **Greywater collection and use:** Installation of diversion systems to redirect used wastewater for future use, such as for landscaping.

- **Drain water heat recovery systems:** Heat recovery systems capture heat in wastewater from appliances such as showers and dishwasher, before the water (and the heat) goes down the drain. The heat is extracted and used to preheat supply.

- **Efficient plumbing layout and hot water circulation:** Minimizing pipe runs and bends to reduce friction, and locating hot water sources as close as possible to end use.

Part of the job growth in the plumbing trade will be linked to the growing concern about water use, particularly in drought-stressed areas of the country. These concerns will require that existing systems be retrofitted to conserve scarce water supplies. The table below identifies resources that may offer networking and training opportunities for those in the plumbing trade.

Originating in Australia, the Green Plumbers Program is a national training and accreditation program for professional plumbers managed by the International Association of Plumbing and Mechanical Officials (IAMPO). The focus of the training is on upgrading skills and awareness of water efficiency and conservation, and the role of the plumber today.[13] Accreditation training consists of courses on environmental and technical issues; courses can be taken online.

As with HVAC and electrical trades, there are multiple unions, associations, and organizations that provide resources (including training) to those in the plumbing trades. Table 8.3 below identifies some of these.

Table 8.3 Resources of Special Interest to Plumbers

Plumbing-Heating-Cooling Contractors National Association (PHCC) *www.phccweb.org*	A membership organization made up of both open and union shops including plumbing and HVAC contractors and manufacturers, PHCC promotes education and training, sponsors apprenticeship and journeyman training, and advocates for safe sanitation and the development of better plumbing appliances and fixtures. It also offers print and online periodicals, meetings, and events, and sponsors online teaching programs and a Green Infrastructure Guidelines Certification Program.
United Association (Union of Journeymen and Apprentices of the Plumbing and Pipefitting Industry)—UA *www.ua.org*	A union representing plumbers, fitters, welders and HVAC service techs, UA provides training for their members in green skills, including the Green Systems Awareness program.
Mechanical Contractors Association of America (MCAA) *www.mcaa.org*	A membership organization for firms working in heating, air conditioning, refrigeration, plumbing, piping, and mechanical service, MCAA offers education, including webinars. See its website for local affiliates.
GreenPlumbers *www.greenplumberstraining.org*	GreenPlumbers® is a training and accreditation program that promotes the use of energy-efficient and water-saving technologies. See IAMPO.
International Association of Plumbing and Mechanical Officials (IAPMO) *www.iapmo.org*	IAMPO coordinates the development and adaptation of plumbing, mechanical, and solar energy codes and publishes the Uniform Plumbing Code (UPC) and the associated codes, the Uniform Mechanical Code (UMC) and the Uniform Solar Energy Code (USEC). In 2011, it acquired the North American rights to the GreenPlumbers Training and Accreditation Program.

Summary

The MEP trades play a vital role in the design and construction of green buildings. In addition to important input during the design phase, the mechanical, electrical, and plumbing trades (along with other specialty trades) are in the trenches (sometimes literally), performing the critical hands-on fieldwork that can make or break building performance. Energy and water sources, uses and disposal, indoor air quality, human comfort, and system controls all fall within the scope of MEP experts.

It is not just the MEP contractors who are impacted by green construction. The next chapter explores how green products, material handling and waste management, site procedures, and code and regulatory expectations are changing the roles of other trades, too.

Glossary

Air changes—how much air circulates in and out of a room.

Air quality—a measurement of the pollution in the air.

Capacity—the amount of energy such as heating or cooling that a system can provide under optimum conditions.

Demand—the amount of heating or cooling a building needs; also called "load."

Greywater—wastewater that has not been generated by toilets or urinals.

Heating and cooling loads—the amount of heating or cooling a building needs; also called "demand."

HVAC(R)—heating, ventilating, air conditioning (refrigeration).

LED—a lighting device that uses semiconductors called light-emitting diodes to produce light.

Load calculations—the process used to determine heating and cooling demand.

MEP—an acronym standing for the mechanical, electrical, and plumbing trades or services.

Merit shop ("open shop")—a firm or organization that pays workers according to the laws of the state and federal government and the individual's abilities; workers are not required to be in a union or pay the union dues.

Procurement—the process of obtaining goods and services.

Zero net energy (ZNE) **building**—a building that produces, on average, as much energy as it uses.

Oregon Dept. of Transportation

Green Construction and the Trades

Introduction

In the shift to green construction, even workers whose current skills may not dramatically change will be faced with unconventional ways of thinking about how they do their work and about how their work may contribute to meeting project performance goals. As noted elsewhere, green projects ideally utilize collaborative approaches to design and construction and this requires some understanding among all the trades. This chapter is intended to assist in this understanding.

As the reader discovered in Part 1, high-performance projects require a level of care among all the members of the construction team that goes beyond what may be required by code. Although the best contractors never accept marginally installed systems, green projects demand very careful and thorough work by all members of the construction team as well as an understanding of how construction practices can affect the eventual operation of the building. Even a relatively minor slip-up can have an impact. Examples of how small actions can have large negative impacts are: a drywaller who inadvertently slashes a vapor barrier with a utility knife to make drywall installation easier might compromise the tightness of the building and cause unacceptable levels of air leakage; a framer who leaves gaps in the sheathing, assuming it will just be covered by siding, may be reducing the energy efficiency of the **building**

envelope; or a carpet installer who uses an adhesive that contains disallowed synthetic chemicals, could threaten the building certification. On a green project, key products, assemblies, and systems and the people who install them are viewed as contributing parts of the whole, with each playing an important role in the success of the project.

Andrea Young

The general contractor develops a strategy to ensure that everyone on the team understands project goals and objectives. This understanding will help prevent situations such as the previous examples and can encourage everyone on the team to contribute to meeting performance objectives. For example, if the framers understand energy efficiency goals, they might suggest alternative ways of framing that leave more room for insulation, or the masons might recommend a product comparable to what is specified but with a higher recycled content, or the floor covering contractor might switch suppliers in order to procure materials that meet the requirements.

Additional trade requirements might include special documentation and extra submittals to meet the requirements for a green building certification program such as LEED. Documentation might include lists of salvaged, recycled, and local materials used; product verification such as FSC-certified wood; chemical content of materials and products used; and material waste management procedures.

A working knowledge of cost, selection, installation, and repair of new green products, systems, and materials will become a requirement for many specialty trades. But for most, the biggest change may be the adoption of onsite procedures designed to lessen the environmental impact of construction practices. For example, specialty contractors may work with the general contractor to develop recycling plans for materials such as brick and concrete that ordinarily would be landfilled; or workers used to using large amounts of water to clean equipment might be asked to conserve.

Although each job is different, there are general principles and approaches common to all green projects. In Chapters 11 and 12, we'll review credentialing and continuing education. There are many organizations and trade associations that may be useful to anyone, however; see Table 7.1 in Chapter 7 for a sampling.

The construction of almost any building requires more than just the mechanical, electrical, and plumbing trades, of course. As noted in the last chapter, there may be dozens of different specialty trades on a single job hired for their focused expertise. Discussed in the following are trades most likely to require enhanced skills on green projects. As in the last chapter, after each trade is a list of unions, trade associations, and organizations of interest to that trade. Not all of these resources are currently active in promoting green construction and some do not yet offer much information on the subject. This situation is likely to change, however, as green construction gains prominence. Further, some of the listed associations have local chapters that can provide opportunities for networking with people in your area in your trade who have experience or interest in green projects. Local trade associations are one of the best ways to find them.

Carpentry

Carpenters construct, install, and repair structures and fixtures made from wood and other materials. They make up the largest group of trade workers and are sometimes divided into separate subcategories including framers, formwork carpenters, trim and finish carpenters, and others. Each has a different function depending on the size and complexity of a project.

As carpenters typically deal with wood (the majority of residences, for example, are built primarily of wood), carpenters on green projects are concerned with issues regarding wood sources and treatment, including: Is the wood from environmentally damaging clear-cut forests? Has it been treated with harmful chemicals? Do the job specifications require that wood be certified, such as through the Forest Stewardship Council (and its FSC label)?

In the course of their work, carpenters buy and use miscellaneous products such as adhesives and sealants that often contain toxic chemicals such as volatile organic compounds (VOCs). As noted earlier, green projects may place restrictions on the use of certain chemicals. Carpenters will need familiarity with the products they use, know the available alternatives, and understand the installation, cost, and possible warranty implications.

Carpenters might be asked about (or might recommend) unconventional framing to reduce waste and to accommodate high-performance products, assemblies, and systems such as extra or unusual types of insulation, unconventional HVAC ducting, double-stud framing, or structural insulated panels (SIPs).

As with several other trades, carpenters may need to work with other trades to minimize air and moisture infiltration through the installation of highly efficient air and moisture barriers at all susceptible points, including doors, windows, and other penetrations. This requires an understanding of the role between thermal breaks and energy performance.

The carpentry work on conventional projects typically results in significant quantities of waste. Minimizing waste, recycling when possible, and disposing when necessary means that carpenters on green projects must know the recycling requirements and procedures on the job site.

Table 9.1 Resources of Special Interest to Carpenters

United Brotherhood of Carpenters (UBC) *www.carpenters.org*	UBC is one of North America's largest building-trades unions, with nearly a half-million members in the construction and wood-products industries. It has a green training program. See its website to locate regional councils and training centers.
Associated General Contractors of America (AGC) *www.agc.org*	A membership organization for contractors working in the commercial sector of the industry, AGC has over 90 chapters around the country and offers training and a Green Contractor Certification, *www.greenconstructionatwork.com*
Associated Builders and Contractors (ABC) *www.abc.org*	A trade organization that represents **open-shop** (merit/non-union) construction firms that work primarily in the industrial and commercial sectors, ABC Activities include workforce development, including green technology credentialing through its educational affiliate, the National Center for Construction Education and Research (NCCER), *www.nccer.org*
National Association of Home Builders (NAHB) *www.nahb.org*	A trade and membership association with more than 100,000 members, NAHB provides green training and other services, and, with the International Code Council, developed the National Green Building Standard for residential projects.

NAHB is an example of one of several good resources for carpenters and others who work in residential construction and remodeling. In addition to the National Green Building Standard that it developed with the International Code Council (discussed in Chapter 4), NAHB offers several green training programs to prepare builders for work in green construction (see *www.NAHBGreen.org*). The Certified Green Professional (CGP) is a two-course program that teaches builders strategies for incorporating green principles into their work, and the Master Certified Green Professional (Master CGP) offers training for more advanced workers. NAHB and its associated organizations, the Home Builders Institute (*www.hbi.com*) and the Home Innovations Research Labs (*www.homeinnovation.com*), are good resources.

Finishing trades: painters, drywall installers, and floor coverers

Workers in this category finish the surfaces of floors, walls, and ceilings and include, among others, painters, drywallers, and floor-covering installers. These workers apply plasterboard or other wallboards or acoustical tile to ceilings and walls; install carpets, tiles, and other floor coverings; hang decorative wall coverings such as wallpaper; and paint walls and ceilings, equipment, buildings, and other surfaces.

Painters

Painters are one of the finishing trades. They apply paints, stains, varnishes, and other finishes and, when necessary, remove grease and old finishes, and fill cracks and nail holes. When selecting materials and products, they typically consider durability, ease of handling, and method of application.

Toxic volatile organic compounds (VOCs) are contained in a wide array of products used by painters, including paint strippers, solvents, and thinners, as well as paints, lacquers, and more. VOCs are used to bind things together (as resins and pigments do in paints, for example) so they can be applied. This group of chemicals are volatile because they tend not to stay in a solid state and can vaporize—called **off-gassing**. This can happen when a product is used (such as caulks and adhesives), when a material such as paint dries, and even while it is stored. VOCs can continue vaporizing for months.[1] If the reader is familiar with the smell of a newly painted room, this is the smell of off-gassing. Even though many of us enjoy the smell of fresh paint, VOCs can cause an array of health problems and, when chemicals vaporize into the air, construction workers and, later, building occupants can inhale them.

Although the federal government caps the amount of VOCs in paint, some products use less and some eliminate VOCs entirely (at least from the base paint; pigment may add VOCs). Green projects typically avoid products with VOCs and painters using these products will need to understand how their use may vary from those that incorporate VOCs. For example, non-VOC paints may not provide the same level of coverage as conventional paints.

In addition to product choices, painters on green projects will be required to follow disposal and recycling procedures as required by the contract documents and by the general contractor.

Drywall installers

Drywall installers apply and tape wallboard to ceilings or interior walls of buildings. Drywall (also called gyp-board, wallboard, sheetrock, or sometimes just "rock") is the most common interior finish material for ceilings and walls and is made of a gypsum panel sandwiched between two heavy sheets of paper. Beyond the basic product, there are different types of drywall for different applications. For example, some drywall is treated with biocides to resist mold, some drywall is moisture resistant, and some has acoustic characteristics.

Most of the drywall on the market is made with recycled gypsum and recycled paper, but additionally contains a variety of polymers, binders and chemicals, and is not free of toxic materials. Standard drywall is typically made with at least some synthetic gypsum, which contains mercury and other heavy metals that can leach into the soil when the drywall is landfilled. Adding to the problems, when cut, gypsum drywall releases carcinogenic crystalline silica dust, which puts installers at risk.[2]

David Stewart-Smith

There are a variety of alternatives to standard drywall. For example: some drywall is made with recycled wood waste dust and minerals, instead of gypsum; some drywall is not paper-faced and is therefore less prone to mildew and mold and does not have toxic biocides added; and some drywalls are mercury free, and have no VOCs.

In any application, when there is excessive moisture vapor in a building, drywall is prone to mold and mildew. This tendency is exaggerated in green buildings that typically have exceptionally tight envelopes, designed to inhibit air and moisture infiltration. To avoid later problems, it is critical that drywall be properly installed and sealed and that all moisture barriers in the building are effective (see Chapter 2).

Floor Coverers

Carpet and flooring installers work with a variety of floor coverings, and their work includes preparing a smooth surface, filling cracks or waterproofing surface as necessary, laying out and cutting material, gluing, binding the edges, and joining carpet pieces together.

On green buildings, these tradespeople will be concerned with product content. For example, many conventional flooring products contain toxic materials and VOCs such as vinyl chloride, used to make vinyl and PVC and linked to numerous cancers.[3]

Contractors on a green project will be asked to procure and install non-toxic flooring such as bamboo, cork, and linoleum (made from linseed oil), carpet made from natural materials such as wool, jute, and sea grass, hardwood from a certified source such as FSC, or recycled products such as wood and tiles. The adhesives used may also have specific content requirements.

In addition to procurement requirements, all the trades, including flooring installers, will need to understand documentation and recycling and waste disposal parameters.

Some of these organizations have local chapters and most have resources available to members and others. Painting and Decorating Contractors of America (PDCA), for example, also has a training arm, Contractor College, that offers more than 180 online classes, including some that would be helpful for those interested in learning about the impacts of sustainability principles on their work. Examples of their classes and brief presentations include: Benefits of High-Performance Gypsum Panels for Moisture Management and Project Scheduling, Successful Management of LEED Projects, and Creating Healthy Living Environments with New Paint Technology.

Table 9.2 Resources of Special Interest to the Finishing Trades

National Tile Contractors Association (NTCA) *www.tile-assn.com*	A trade association for installers of ceramic tile and natural stone, NTCA focuses on education and training and offers a variety of resources.
Painting and Decorating Contractors of America (PDCA) *www.pdca.org*	PDCA is a trade association that serves the coating and wall covering industry with standards, training, and advocacy. Contractor College is its training center and offers multiple programs on green aspects of the trade, *www.contractorcollege.org*
Association of the Wall and Ceiling Industry (AWCI) *www.awci.org*	A trade association for wall and ceiling contractors, manufacturers, suppliers, and distributors, AWCI offers resources including magazines, newsletters, and product catalogs.
Certified Floorcovering Installers Association (CFI) *www.cfinstallers.com*	CFI is a trade association for floor installers that offers professional certifications and hands-on training courses.
Flooring Contractors Association (FCICA) *www.fcica.com*	A trade association representing the commercial floor covering industry, FCICA provides newsletters, magazine, webinars, and floor-covering training.
International Union of Bricklayers and Allied Craftworkers (BAC) *www.bacweb.org*	BAC is a union representing bricklayers, stone and marble masons, cement masons, plasterers, tile-setters, terrazzo and mosaic workers, and pointers/cleaners/caulkers.

Glaziers

Glaziers are responsible for selecting, cutting, installing, replacing, and removing all types of glass, including window glass, shower doors and mirrors, glass for tabletops, and display cases, or, in a commercial project, installing items such as heavy, decorative room dividers or security windows, glass panels, or curtain walls. Glaziers are key players in maximizing energy efficiency through the installation of new window and door products.

Leaky, single-glazed windows are recognized as being very energy inefficient and typically responsible for a large percentage of a building's total heat loss and an overall lowering in the **R-value** (a measure of resistance to heat flow) of a wall.[4] New window products have been developed to respond to the requirement that windows do not allow excessive heat to escape in the winter or unnecessarily heat up rooms in the summer. Consequently, glaziers

THE TRADES AT WORK

Window replacements for the Empire State Building

Luigi Scarantino

Poorly insulated or installed windows and doors can be major sources of energy loss (and energy costs) for a building, and owners are doing something about it. As noted in Chapter 4, New York's 80-year-old Empire State Building recently went through a $550 million dollar renovation, part of which was to improve energy efficiency and to attain LEED certification. Multiple efforts included equipment upgrades and opening up subdivided spaces to increase natural light, as well as the renovation of each of the building's 6,500 windows. The existing double-hung windows were turned into super-insulated glazing units with suspended, coated film, with a mix of krypton/argon gas inserted between the glass and the film. The "remanufacturing" of the windows occurred on-site, improved the thermal resistance of the glass, and cut the unwanted summer **heat gain** by more than half; 96% of the original glass and window frames were reused in the project.[5]

should be familiar with a wide variety of products. Among those commonly used are: double- and triple-glazed windows, **low-E glass** coatings that reflect long-wave heat energy and improve insulating characteristics, and gas fillings such as argon or krypton that boost energy efficiency.

Glaziers should understand the relationships between glass, spacer material used between different panes of glass, frame construction, and thermal characteristics, and know the roles that conduction, convection, and air leakage play in energy performance. The importance of proper installation, the role that sealing against moisture and air leaks plays in performance and durability, and the need for effective closing mechanisms are all part of the glazier's knowledge. Prevailing winds, building orientation, and the benefits of using certified wood products all feature into the glazier's approach, as do durability and recyclability.

Glaziers benefit from the increasing demand for environmentally conscious green construction, and, like many trades, need familiarity with new products and their cost and installation requirements. As noted, there are many ways for builders to get information on green principles. For information specific to glaziers, there are multiple membership associations, manufacturers, and organizations that provide networking and, in some cases, educational opportunities. Table 9.3 offers a sampling.

Table 9.3 Resources of Special Interest to Glaziers

Painting and Decorating Contractors of America (PDCA) *www.pdca.org*	PDCA is a trade association that serves the coating and wall covering industry with standards, training, and advocacy. Contractor College is its training center; it offers multiple programs on green aspects of the trade, *www.contractorcollege.org*
Window & Door Manufacturers Association (WDMA) *www.wdma.com*	WDMA is an industry association that provides information, advocacy, and product certification for window and door manufacturers.
National Fenestration Rating Council (NFRC) *www.AmericaGlassAssn.org*	NFRC is a nonprofit that rates the energy performance of windows, doors, and skylights. It has certification and membership programs that can provide networking opportunities.
American Architectural Manufacturers Association (AAMA) *www.aament.org*	AAMA is a trade association for the fenestration industry: windows, doors, skylights, curtain walls. Members include architects, manufacturers, and builders. AAMA writes standards and codes and offers a variety of resources.

Insulation installers

Insulation is a material or product that prevents the transfer of heat (or sound), and in buildings is applied around pipes and ducts, under floors, in ceilings and walls, and other places. Although most materials have some insulating value, most do not have sufficient thermal or acoustic resistance to be useful as an insulating material; copper is an example. There are however multiple materials that, when properly installed, provide effective insulating values. Cellulose, fiberglass, and various types of foam are examples. Insulation is installed in different ways: some loose-fill insulation such as fiberglass or cellulose is blown in, fiberglass or cotton batts are stapled or laid in place, and foam boards are typically nailed in place.

As noted in earlier chapters, the resistance to heat flow is given a rating called an R-value, which is a measurement derived from standardized tests: the higher the R-value the better the insulating characteristics. R-value depends on the type of insulation, its density, and its thickness (for example: 1 inch of closed-cell polyurethane foam has an R-value of approximately 6 per inch; fiberglass and cotton batts each have an R-value of around 3.5 per inch).[6] Improper installation of insulation (such as fiberglass that is stuffed too tightly between studs) will result in a decrease in performance.[7]

Proper insulation is critical for energy efficiency, and new products and creative construction procedures are being developed in response to strengthened energy standards and codes. Continuous insulation at wall assemblies is one example. Instead of the conventional approach of filling the cavities between structural members with insulation that offers multiple avenues for air and heat leaks, the insulation is continuous across all structural members. As there are no **thermal bridges** (areas of increased heat loss such as a stud), the energy performance of the building envelope is improved.

In addition to new ways of installing insulation, workers in this trade need to know the performance of, and installation techniques for, new insulating products such as recycled denim, vacuum insulation panels (with an R-value of 30 per inch), ultra-low-density aerogels, soybean-based spray foam, and more. (Yes, seriously, denim and soybeans can be used to make building materials.)

Table 9.4 Resources of Special Interest to Insulation Installers

North American Insulation Manufacturing Association (NAIMA) *www.naima.org*	NAIMA is a trade association with a useful website and information on sustainability and energy efficiency.
Insulation Contractors Association of America (ICCA) *www.insulate.org*	ICCA is a trade organization for residential and commercial insulation installers.
National Insulation Association (NIA) *www.insulation.org*	A trade association representing both union and non-union contractors, distributors, and manufacturers primarily in commercial and industrial construction, NIA sponsors annual conventions and training programs and its website has links to insulation associations around the country.
International Association of Heat and Frost Insulators and Allied Workers (AWWIU) *www.insulators.org*	AWWIU is a trade association with updated apprenticeship training and information on green construction.
Air Barrier Association (ABAA) *www.airbarrier.org*	ABAA is an association that provides information on air barriers and building envelopes.

The reader can find listings for other energy and environmental nonprofits and organizations of interest to insulation installers through the North American Insulation Manufacturers Association website. Listed groups are sources of information on tax credits, insulation to improve energy performance, and more.

Roofers

Roofers work on the installation of new roofs and the repair and renovation of existing roofs. If needed, roofers also replace old materials with new, solid structures. Roofers deal with a variety of materials including tar, asphalt, tile, rubber, and metal to protect a structure and its contents from water damage. For many jobs, roofers must remove the existing materials before laying down a layer of fresh tarpaper and installing new materials using either staples or nails. Often, roofers must replace wood on the roof that is damaged due to weather exposure and rot.

In addition to cost, installation, and warranty concerns, roofers on green projects will emphasize durability, recycled content, and product recyclability.

As with all workers on a green project, waste management and recycling strategies will be part of the roofer's concern and responsibilities.

Roofers on high-performance buildings may be engaged in the installation of roof-mounted solar photovoltaic arrays that present multiple potential complications of which the roofer should be aware: Can the roof carry the load? (Solar arrays typically add 3 to 4 pounds per square foot.[8]) Given the added traffic on the roof surface to maintain the panels, how will this impact roof durability? How will existing roof warranties be impacted? Will any required roof penetration, such as electrical conduits, compromise the roof, and are

THE TRADES AT WORK

Green roofs

The installation of living (green) roofs on new residential and commercial construction as well as on existing buildings provide job opportunities for multiple trades including roofers, plumbers, landscapers and others. Because living roofs provide insulating benefits as well as reduce stormwater runoff and the loads on sewage systems, cities throughout the United States have converted existing traditional roofs into those with vegetative cover. Chicago was an early leader in this effort and among almost 400 green roofs is the 20,300 square foot green roof on the 1911 City Hall shown here. The city compared surface area temperatures on the City Hall green roof and found that on a typical summer day it was almost 80 degrees Fahrenheit cooler than adjacent conventional roofs, which meant significantly lower cooling demands.[9]

Conservation Design Forum

Some property owners are discovering that green roofs offer more than energy conservation and water management benefits. There are examples of commercial enterprises that are taking advantage of overhead landscapes. A café in Long Island City NY, for example, makes its sandwiches and salads from vegetables grown on its roof and sells produce to the community.[10]

special flashing techniques required by the roofing contractor? Will drainage be impacted?

A small but increasing number of buildings now has a **green (living) roof** that incorporates landscape into the roofing system. As noted in Chapter 2, vegetative roof systems include a waterproofing layer, a root barrier to prevent roots from growing too far down, a drainage and irrigation system, and a suitable growing medium for plants. In addition to installation and maintenance job opportunities, living roofs provide multiple building-specific and community benefits including: improved insulating value and energy efficiency, stormwater management due to absorption of excess water by plants, improved air quality, increased biodiversity, and more.[11] Those installing green roofs require knowledge and expertise typical of roofers (understanding non-living elements such as the costs and installation issues with water proofing, loads, and warranties) as well as expertise in the "living" roof components such as water management, growing media, plants, and maintenance.

Because many green buildings include rooftop installations such as solar panels or green roofs, roofers face a range of challenges. These include structural considerations, knowledge of applicable codes, accessibility for maintenance of the green system, warranty concerns, and more. For those interested in getting maximum speed on green roofs, GRHC (see Table 9.5) has a helpful website that includes an overview of the field, including definitions, projects, conferences and events, a bibliography, and more.

Table 9.5 Resources of Special Interest to Roofers

National Roofing Contractors Association (NRCA) *www.nrca.net*	NRCA is a nonprofit association that represents all segments of the roofing industry, including contractors, manufacturers, distributors, engineers, building owners, and others. It sponsors EnergyWise Roof Calculator Online, a Web-based application to evaluate thermal performance and energy costs, and offers classes in rooftop photovoltaic systems.
Green Roofs for Healthy Cities (GRHC) *www.greenroofs.com*	GRHC is a trade association that offers a range of services and information on green roofs and courses in over 30 cities nationwide.
Single Ply Roofing Industry (SPRI) *www.spri.org*	SPRI is a trade association representing sheet membrane and component suppliers to the commercial roofing industry.

Other specialty trades and green construction

Carpenters, roofers, insulation installers, glaziers, painters, and drywallers are not the only specialty tradesmen on the job. On some projects, there may be dozens more. An emphasis on building performance requires that many of these workers adapt to new approaches to their work. For example:

Masonry tradespeople

Masonry tradespeople (bricklayers, cement masons, and others) working on green jobs are likely to be involved with materials and assemblies incorporating characteristics that extend beyond durability. Products that use less energy to produce and improve building energy performance (for example, masonry anchors that reduce thermal bridging); mortars, grouts, stucco, and concrete blocks that incorporate less energy-intense alternatives to cement such as fly ash; aggregates made from recycled waste and slag; and products that are lightweight or locally sourced may all be part of a green building. Tightening energy codes that impact masons (for example, requiring continuous insulation over certain masonry units), designs that utilize masonry as integral components of a building's heating and cooling loads, and alternative foundation and wall systems (such as insulating concrete forms) to improve building energy efficiency are part of today's green construction procedures. Efforts are being made to expand the profile of these trades in green construction. The Bricklayers and Allied Craftworks union (BAC) and the International Masonry Institute, for example, work with manufacturers to promote sustainability and create jobs among their workers.[12]

Landscape contractors

Landscape contractors play important roles in the development of green projects. The elimination of invasive plants, the installation and maintenance of native and adapted drought-tolerant plants, the selection and installation of appropriate plants on living roofs, green infrastructure that includes products such as natural drainage areas, and greywater irrigation systems may all be part of a landscaper's scope of work.

Green landscaping

As many parts of the U.S. experience severe or extreme drought, public and private landowners are adopting policies and design approaches to conserve water. As a result, landscape contractors need to adapt to a variety of new approaches and project requirements. These approaches may include the removal of water-intensive plantings (including turf) and the installation of hardy, drought tolerant plants that can survive with little or no water; the installation of drip irrigation systems; the use of porous asphalt and concrete; and the design and installation of rainwater catchment systems. In addition to voluntary performance goals, some municipalities, for example San Francisco, also have green landscaping ordinances that require compliance. These ordinances address exterior water use, hard-surface permeability requirements and more.

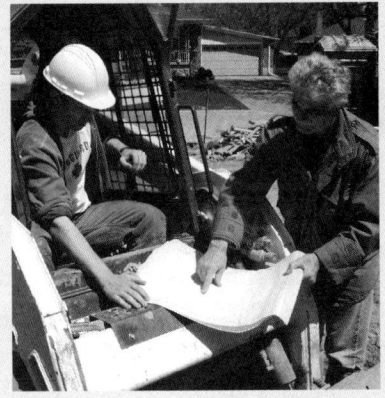

Ethan Drinker, courtesy of Coldham & Hartman Architects

Heavy equipment operators

Heavy equipment operators working on green projects need heightened sensitivity to habitat protection and restoration, and need to be proactive in minimizing soil compaction, erosion, and water runoff. There are regulations in place to reduce the pollution emitted by diesel engines, but the Environmental Protection Agency also advises owners of older equipment to install soot-reducing filters, to use cleaner fuels, to reduce engine idling, and more.

Equipment operators may also be required to use biodegradable hydraulic fluids and diesel injectors, and may be required to develop measures to reduce oil spillage, to reuse equipment components, and to recycle all waste fluids.

Laborers

Although not considered a separate specialty trade, laborers are important on any jobsite. They perform a variety of low-skilled and semi-skilled tasks on a construction site and often provide assistance to specialty contractors such as rough carpenters, plasterers, and masons. Their work may include using, supplying, or holding materials or tools; erecting scaffolding; cutting wood; and cleaning work areas and tools. Depending on the type of project, laborers may work with a wide range of tools and materials. Although no specific training is required for laborers on green jobs, they need to be aware of a variety of environmentally sensitive procedures such as material recycling and erosion control during construction.

Other industry workers

There are many individuals involved in construction who perform tasks that are important beyond the physical work. Some of these workers are also impacted by the growth of green construction, as in the following categories.

Manufacturers/product representatives and suppliers

This group includes the individuals and companies that make up the product manufacturing and supply segment of the construction industry. Product representatives, suppliers, and distributors who furnish products (but typically not labor) to contractors and subcontractors are sources for up-to-date information and cost data and, once construction is under way, can provide a range of services to the contractor. These services might include technical assistance as well as installation advice and inspections, and operational and maintenance training for the owner's facility manager. Many high-performance products, such as solar panels, wind turbines, and super-efficient pumps and equipment, for example, may be unfamiliar to installers and end-users and require information and/or training from product representatives.

Testing, inspection, and commissioning agents

Testing and inspecting occur multiple times in construction. In addition to code and regulatory inspections, there are other tests that are required. Some are required by law (such as testing steel bolt connections or welds), some by the contract documents (such as air leakage tests to ensure doors and windows meet performance requirements), and still others may be completed as part of a contractor's quality control measures. Testing is typically done by independent testing agencies and may be based on calculations or analysis of data or on physical tests conducted during manufacturing (such as steel strength tests) or in the field (such as slump tests to measure concrete design mix). Agencies such as ASTM International (formerly known as the American Society for Testing and Materials) may certify performance criteria for specified products or materials.

Darren Holden

Before a site can be occupied or used, it must be inspected and certified by the agency having jurisdiction over the project (such as the local building department) and any other jurisdictional agencies. Inspections are performed to verify that the project and its components are in full compliance with codes and regulations. To be effective on high-performance buildings, inspecting agents need to be up-to-date on changing codes and regulatory requirements and the products, systems, and assemblies incorporated into a non-conventional structure.

Many projects include **commissioning agents**, who are typically hired by the owner to verify that specific systems are installed properly and are working as designed. Commissioning agents often review operations and maintenance information for the owner, may review drawings and other documents, and ideally is on board throughout construction. Projects seeking green building certification such as LEED are required to do **commissioning** during occupancy to verify that the total project (not just individual assemblies or systems) is performing as intended. Some private building certification programs as well as green codes (such as California's statewide building energy standards code, **CALGreen**) require commissioning and it is becoming increasingly common as a standard practice.[13]

The adoption of green protocols and requirements at all levels of the process is dictating that inspectors be thoroughly familiar with new green codes and ordinances as local jurisdictions and states adopt them. As noted, green rating systems such as LEED have specific inspection requirements to verify building performance.

Environmental health professionals/ indoor air quality managers

This category represents a collection of professionals who work in many industries, including construction, to monitor the effects of hazardous materials. These workers set up equipment to test water, soil, and air quality; analyze results; assist in the design and implementation of mitigation and monitoring efforts; and may be involved in controlling the sources of pollution. They review and analyze work environments and conduct inspections to verify compliance with regulations and laws governing workplace health and safety, including regulations enforced by OSHA. Increasing demand for safe and healthy work environments creates demand for these professionals.

Facility and building managers

Individuals in these positions are employed by the owner to ensure that all systems are operated and maintained properly in a building, plant, or complex. Facilities managers typically become involved at the end of a project, and the GC provides them with operations information prior to occupancy. If the building is green or has unconventional equipment, products, and systems, the facility manager will typically receive training on their proper operation and maintenance. As discussed previously, all systems must be operated and maintained properly for a building to meet performance goals. The facility manager is typically the responsible party. In addition, the facility manager may be required to explain green systems and behavioral procedures (such as shading or occupancy controls) to the building users.

Summary

All workers on high-performance building projects, in all sectors of the construction industry, must understand how a green project differs from a conventional project. Everyone, not only those in the mechanical, electrical, and plumbing trades, is impacted. An increasing emphasis on energy and water efficiency, site utilization, and environmental impacts requires workers to learn new ways of thinking about and approaching their work. Even those whose current skills may not change dramatically will need to understand *why* they're doing things the way they are on a green project. The attitude "Hey, we've always done it this other way and its been good enough" doesn't acknowledge that maybe the old way *wasn't* good enough. Some of the changes that all workers are likely to face include:

- Increased cooperation between the trades, with an understanding of how the work of one trade might negatively (or positively) impact the work of another

- Understanding the role of a trade in meeting overall building performance goals

- Keeping up-to-date with codes and standards that are continually changing and tightening

- Understanding expectations regarding construction work standards and on-site procedures such as the conservation of existing site resources, waste management procedures, and procurement requirements

- The possibility of increased documentation and submittal requirements for projects that are attempting to be certified under one of the green building rating programs

Glossary

CALGreen—California's statewide building energy standards code.

Commissioning—a process of verifying that a building and all its systems and equipment are installed as specified and the building is operating at optimal performance. Commissioning can occur during design, construction, and operation.

Commissioning agent—member of the project team who coordinates the commissioning process.

Facility manager—employed by the owner to ensure that all systems are operated and maintained properly in a building, plant, or complex after occupancy.

Green Roof—a roof that is partially or completely covered with vegetation; also known as a living roof.

Insulation—a material or product that prevents the transfer of heat (or sound).

Low-E glass—glass with a coating that reflects long-wave heat energy and improves insulating characteristics.

Off-gassing—the emission of noxious gases, as from building materials.

R-value—a measure of resistance to heat flow; the higher the R value the greater the insulating value.

Solar heat gain—the increase in temperature in a space, object or structure that results from solar radiation.

Thermal bridge—an area or material that has significantly higher heat transfer capability than the surrounding area, resulting in heat loss.

Susan Bilo

Renewable Energy and the Trades

Given the growth of renewable energy systems, the energy sector of the construction industry provides multiple opportunities for workers in the construction industry not only for designers and engineers, but also for contractors and project managers, specialty tradespeople, estimators, inspectors, auditors, and more. Although much of the construction of renewable energy systems requires traditional skills such as electrical, plumbing, and roofing, some specialized knowledge is often required. This is true for **utility-scale solar and wind farms**, for example, with large power-generation machinery located high above the ground. But even much smaller rooftop solar systems, generally considered simpler than wind power systems,[1] typically require that installers have specialized training. Once operational, technicians are required to monitor power generation and distribution, and electricians, plumbers, pipefitters, and steamfitters are required to operate and maintain the systems.

Renewable energy systems

As noted, owners of green buildings strive to eliminate or reduce the use of fossil-fuel-based energy (coal, oil, and natural gas) by reducing demand and by relying on renewable sources that are replenished or that restore themselves over short periods of time. These energy sources, including solar and wind, are abundant and freely available (although a "free" fuel doesn't mean a fuel without cost; see chapter 2 regarding the link between water and energy).

For example, there is enough solar energy falling on the earth in one and a half *hours* to match total worldwide energy consumption for a *year*.[2] Closer to home, "the sunshine that falls on Texas each month has more energy than all of the oil that has *ever* been pumped out of the state."[3] Harnessing this energy is a different matter and the world is trying to economically capture, convert, and effectively distribute it.

Renewable energy sources do not represent a large percentage of U.S. power. In 2014, just under 9.8% of all the energy consumed in the United States was from **renewables** (up from 8.2% in 2008) and accounted for about 13% of electrical generation.[4] But these figures are increasing and, according to several sources, including the Energy Information Agency, the use of renewables is anticipated to continue growing.[5]

Solar photovoltaic systems are the fastest growing source of electricity in the United States.[6] But solar energy is not the only renewable, others include:

- Wind

- Geothermal

- Hydropower

- Bioenergy

Each of these types of energy have different characteristics and cost/benefit implications. Systems fueled by renewable energy can be designed to satisfy a variety of needs for different applications and building types. Solar and wind-based systems, for example, can be effectively utilized to heat, cool, and light a single-family residence or a commercial office building. On a larger scale, solar and wind energy can also be harnessed to fuel complex, utility-scale **power plants**, capable of generating sufficient electricity for thousands of homes.

Let's look briefly at each of these renewable energy sources.

Solar energy systems

The sun's energy can be captured and used as heat (**thermal energy**) or it can be converted into electricity. The types of solar heating systems range from very simple "passive" systems with little or no mechanical parts to huge and very complex solar "farms" capable of generating hundreds of megawatts of electricity. Solar technology falls into two broad categories: photovoltaic systems that use semiconductors to directly convert the sun's energy into electricity and solar thermal systems (also called solar hot water systems) that convert the sun's energy into low-temperature heat for space and water heating or to super-heat water used for the generation of electricity.

Photovoltaic (PV)

The majority of solar energy technologies on the global market today are photovoltaic (PV), whereby an electric current is produced in a material when exposed to light.[7] There are different types of PV systems, with different equipment, and these can connect with or be independent of an existing power grid such as those operated by utility companies. PV systems are used in small-scale applications such as a single house, or can be installed in very large, utility-scale arrays that generate large amounts of electric power.

PV technology is based on the ability of certain materials (primarily silicon but also thin-films) to act as tiny semiconductors. When sunlight (which contains energy) strikes a cell, its energy is converted into electric current, which, depending on the specifics of the system, can be used directly or fed into a power grid for future use. We'll look briefly at the three common applications of PV technology:

- Flat plate PV

- Building-integrated photovoltaics

- Concentrating PV (CPV)

Flat plate PV systems have been around since the 1950s and 60s and today are used extensively on residential and commercial structures; they can be seen in communities throughout the country. Flat plate PV systems utilize an arrangement of photovoltaic cells mounted on a rigid flat laminate and covered with a transparent (tempered glass) top. The cells are freely exposed to incoming sunlight and generate electricity. Arrays of flat panels (modules) are often secured to roofs but may also be ground-mounted.

Installation of flat plate PV panels

Installers and technicians working in this field typically have experience as electricians, plumbers, roofers, or construction workers and incorporate many traditional technical skills such as electric motor control, wiring, piping, and power distribution. Specialized skills typically include a general understanding of solar technologies as well as specific requirements for the safe installation, maintenance, troubleshooting, and pricing of systems,[8] plus knowledge of local building codes and ordinances, the National Electric Code, and sometimes of federal, state, county and local grants, subsidies, and rebate programs that

USMC

A worker installs a rooftop PV solar array.

can help offset the cost of the installation. A solar flat plate PV system includes more than just modules, and workers in the industry are familiar with other system components including mounting systems to affix modules to roofs and other surfaces, wiring and interconnection cables to connect the panels other electrical components of the system, switches, solar inverters to convert the direct current (DC) output of a PV panel into alternating current (AC), and, for some installations, optical lenses, mirrors, and more.

In addition to specialty tradespeople, career opportunities in solar energy include manufacturing and sales, customer support, software applications development, system design, engineering, and project management. Solar financing, vital to industry growth, is undergoing rapid change and requires skilled people.

Flat plate systems may be connected to a power grid or may be designed to operate independently (typically, with batteries to store the electricity for night and other times when power is not being generated). If a flat plate system is connected to a power grid, no electricity will be required from the utility company as long as there is enough electricity flowing in from the PV system.

If the solar system is generating more power than is being used, the excess will flow back into the grid, turning the electric meter backward. (In the 40+ states that allow **net-metering**, all power goes in and out through a single meter and the customer pays only for the *net* electricity used.)

Building-integrated photovoltaics (BIPVs) integrate solar cells directly into building materials and are an exciting new type of PV technology. Because PV systems can be fabricated in different forms, they may be integrated into glass, shingles, tiles, and other products and assemblies that allow building components to double as solar collectors. Potential on-site power sources include: glazing systems that incorporate solar cells; roofing systems that incorporate BIPV shingles, tiles, and metal; and curtain walls. Although BIPV technology has tremendous potential, it is relatively new and therefore still expensive; cost is falling as demand increases, however.[9]

Concentrating photovoltaic (CPV) systems also directly convert sunlight into electricity but use lenses or mirrors, instead of flat plate collectors, to focus sunlight onto a small area of highly efficient semiconducting material such as silicon (called cells). By concentrating sunlight on a small area, CPV systems can generate the same amount of power with less materials and with a smaller footprint than non-concentrating-type systems. But, as diffuse light can't be concentrated, they are most efficient in full sunlight, which limits where they can be installed.

Despite restrictions on location and costs, there are CPV systems in place around the world, and the global market is expected to grow substantially between 2013 and 2020.[10]

A CPV installation consisting of 500 pedestal assemblies, each of which contains 7,560 lenses that concentrate sunlight.

Dennis Schroeder/NREL

A quick look at units of measurement

Energy and **power** are often confused and sometimes used interchangeably. But they're different and are described by different units of measurement that are important to keep straight.

Energy is the ability to do work: to drive a truck down a highway, to push a sofa across a room, to light a filament in a bulb. Energy is typically measured in kilowatt-hours (kWh). Power is the *rate* at which energy (work) is produced or consumed and is measured in watts (W), kilowatts (one thousand watts, kW), mega-watts (one million watts, MW), and gigawatts (one billion watts, GW).

Let's use a 100-watt light bulb as an example of how power and energy relate to each other. We know that a 100-watt bulb gives off more light than a 60-watt bulb (it has more power). We also understand that the light doesn't get brighter the longer the lamp is turned on. This is because a 100-watt bulb is designed to put out 100 watts of power and no more. The quantity of energy consumed or light generated by the bulb is a function of the bulb's power (its wattage) and how long the bulb is on (time). The formula for this is Energy = Power × Time. If our 100-watt bulb is left on for one hour it will produce 100 watts × 1 hour of light (and heat) energy; the unit of measurement is 1 watt-hour of energy. If left on for 10 hours, the same bulb will still have a power output of 100 watts but will produce 10 times as much energy, or 1,000 watt-hours. (Instead of saying 1,000 watt-hours, we say 1 kilowatt-hour or 1kWh. This unit of measurement for energy may be familiar to the reader as utility companies use kWhs to bill customers for electricity usage.)

One hundred watts is the unit of measurement that describes the *capacity* of the bulb—the maximum power output possible. No matter how long the bulb is turned on it will never run at more than 100 watts. The concept of capacity is important when sizing heating and cooling systems. A 5 kilowatt (5kW) solar system for example, has the capacity to put out 5 kilowatts of power under ideal conditions (the brightest sun, the perfect orientation, etc.). But as ideal condi-tions don't last 24/7 (it gets dark, after all) the total energy that the system is able to generate is less and the system designer will match the system's anticipated energy output to the needs of the building occupants, called the **load** or **demand**.

(continued)

(There are multiple resources available on how to calculate heating and cooling loads. For an overview, see *HVAC Design Done Right,* by Allison Bailes writing for the Energy Vanguard Blog.)

Another common unit of energy measurement is the BTU, British thermal unit (a unit of energy equivalent to the heat produced by a single kitchen match and measured in watts). This is a unit most often used to measure heating and air conditioning equipment and systems. As with the previous examples, BTU is an expression of a theoretical maximum power output: the higher the BTUs, the more powerful the heating or cooling system.

Energy comes in many different forms—heat, light, motion, and more—and a characteristic is that it can be converted from one form into another. For example, boilers, power plants, and wind turbines, take energy in one form (e.g., gas or coal or wind) and turn it into another (e.g., heat or electricity). When we talk about producing or consuming energy, what we're talking about is the rate at which energy is converted from one form into another.

(For information on where our energy comes from and how we use it, see Appendix B.)

Solar thermal

Unlike photovoltaic systems, which convert radiant solar energy directly into electricity, solar thermal systems use the sun's energy to heat a working fluid (water or another fluid) or air. In small residential or commercial applications, the heated water or air is used directly to heat or cool buildings or domestic hot water; in community-scale applications, heated water is used to create steam that drives generators to produce electricity.

As with PV systems, there are different types of solar thermal systems: some are quite simple and suitable for a residential-scale installation; some are large and complex systems that generate power for entire communities; some systems are "passive" and rely on natural convection to circulate heated air or water while others are "active" and include pumping mechanisms; some systems are hooked up to batteries; and others are connected directly to a power grid. There are three primary types of solar thermal systems:

- Flat plate thermal collectors
- Evacuated tube collectors
- Concentrating solar power (CSP)

Flat plate thermal collectors: In a common type of flat plate thermal collector, sunlight passes through glazing and strikes a metal absorber plate, which heats up, changing solar energy into heat energy. The heat is transferred to a working fluid passing through pipes attached to the absorber plate. The heat may be used for space heating, domestic hot water, or cooling with an absorption chiller.

The main use of this technology is in residential buildings where the demand for hot water has a large impact on energy bills. (Some professionals conclude that the falling price of PV systems makes residential thermal flat plate systems less competitive.[11]) Commercial applications include Laundromats, car washes, military laundry facilities, and eating establishments. The technology can also be used for space heating if the building is located off-grid or if utility power is subject to frequent outages.

Evacuated tube collectors are a more recent technology than flat plate collectors and a more efficient means of capturing the sun's energy for space and domestic hot water heating. Several types are available, with the common element being a glass tube surrounding an absorber plate. A collector contains several rows of glass tubes connected to a header pipe on a frame. Each tube has the air removed from it (evacuated) to create a vacuum that provides excellent insulation. Inside the glass tube, a flat or curved aluminum or copper fin is attached to a metal pipe. The fin is covered with a selective coating that transfers heat to the fluid that is circulating through the pipe. An advantage of this type of collector is that because of the technology and a greater surface area exposed to the sun than flat plate collectors, it can capture sunlight early or late in the day and, even during overcast days.

Concentrating solar power (CSP): Other solar thermal systems are more complex and use solar energy to create steam to power conventional generators for the production of electricity. **Concentrating solar power (CSP)** systems (not to be confused with concentrating photovoltaic systems, CPV) use a mechanism to reflect sunlight onto a focal point. Unlike CPV systems that directly generate electricity, a CSP system concentrates solar heat to create steam to run a turbine that generates electricity. Most CSP systems use parabolic troughs, with long, curved mirrors that move to follow the path of the sun.

CSP systems are more common than Concentrating PV systems, which convert sunlight directly into electricity.

There are utility-grade CSP "farms" and three of the five largest in the world are located in the United States, the largest of which is the 377-megawatt Ivanpah Solar Electric Generating System in the Mojave Desert of California. (Interestingly, Google has a substantial financial stake in Ivanpah.[12]) More than 170,000 movable mirrors (called heliostats) focus sunlight on three 450-foot towers filled with a heat transfer fluid, raising temperatures to more than 1,000 degrees Fahrenheit and producing steam that spins turbines that generate electricity. After the facility is fully operational, it is estimated the project will produce hundreds of megawatts of electricity annually, add $400 million in local and state tax revenues, and produce $650 million in wages over its 30-year life. The majority of the equipment used to construct the solar thermal power generation plant is sourced domestically, too, creating additional jobs.[13]

As with PV systems, energy generated from CSP systems can be used at or near the point where the energy is needed, or the energy can be transmitted and distributed over wide geographic areas.

There are many national and local groups and organizations that provide extensive information about solar systems; Table 10.1 identifies several prominent ones.

Gilles Mingasson/Getty Images for Bechtel

The Ivanpah Solar Electric Generating System arrays in California's Mojave Desert

In addition to the websites identified in Table 10.1, there are many other organizations, blogs, magazines, and books freely available (Vote Solar, the Solar Foundation, Solar Electric Power Association, and Rocky Mountain Institute are a few). In addition, local community colleges, nonprofit organizations, builders exchanges, and chapters of national organizations such as USGBC may conduct local or online classes that would be helpful.

Table 10.1 Resources of Special Interest: Solar Energy Systems

Solar Energy Industry Association (SEIA) *www.seia.org*	This national trade association offers a variety of helpful information including news articles, a job board, information regarding legislation, training opportunities, certifications, and more. Its National Solar Database provides comprehensive information on solar companies operating in the United States.
Interstate Renewable Energy Council (IREC) *www.irecusa.org*	A nonprofit that provides links to helpful databases, training providers, and available incentives for renewable energy systems, IREC publishes multiple news publications on issues of interest to the industry and, in partnership with the American National Standards Institute (ANSI) provides standards for solar and renewable energy training programs.
Office of Energy Efficiency and Renewable Energy (EERE) *www1.eere.energy.gov*	An office of the U.S. Department of Energy, EERE is an excellent source of information, initiatives, and data on solar applications nationwide. EERE's site,"Energy Basics," is a good resource for all types of renewable energy information; website includes a comprehensive glossary.
International Solar Energy Society (ISES) *www.ises.org* American Solar Energy Society (ASES) *www.ases.org*	ISES provides information on renewable energy issues worldwide, has a network of student and young professional ISES members, publishes a scientific journal (*Solar Energy*), and issues reports and newsletters on the industry. Its U.S. section is the American Solar Energy Society (ASES), which was established in 1954. There are independent chapters of ASES (for example NorCal Solar, *www.norcalsolar.org*) serving most of the United States. Each chapter has its own membership and dues structure.
International Society of Sustainability Professionals (ISSP) *www.sustainabilitypro-fessionals.org*	ISSP is a nonprofit educational organization that offers workshops, information, and links to local professionals.
Bureau of Labor Statistics (BLS) *www.bls.gov*	This U.S. Dept. of Labor bureau includes information on renewable energy and job opportunities in the field.

Wind powered systems

Wind powered systems use turbines to convert the kinetic (motion) energy present in wind into energy that can be used for tasks such as grinding or pumping, or that can be used to spin a shaft, which connects to a generator that makes electricity.[14]

The central component of a large wind energy system is the turbine, which consists of three major components—the blades, a tower (for a small installation this is a metal frame), and a power drivetrain housed in a nacelle—each of which is designed and manufactured separately and installed on-site. Modern turbine blades are made of fiberglass and can be more than 200 feet long; towers comprise several steel segments placed atop one another; and the nacelle is a rectangular enclosure assembled on top of the tower and contains a rotor shaft, gearbox, generator, and other electromechanical components. The nacelle also contains electronic components, sensors, and control systems that allow the turbine to monitor changes in wind speed and direction, yaw (position) the turbine relative to wind direction, pitch the blades, vary the rotational speed, and control power production. The most common wind turbine configuration is a three-bladed horizontal-axis type (see photo).[15]

Wind turbines are available in a range of power capacities (as noted, capacity indicates how much power can be generated in ideal conditions). Small wind turbines are rated up to 100 kilowatts and are typically used for residential, farm, and small business applications as stand-alone or distributed grid-connected systems. Midsize wind turbines are rated above 100 kW and up to 1,000 kW and are used for larger industrial and community-based installations, and utility-scale systems use much larger, multi-megawatt-size wind turbines. Systems can consist of a

Wind turbines at the Forward Wind Energy Center in Wisconsin

Ruth Baranowski

single turbine, powering an individual facility or community, to a multi-wind-turbine array that feeds bulk electrical power into a utility power grid, just as with conventional power plants or solar farms.

The process of getting energy from the wind into the home or business is complex and involves many steps and players, including those directly employed in the trades, many of whom come from conventional trades but with enhanced or specialized training.[16] A 2012 report, *American Wind Farms,*

THE TRADES AT WORK

The manufacture and installation of wind systems

The manufacture of the components that make up a wind system—the blades and tower, the power equipment and electronics, gear housing, braking and power couplings, and more—requires workers in many different occupations, including machinists, machine tool operators, assemblers, welders, quality-control inspectors, and industrial production managers.[18] During installation, specialized construction workers and heavy equipment operators build access roads and foundations for the towers, stack the tower segments atop one another before adding the nacelle and blades to the top of the turbines, and connect the wiring. Specially trained electricians are required to complete the electrical installation of each wind turbine, connect individual wind turbines to the power collection system and substation, and connect the substation to the utility grid.[19]

Technicians and electricians are required to repair and maintain the operational turbines and ensure that electric motors, lighting and wiring, generators, communications systems, energy transmission systems, and machinery controls are working efficiently.[20] These technicians climb up and down the ladders housed within the tower to reach the nacelle and blades. On the top of turbines, they perform preventative maintenance and do routine checks and repairs.[21]

Work on the nacelle of a 2.3 MW, 260 foot high wind turbine

Dennis Schroeder/NREL

reports that every 250-megawatt wind farm creates several hundred construction jobs.[17] In addition, the development process involves analysts, engineers, technicians, machinists, assemblers, and other trade workers who are employed during the manufacturing phase.

Utility-scale wind farms are found in multiple states including California, Texas, Oklahoma, Iowa, Indiana, Oregon, and elsewhere.[22] (Iowa gets the highest percentage of its power from wind than any other state—almost 30%.[23]) The largest wind farm in the United States is the Alta Wind Energy Center (AWEC) in Tehachapi Pass in Kern County CA, which, when completed, will have a generating capacity of 1,550 megawatts (MW), large enough to supply power to 1.2 million people in 450,000 homes.[24]

Concerns about large-scale wind farms

Wind systems have their critics. Among concerns is that the capacity of a wind turbine typically doesn't take into account the amount of outside electric power required to operate the turbine, which includes power to maintain proper positioning of the blades and power for lights, controllers, monitoring, and data collection, and more. Some critics claim that because wind is highly variable, the actual capacity of a turbine may be much lower than advertised and that large-scale wind farms actually use more energy than they generate. Other concerns include the large footprint required for a wind farm, and some object to the aesthetics and noise and the fact that birds can be hurt by the blades.[25] Many professionals working with wind technologies argue that these concerns are myths and, furthermore, do not take into account the many benefits.[26]

Wind energy currently provides about 5% of U.S. electrical supply. Wind power is one of the fastest growing sources of new electricity capacity and the largest source of new renewable power generation added in the United States since 2000.[27]

Although not all sites are well suited for wind systems (the topography or other structures interfere, or there is a lack of wind), they can be installed on buildings and built on land or offshore, and there are even airborne wind systems.

Wind systems take flight

Not all wind systems are earthbound; research and development is being done on airborne systems. The Makani Airborne Wind Turbine (AWT), created by an Oakland CA–based company (and owned by Google X) is one. It is a tethered "kite" fitted with turbines, and generates power by flying in large circles. Operating at 1,000 feet, where the wind is stronger and more consistent than on the ground, the AWT mimics the speed and motion of a conventional wind turbine's aerodynamically effective blade tips. The kite eliminates 90% of the material used in conventional wind turbines (such as the tower) and can be used offshore above deep water. The power generated by the blades flows down the tether into the existing grid.[28]

Makani Power

Makani airborne wind energy prototype

Although U.S. wind power is currently experiencing strong growth, its success is tied, in part, to competing energy costs and the uncertainty of federal tax incentives.[29] The federal production tax credit (PTC), which provides a 2.2-cent per kilowatt-hour benefit for the first 10 years of a facility's operation, has been a major driver of wind power development over the past decade. But Congress has gone back and forth between expiring and extending the PTC; it has extended the provision five times and has allowed it to sunset on four occasions. This on-again/off-again status contributes to a boom-bust cycle of development that plagues the wind industry.[30]

As noted, the Department of Energy's WINDExchange website is a helpful source of information on wind systems. Its map of Wind Energy Education and Training Programs identifies education centers in each state. An interactive map enables the user to hover over a state and training locations, with links to information.

Table 10.2 Resources of Special Interest: Wind Energy Systems

American Wind Energy Association (AWEA) *www.awea.org*	A national trade association, AWEA offers a variety of information on wind energy, publishes a membership directory, and hosts the annual WINDPOWER conference.
Global Wind Energy Council (GWEC) *http://www.gwec.net/*	Members include all the world's major wind turbine manufacturers. GWEC provides news, information, publications, and job listings for wind farm and wind energy jobs worldwide.
U.S. Department of Energy WINDExchange *http://apps2.eere.energy. gov/wind/windexchange*	WINDExchange provides publications, webinars, podcasts, maps of wind resources, and a locator map of wind education and training programs in the United States.
National Wind Technology Center *wwwnrel.gov/wind*	This Department of Energy center located at the National Renewable Energy Laboratory provides research and development expertise assistance to other agencies and universities in wind and water power technologies.

Geothermal systems

Geothermal systems produce energy using the heat of the earth. Deep within the earth, molten rock (magma) heats underground water, some of which reaches the earth's surface as hot springs or geysers and some of which stays underground, trapped in reservoirs. This geothermal energy (*geo* = earth and *thermal* = heat) can be used in many ways, from large power plants that generate electricity to small-scale systems that use the hot water directly to heat buildings.

Geothermal power plants use steam as fuel for the generation of electricity. There are different types of geothermal power plants: sometimes steam from the earth is used directly; sometimes steam is created from the naturally occurring super-heated water located in the underground reservoirs. In all cases, however, steam is used to turn a turbine connected to a generator that changes the energy of motion from the turbine into electric energy that is fed into the power grid.[31]

Geothermal resources are concentrated in the West; Nevada, Utah, and California have the highest installed capacity, but geothermal power plants are located in more than a dozen other states.[32] The first and largest U.S. plant is located at the Geysers, north of San Francisco, and has been producing electricity since 1960; it has a capacity of almost 2,000 megawatts, comparable to the largest wind farm.[33] Due to untapped potential and several state policy changes and initiatives, the number of plants and additions to existing facilities is expected to grow substantially in the next two decades.[34]

A note about geothermal heat pumps

Unlike traditional geothermal systems, which use hot water and/or steam as a high-temperature fuel source for generating electricity, ground-source heat pumps, confusingly referred to as geothermal heat pumps, use the earth (and its constant ground temperature) as a giant heat exchanger. Electricity typically powers the circulation of water or antifreeze through pipes buried underground. During the winter, the fluid collects heat from the earth and carries it via the fluid circulating in the pipes, through the system and into the building. During the summer, the system reverses itself by pulling heat from the building, and dumping it in the relatively cooler earth.[35] Ground-source heat pumps operate like air conditioners or refrigerators and require electricity to operate (a compressor is the biggest load[36]) and some experts consider it inaccurate to refer to them as renewable energy systems.[37]

Although traditional geothermal has many benefits—it utilizes a virtually unlimited energy source that is clean and available 24/7, and creates no emissions—it also has potentially damaging consequences. These include possible seismic activity caused by drilling, threats to groundwater, and the potential for long-term changes to ground temperatures.[38]

As with any large power plant, the development of a geothermal plant can take many years, from exploratory work through construction, and requires workers from a variety of construction trades: crews to clear the land; equipment operators to build roads and transmission lines; drilling crews to drill the wells; cement workers, plumbers, pipefitters, welders, and steamfitters to install, maintain, and repair the pipe systems that carry hot, high-pressure fluids up from the wells; and electricians to hook up the plant's electrical components. Once the plant is running, operators and technicians remain on-site to monitor the plant and resolve any problems.[39]

Table 10.3 Resources of Special Interest: Geothermal Energy

Geothermal Energy Association *www.geo-energy.org*	A trade association composed of U.S. companies that support the expanded use of geothermal energy, it has a list of member companies with addresses and contact names.
Geothermal Technologies Office, U.S. Department of Energy *www.energy.gov/eere/geothermal*	This government office has multiple resources on geothermal: publications, information resources, and more.
International Ground Source Heat Pump Association (IGSHPA) *www.igshpa.okstate.edu*	IGSHPA is a nonprofit group supporting the ground-source heat pump industry with publications, information, research, and more.
Geothermal Heat Pump Consortium (GEO) *www.geoexchange.org*	GEO is a nonprofit trade association that promotes the manufacture, design and installation of geothermal systems. Its website offers a directory of contractors/service providers by state.

Hydropower

The word "hydropower" describes systems that use the energy of moving water to produce electricity. As noted, a traditional geothermal power plant uses steam to turn a turbine that then powers an electric generator. Hydroelectric systems use the motion of water to do the same thing. At its smallest scale, a hydro system can power a single home; the largest systems generate thousands of megawatts of power for entire communities.

There are multiple types of hydro systems. The largest require that a suitable river be dammed; in many of these systems, water is stored behind the dam in a reservoir and released as needed to drive a turbine that operates a generator.[40] The largest reservoir hydroelectric plant in the United States is the 6,800-megawatt Grand Coulee Dam, on the Columbia River in the Northwest. This huge dam and reservoir (the largest of 11 dams on the Columbia River[41]) provides electricity as well as irrigation and flood control. It is massive in scale—550 feet high and 500 feet wide—and took thousands of workers nine years to construct.[42] (It's interesting to note that this project is dwarfed by the 22,500-megawatt Three Gorges dam in China, the world's largest, which was completed in 2012.[43])

Smaller hydro systems, called run-of-river or in-stream systems, are less invasive than large plants. They require a relatively small water flow and no dam, and can be used to generate enough power for a large home, or for pumping water.[44] These systems typically require pumps, piping, a turbine, an alternator or generator, and wiring. They can be stand-alone or grid-connected.

About 7% of electric energy production in the United States, enough to power approximately 20 million homes, is currently from hydropower, and production is increasing (primarily from the upgrade to existing facilities). In the past ten years the technology has seen a significant increase in the amount of power generated at hydro facilities,[45] with approximately $6 billion invested in refurbishments and upgrades to existing plants.[46] Hydropower facilities are located throughout the country; the top five states by installed hydropower capacity are Washington, California, Oregon, New York, and Alabama, and 11 states receive greater than 10% of their electricity from hydropower.[47]

Water motion is a renewable energy source and has multiple benefits, including the ability to provide clean, efficient power. Large hydroelectric plants draw criticism, too, however, and some critics argue that very large dams can be environmentally damaging and disruptive to riverside communities. A movement toward "sustainable hydropower" is urging extreme care in planning, siting, and operating both small and large dams within an overall system that seeks to balance a range of resources and values.[48]

Table 10.4 Resources of Special Interest: Hydropower

Hydropower Reform Coalition *www.hydroreform.org/*	This coalition provides information on how dams and hydropower projects can be operated differently to reduce their adverse impacts.
National Hydro Association (NHA) *www.hydro.org*	A nonprofit working to develop hydropower, NHA is a good source of information.
International Hydropower Association (IHA) *www.hydropower.org*	Created under the auspices of UNESCO in 1995, IHA was founded to advocate for sustainable hydropower. Their blog has up-to-date information on what's happening around the world in hydro.
National Wind Technology Center *www.nrel.gov/wind*	A This Department of Energy center located at the National Renewable Energy Laboratory provides research and development expertise assistance to other agencies and universities in wind and water power technologies.

R&D is finding new ways to use water motion to generate power.

Hydropower covers more than conventional hydroelectric plants and in-stream systems. A variety of technologies under development that use motion energy to generate power are likely to become increasingly important. These systems include ocean wave and tidal systems that convert wave and tidal energy into electricity.[49] To date, few of these projects have been built anywhere in the world. In the United States, pilot projects are under way and the Federal Energy Regulatory Commission has approved preliminary permits for a handful of projects in Arkansas, Alaska, New York, California, and Michigan.[50]

Bioenergy

Bioenergy describes energy that is obtained from biologically derived material called **biomass**. Electricity can be generated from construction and demolition waste, scrap lumber, wood and agricultural crops and waste, corn kernels and stalks, perennial grasses, and other organic materials, all of which are biomass. All of these materials store energy from the sun that can be released in a number of ways, including burning to produce heat or electricity, or converting it into liquids such as ethanol, biodiesel, or gas.[51] The majority of biomass energy systems are currently used to create ethanol for the transportation industry, but it is also used to generate heat and electricity.

There are different types of bioenergy systems, ranging from residential-scale heating stoves and boilers to large power plants capable of generating many megawatts of electricity. Power plants fueled with biomass were first built in the United States in the 1980s; as of 2012, there are more than 100 biomass power plants, located in more than half the states.[52]

Bioenergy power plants have many benefits, including the ability to be reliable disposal systems for potentially dangerous waste materials. For example, millions of pine trees killed by the Mountain Pine Beetle have been used to fuel an 11.5-megawatt biomass plant in Gypsum CO, thus safely reducing fire hazards as well as providing heat and light for thousands of homes.[53] As with any large power plant, the development of biomass plants creates jobs in the

Table 10.5 Resources of Special Interest: Bioenergy

Biomass Energy Resource Center (BERC) *www.biomasscenter.org*	A nonprofit organization located in Vermont, BERC works to advance community-scale biomass. Its website includes a resource library and an extensive glossary.
National Renewable Energy Laboratory (NREL) *www.nrel.gov/biomass.html*	NREL is the only federal laboratory dedicated to R&D, commercialization, and deployment of renewable energy technologies. See its website for information on its bioenergy research program, plus biomass energy maps.
National Resources Defense Council (NRDC) *www.nrdc.org/energy/renew-ables/biomass.asp*	NRDC has lots of helpful information on renewable energy, including overviews, state profiles, and energy maps. Its section on biomass includes explanatory information plus other resources.

construction industry: several hundred tradespeople are required during construction, plus full-time managers and technicians once the plant is operational.

But biomass can also have negative impacts.[54] An April 2014 report from the Partnership for Policy Integrity, for example, calls biomass electricity "the new coal" because of its potentially damaging environmental effects, including pollution from burning.[55] Efforts are under way to develop new sources of biomass fuels such as switchgrass, fast-growing trees, crop residues, algae, and clean municipal wastes. New technologies to economically convert biomass into advanced biofuels, and new or expanded infrastructure may be needed to deliver these fuels to consumers.

Summary

Compared to fossil-fuel-based energy sources, renewables do not currently provide a large portion of the energy that we generate or consume, but the portion is growing. At least in the short term, solar and wind systems are expected to lead this trend: for example, electricity generation from wind increased from about 6 billion kilowatt hours in 2000 to roughly 168 billion kilowatt hours in 2013.[56] The growth of the solar industry is also impressive: from 2012 to 2013, it grew by 53%. As noted, this translates into direct work in construction, often for those with experience in traditional trades such as electricians, plumbers, and roofers. In addition, an increase in the development of renewable systems will result in increased numbers of workers in manufacturing, computer-controlled machine tool operators, machinists, assemblers, welders, glaziers, coating and painting workers, and others, in addition to quality-control inspectors, energy and performance auditors, product testers, and more.

The next chapter reviews professional certifications that can provide industry workers with the skills and credentials they need to be successful employees on projects that utilize renewable energy.

Glossary

Biomass—any organic matter that can be burned for energy.

British thermal unit (BTU)—a unit of energy equivalent to the heat produced by a single kitchen match and measured in watts.

Building-integrated photovoltaics (BIPVs)—systems that integrate photovoltaic solar cells directly into building materials.

Concentrating photovoltaic (CPV) systems—systems that generate electric power by concentrating sunlight or thermal energy on photovoltaic cells. Not to be confused with concentrating solar power systems.

Concentrating solar power (CSP) systems—systems that use a mechanism to reflect sunlight onto a focal point to create heat or steam. Not to be confused with concentrating photovoltaic systems.

Energy—the ability to do work. Different forms of energy can be converted to other forms, but the total amount of energy remains the same.

Evacuated tube collectors—solar thermal systems that use glass tubes surrounded by absorber plates.

Flat plate PV system—a group of solar photovoltaic panels connected together.

Geothermal systems—systems that produce energy using the heat of the earth.

Hydropower—systems that use the energy in moving water to do mechanical tasks or to produce electricity.

Net-metering—the practice of using a single meter to measure consumption and generation of electricity by a small generation facility (such as a house with a wind or solar photovoltaic system); the net energy produced or consumed is, respectively, sold to or purchased from the power provider.

Photovoltaic array—a group of solar photovoltaic modules connected together; also called flat plate PV panels.

Photovoltaic panel (also called a flat plate PV panel)—an arrangement of photovoltaic cells mounted on a rigid flat surface with the cells exposed freely to incoming sunlight and a transparent top.

Photovoltaic (PV) systems—systems that use semiconductors to convert the sun's energy directly into electricity.

Photovoltaic (solar) cell—treated semiconductor material that converts solar energy to electricity.

Power—the rate at which energy (work) is produced or consumed measured in watts (W). See energy. Energy and power are often mistakenly used interchangeably.

Power plant—an installation where electricity is generated for distribution.

Renewables—energy generated from continually replenishing natural sources.

Solar farm—multiple solar panels that are grouped together into a single power plant.

Solar flat plate thermal collectors—panel systems that use the sun's energy to heat a fluid or air.

Thermal energy—energy in the form of heat.

Wind farm—multiple wind turbines that are grouped together into a single power plant.

Wind powered systems—systems that take the kinetic energy present in wind and convert it into mechanical or electric energy.

Green Professional Credentials

Green buildings often don't look unconventional, but their specialized designs and materials require workers in all phases of the process—manufacturing, design, construction, operation, and demolition—to understand how green principles translate into design and construction practices. As sustainable buildings become more commonplace, a skilled green work force becomes more necessary.

How do workers show they have the skills required in today's green marketplace? One way is to have a green professional credential. A credential is a formal recognition that an individual has attained a certain level of understanding or accomplishment in a field.

There are different types of credentials. This chapter begins with an overview of three: licenses, certificates, and academic degrees. Not all credentials are directly applicable to green construction. The focus of this text is on those that are.

Introduction to credentialing

Credentialing is the umbrella term used to describe a process whereby a qualified agent (such as a state license board, a nonprofit, a school, or another organization) grants recognition that an individual has met certain criteria

> Not all credentials are equal or have the same value.

and, typically, passed an assessment test. **Credentials** are not all the same: in addition to the designating party, some indicate the holder has broad knowledge whereas others are more narrowly focused; some are given only after a significant commitment of time and resources and others can be obtained online. Credentials also have different qualification requirements, legal implications, continuing education requirements, and marketplace value. All of them include a time and cost commitment from the individual. Because there is no single government agency or private organization responsible for credentialing, government agencies and other credentialing organizations are free to set and regulate their own programs.

A central difference between credentials is their legal significance. Unlike certificates and academic degrees, for example, a license is a legally required credential for those performing certain tasks on certain projects in certain jurisdictions. Architects, engineers, general contractors, HVAC contractors, and electricians are examples of professionals that typically need to be licensed. Certificates and academic degrees are voluntary and, although they may be required in order to secure a license (or a job), they are not legally mandated. Although these three credentials—licenses, certificates, and academic degrees—have different requirements and provide different benefits, all involve a financial and time commitment. Some have additional, ongoing educational requirements.

Licenses

To protect public health, safety, and welfare, states have enacted laws that specify licensing requirements for various professions, including construction. As noted, a **license** is a permit from an authority (generally, a government entity such as a state licensing bureau) that is issued based on experience and/or tested knowledge.[1] Requirements regarding *who* needs to be licensed, *when* a license is required, and *how* one gets licensed vary greatly from state to state. In construction, the type and dollar value of a project are typically what determine whether a contractor needs to be licensed. Commercial projects, for example, usually have licensure requirements different from residential projects. In some states, any project that costs more than a few hundred dollars will require a licensed contractor; in other states, the threshold value of work is many thousands of dollars.

Licensing requirements are typically defined by individual states through the secretary of state, a department of labor, or a similar authority. The state determines qualifications, testing requirements, and conditions under which a license is required. Most states differentiate between general building contractors and specialty contractors, but, not surprisingly, this, too, is variable between jurisdictions. A few states have many different specialty license categories. California is an extreme example with three classifications for general contractors and over 40 specialty classifications including everything from ironworkers and plumbers to glazers and awning installers. Other states require licenses in only a few categories; the most common classifications are electrical, mechanical, and plumbing. Those contemplating doing construction work should educate themselves regarding local and state licensing requirements.

Ron de Vries

Although familiarity with sustainability principles is becoming commonplace for many management-level workers (for example, project managers and job superintendents), no states currently have special green licensing requirements.

Certificates

A **certificate** is a voluntary non-degree credential. Professional organizations, private for-profit and public schools, trade associations and unions, and community colleges issue certificates. The guidelines for certification are set by the designating organization or agency. Unlike licensure, an individual is not required to have a certificate in order to engage in an occupation, but a certificate indicates a level of accomplishment.

Academic degrees

Academic degrees include associate, bachelor, masters, and doctoral (PhD) degrees. Associate degrees (AA and AS) require more classroom credits than do certificates, typically two years of full time study; they are primarily awarded by two-year colleges and technical schools. Associate degrees are offered in many aspects of construction, including electrical and power installation, plumbing, masonry, management, and much more. There are now schools, such as Salt Lake Community College in Salt Lake City UT; Crowder College in Neosho MO; Delaware Technical Community College in several locations in Delaware; and many more that offer degree programs in various aspects of sustainable construction.

The next degree level, the bachelor's (or baccalaureate) degree, has two types: a bachelor of arts (BA) and a bachelor of science (BS) for more technical occupations such as engineering and construction management. Bachelor degrees generally require four or five years of study. Beyond these degrees are graduate degrees—master's and doctorates—that require substantial time in addition to the undergraduate degree programs. Most jobs in construction do not greatly benefit from a bachelor's or graduate degree, although a current trend in the industry is for increased levels of education, especially for those in management positions such as project managers or job superintendents. Many of these workers may have a degree in construction management or in business.

As noted, there are no specific professional licensing or certification requirements for those working in green construction. There are, however, many types of green credentials, including certificates and academic degrees, which can provide confidence to an employer that a worker has certain enhanced skills. For a growing number of jobs, this confidence is beneficial, and sometimes a job requirement.

Green credentials

There are no mandatory green credentials; no laws require a special license, certificate, or degree in green construction. As noted, a green credential may be a job requirement and, in response to increasing interest in sustainability and a work force familiar with green principles, the number of green certification programs, offered by different organizations, with different emphases, is growing. Some, such as the professional LEED credentials awarded by the Green Building Certification Institute (which also administers the LEED building rating systems) and the Green Globes Credentials administered by the Green Building Initiative (which administers the Green Globes building rating systems), require a high level of skill, continuing education, and periodic renewal. These credentials typically require broad understanding of green principles. Some certificates are narrowly focused on a specific aspect of green construction and require intensive short-term training. Certifications in solar PV installation or wind system installation and maintenance are examples. Other certificates may require as little as completion of a workshop or seminar.

Programs are offered through a variety of venues: community colleges, associations such as the Green Building Initiative, ASHRAE, the National Association of Home Builders, and others as well as trade unions, for-profit training organizations, and technical schools.

A problem with terms

The reader should note that the language used for assessing a building or a system sometimes mirrors that used for assessing individuals. This chapter regards certification as one of the ways a worker can receive validation that they have achieved a certain level of accomplishment. The National Home Builders Association and Green Advantage are two programs that assess and certify individuals. But, as discussed in Chapter 4, some programs, such as the Living Building Challenge, LEED, and Energy Star, assess and certify *buildings* or *systems*. While the terms vary, the idea is the same: whether for people, specific systems, or entire buildings, a certification, credential, rating, or assessment provides the industry and others with tools to judge performance.

There are multiple professional credentials and certifications geared toward those in the design and construction industry. As the LEED professional credentials have made the largest impact in the market, they are explored in some detail here.

LEED professional credentials

As discussed in Chapter 4, the incorporation of green principles into new and renovated buildings has led to the development of building rating systems to measure green methods and practices. Some building rating systems, such as LEED, also offer opportunities for industry professionals to earn a credential that provides them with expertise in the implementation of a rating system and allows them to demonstrate understanding of green best practices and familiarity with the evolving building certification systems.

The Green Building Certification Institute (GBCI), which administers the LEED rating systems, administers three categories of broad-spectrum professional credentials:

- **Green Associate** (GA)—an introductory level credential

- **Accredited Professional with Specialty** (LEED AP)—five professional credentials linked to specific building rating systems

- **Fellow**—the highest level credential, for those with exceptional proficiency and experience

Let's look at each of the three broad-spectrum credentials.

LEED Green Associate (GA) credential

The LEED Green Associate credential is the basic LEED professional credential and can be pursued by anyone working in the field of green building. The credential denotes a basic understanding of green building principles and practices and knowledge of the LEED rating systems. The goal for this credential is to support other professionals working on LEED projects.

A LEED Green Associate reflects knowledge in several categories including:

- LEED strategy and process and the tasks required to implement LEED safely and effectively

- Credit categories (for example, Energy and Atmosphere; Water Efficiency; Materials and Resources; and Indoor Environmental Quality)

- The environmental impacts of a project, codes, and more.

Other than being at least 18 years old, there are no eligibility requirements for candidates who wish to take the LEED Green Associate exam. However, GBCI recommends that candidates have exposure to LEED and green building concepts through educational courses, volunteering, or work experience prior to testing. The GA credential must be renewed every two years.

Accredited Professional with Specialty (LEED AP)

The LEED GA credential is required for those who wish to earn one of the five specialty LEED Accredited Professional (AP) credentials (see "LEED professional credentials" on the next page). In addition to an in-depth knowledge of green principles, the specialty credentials reflect an ability to specialize in a particular LEED rating system.

Evidence indicates that earning a LEED credential increases a worker's employability. The numbers reflect this: a 2014 report from the USGBC states that demand for LEED Green Associates and LEED APs grew 46% between 2013 and 2014. Improved business competitiveness, better communication among clients and teams, and the demonstration of commitment to sustainability all drove this demand on the business side.[2]

LEED Fellows

LEED's third tier professional credential is available to those who are highly accomplished and have 10 or more years of professional green building experience. Fellows are nominated by their peers and the criteria for assessing nominees are based on technical proficiency, education and mentoring, leadership, commitment, and advocacy.

Jocelyn Augustino

LEED also offers two categories of more narrowly focused credentials: LEED for Homes Green Raters and the Green Classroom Professional (GCP). Green Raters assist in the submittal of data and verification for projects pursuing building certification as a LEED Home. The credential is awarded following an examination and

LEED professional credentials: an overview

1. **LEED AP Building Design & Construction (LEED AP BD+C)**

    The LEED AP BD+C credential is designed for those with expertise in the design and construction phases of green buildings serving the commercial, residential, education, and healthcare sectors of the industry. The LEED AP BD+C credential denotes understanding of green building, the LEED Building Design and Construction rating system (LEED BD+C), and the ability to facilitate the certification process.

2. **LEED AP Operations & Maintenance (LEED AP O+M)**

    This credential is for those implementing sustainable practices, improving performance, heightening efficiency, and reducing environmental impact in the operations and maintenance of existing buildings. This professional credential is linked to the LEED for Existing Buildings: Operations and Maintenance rating system.

3. **LEED AP Interior Design & Construction (LEED AP ID+C)**

    The LEED AP ID+C credential is for professionals who are working in the design, construction, and improvement of commercial interiors and tenant spaces. The credential denotes specialized expertise in the LEED for Commercial Interiors rating system.

4. **LEED AP Homes**

    The LEED AP Homes credential is suited for those involved in the design and construction of homes and denotes specialized expertise in the LEED for Homes rating system.

5. **LEED AP Neighborhood Development (LEED AP ND)**

    The LEED ND credential applies to individuals participating in the planning, design, and development of sustainable, pedestrian-friendly neighborhoods. The specialty denotes practical knowledge in the LEED for Neighborhood Development rating system.

internship. The Green Classroom Professional certificate is directed at school administrators and educators, not those in the construction industry, and is designed to provide trained resources to encourage sustainable learning environments and to foster an understanding of sustainable practices among students and others.

Other non-degree green credentials

LEED is not the only building rating system that offers professional credentials focusing on an understanding of the whole building. Some sponsor credentials that, like LEED, are designed to assist in the successful implementation of a particular building assessment program. Examples are the credentials developed by the Green Building Initiative and linked to the Green Globes building assessment systems. Other organizations sponsor credentials that are more narrowly focused, offering certification as a solar PV installer, wind technician, energy auditor, and more.

There are many organizations that offer credentials.

There are many other organizations that offer credentials. They vary in subject and requirements as well as value. Some are national or statewide and others are local. Table 11.1 identifies some of the credentials offered by nationwide organizations, but local and state-run programs exist around the country and readers are advised to check their local USGBC chapter, Builders Exchange, or trade association for help in identifying them.

In addition to the nationwide programs identified in Table 11.1, there are statewide credential programs. The Green Point Rater certificate, provided and overseen by Build It Green, a California-based nonprofit, is one example. The Green Point Rating system is designed for assessing green buildings, with a checklist during the permitting process and verification by a Green Point Rater after completion to verify that all measures are actually implemented during construction. Many jurisdictions, cities, and counties in the state require that new and remodeled residential and commercial projects comply with this rating system. For information on becoming a Green Point Rater, see *www.builditgreen.org/training-events/green-point-rated-training-courses*

In addition to the non-academic certificate programs, two-year community colleges are also important providers of green certification and vocational training to workers in the construction industry. Public institutions have many advantages: they are located in towns and cities across America and typically

Table 11.1 Examples of Green Credentials

CERTIFYING ORGANIZATION	GREEN CREDENTIAL
American Society of Heating, Refrigerating and Air-Conditioning (ASHRAE) *www.ashrae.org*	ASHRAE focuses on building systems, energy efficiency, indoor air quality, refrigeration, and sustainability within the HVAC industry. The organization offers multiple professional certifications on sustainability including: • Building Energy Assessment Professional Certification (BEAP) • Building Energy Modeling Professional Certification (BEMP) • Commissioning Process Management Professional Certification (CPMP) • High-Performance Building Design Professional Certification (HBDP)
North American Board of Certified Energy Practitioners (NABCEP) *www.nabcep.org*	The nonprofit NABCEP works with the renewable energy industry and provides individual certification and company accreditation. Professional certifications include: • PV Installation Professional Certification • PV Technical Sales Certification • Solar Heating Installer Certification • Small Wind Installer Certification
Solar Energy International (SEI) *www.solar-energy.org*	Solar Energy International offers multiple training and certification programs in solar systems, including: • Residential and Commercial Photovoltaic Systems • Battery-based Photovoltaic Systems • Solar Business and Technical Sales • Renewable Energy Applications
Building Performance Institute (BPI) *www.bpi.org*	The Building Performance Institute develops standards for home energy retrofit projects and offers credentials from entry-level to skilled including: • Building Analyst credential • Envelope Professional credential
National Association of Home Builders (NAHB) *www.nahb.org*	The NAHB provides certifications to train those working in residential building to incorporate green building principles into homes. Credentials include: • Certified Green Professional credential • Master Green Professional Certification
Green Building Initiative *www.thegbi.org/professional-certification*	Green Globes has three professional credentials linked to its building assessment programs. • Green Globes Professional (GGP): an online program that trains individuals to assist owners in implementing the Green Globes building rating programs • Green Globes Assessor (GGA): an advanced credential that enables certified holders to perform as third-party assessors on Green Globes building projects • Federal Guiding Principles Compliance Professional (GPCP): a professional credential designed to help federal clients make their buildings more compliant with green regulations

Table 11.1 Examples of Green Credentials *(continued)*

CERTIFYING ORGANIZATION	GREEN CREDENTIAL
Green Advantage *http://greenadvantage.org*	The Green Advantage is an ANSI-approved training and certification for green builders and remodelers that is unaffiliated with a trade association and not linked to its own building rating system. The program offers two credentials: • Green Advantage Certified Associate (GACA): for entry-level workers, tradespeople, vocational students, and pre-apprentices and apprentices • Green Advantage Certified Practitioner (GACP): for construction supervisory personnel, experienced tradespeople, and advanced students
Residential Energy Services Network (RESNET) *www.resnet.us*	RESNET is a nonprofit developer of energy standards and offers several professional credentials focusing on rating and on improving residential energy efficiency: • HERS Raters • Home Energy Survey Professionals • Home Energy Auditors
REGREEN *www.regreenprogram.org*	REGREEN Guidelines, developed by USGBC and the American Society of Interior Designers (ASID), is a resource for green home remodeling. It offers a REGREEN Trained Certificate for those in the residential remodeling sector that addresses the major elements of any green residential renovation project.
Association of Energy Engineers (AEE) *www.aeecenter.org*	AEE is a worldwide membership organization with 95 U.S. chapters that provides information on renewables and other energy sources. It offers multiple certifications, including: • Energy Auditor Certification (CEA) • Building Commissioning Professional Program (CBCP) • Energy Manager in Training (EMIT)
National Registry of Environmental Professionals (NREP) *www.nrep.org*	NREP and its affiliates offer many professional certifications in sustainability including: • Environmental Systems • Auditing • Site Assessment • Indoor Air Quality • Environmental & Safety Compliance • Refrigerant Compliance Manager

offer open enrollment to anyone with a high school diploma; they are more affordable than four-year public universities and colleges; their programs are often designed for older workers, those who are transitioning, and those who are currently working (classes may be at night, on the weekends, and even online); and they typically provide students with opportunities to take individual classes and workshops without pursuing a degree.

A growing number of community colleges offer certificates in aspects of green design and construction. For example, Crowder Community College in Missouri offers students a one-year certificate as a Solar Energy Technician or a Wind Energy Technician; Columbia Gorge Community College in Oregon offers a certificate in renewable energy; Butte Community College in Oroville CA, offers a certificate in Sustainable Construction Planning to prepare students for careers as building inspectors, plan and permit technicians and examiners, and home inspectors; and Cape Cod Community College in West Barnstable MA, has certificate programs in Environmental Site Assessment, Solar Thermal Technology, and Photovoltaic Technology.

David Potter

There are also technical schools that provide hands-on training and certificate programs in green construction skills. Examples are the Career and Technical Education program at Laney College in Oakland CA, and the Wind Turbine Technician program at the Northwest Renewable Energy Institute in Vancouver WA. Technical Schools may be not-for-profit or for-profit. Some partner with businesses or unions to provide targeted skills training, such as the Green Plumbers Training Program, which is partnered with the International Association of Plumbing and Mechanical Officials. Some programs require classroom work; others are completed online.

Green degrees

As noted, academic degrees include associate, bachelor's, master's, and doctoral (PhD) degrees and many community colleges and four-year institutions offer academic degrees (as well as certificates) in areas of renewable energy and green construction. These programs are often offered as specializations within building-related departments such as construction management, engineering, and environmental design. Some institutions have made deep commitments to green programs. For example, at the University of Massachusetts at Amherst, almost a third of the undergraduate majors available are related to sustainability, and Portland State University in Oregon has eight LEED-certified buildings on campus and operates as a living laboratory for students.

For those considering enrolling in a college program there are several references that can provide information on the "greenness" of a college. Some of these expand information beyond classes and green degrees to include institution-wide sustainability efforts and a look at data such as campus energy use and broader student opportunities. Such resources include the *Princeton Review* (*www.princetonreview.com/green.aspx*), *Sierra Club Cool Schools Annual Rankings* (*www.sierraclub.org/sierra/coolschools-2014*), *STARS—The Sustainability Tracking, Assessment & Rating System* (*www.stars.aashe.org*), and *Making a Difference College Guide* (*www.green-colleges.com*).

Is a credential worth the time and cost?

While there is strong evidence that workers need additional skills, hard numbers on the impact of certifications in the construction industry is limited, and much of the reported value is in the form of claims made by the certifying organizations. We do know from surveys done by McGraw-Hill that, given a green market that is expected to grow significantly, nearly half of general contractors are concerned about finding green-skilled employees.[3]

Professional credentials can lead to increased job opportunities.

There is evidence that certification from a reputable organization or association can provide value to a worker. A 2013 survey of energy managers and consultants, contractors, and others conducted by the Association of Energy Engineers, for example, indicated that certification results in higher professional experience and increased job opportunities.[4] Besides providing workers with enhanced skills, many credentials require continuing education as part of a renewal process. In an industry that is always changing, an awareness of changing approaches, practices, and products is particularly important. Additionally, earning a certification can foster recognition of achievement from colleagues and employers.

> ### *Tip*
>
> One way to determine if a credential will help with job searching is to go to job search engines such as INDEED (*www.indeed.com*), GreenJobs.net (*www.GreenJobs.net*), Simplyhired (*www.simplyhired.com*) or Monster.com (*www.monster.com*) and see what qualifications are required for various trades. You can also plug in a specific credential and see what pops up. These are nationwide sites and have job listings from around the country. You'll get a sense of the demand for employees with different credentials.

Getting credentialed is a big decision. It takes a commitment of time and money, and workers want to be sure that it's worth it. The first step is to identify and compare different credentials and determine their costs and benefits. Some considerations when comparing credentials might include:

- Market expectations—What are potential employers expecting? Will the credential result in an increase likelihood of employment and higher wages?

- What will be the costs to you in terms of dollars and time and can they be justified in terms of job pay-off? How long will it take to make back the costs?

- Will the credential enable you to competently perform important additional and helpful services in your trade?

- What is the level of difficulty in getting the credential and what is the process? Are there qualification requirements? Do you have to take classes? Does the credential require an academic degree or can you substitute experience?

- Can any required courses be taken online? If so, is the credential still worthwhile?

- Is there an exam and, if so, how much time will be required to study and to take the exam? (Don't be tempted by a very easy certification process and exam; credentials are typically less valuable if the bar is set too low.)

- Who will issue the credential and are they reputable? For example, is the organization approved by a third party such as ANSI or USGBC, or is the technical school accredited? Check out their website; how long have they been in business, are there reviews, and can you speak to graduates?

- Will having a credential provide you with recognition among your peers?

- Is the credential valid beyond your immediate community?

- How long is the credential valid and is there a financial cost and/or continuing education requirement for renewal?

- Will your increased knowledge provide personal satisfaction?

Summary

As we have learned, the construction industry has changed and grown dramatically over the last few decades. These changes require a work force that can demonstrate that it possesses many unique specialty, technical, and managerial skills. Given this, it is not surprising that half of the industry-wide respondents to McGraw-Hill Construction's 2012 work-force survey find that certification provides a marketplace advantage to firms and allows them to screen employees and reduce training costs. There are marketing advantages, too. Joseph Sapp of the American Institute of Constructors and the Constructor Certification Commission (AIC) states, "The employers (of certified workers) benefit (because) the certification provides a recognized credential within their company that improves marketability to clients. And in turn, clients get an increased level of assurance that their projects are being managed more effectively." Regarding the value of a credential to individuals he explains that "it not only ... sets them apart from other individuals, but it also enhances the individual's personal image as a professional to the employer, the clients and the industry."[5]

Getting a formal credential may be a good investment. It may not always be necessary, however, to make the time and expense commitment required to get a credential. There are training and workshop opportunities, expos and green fairs, blogs, and books that are affordable and accessible. This is the subject of the final chapter.

Glossary

Academic degree—a post-secondary credential offered by colleges and universities.

Certificate—a voluntary non-degree credential.

Credential—recognition by a qualified agent that an individual has met certain criteria and passed an assessment in a subject.

Credentialing—the umbrella term used to describe a process whereby a qualified agent (such as a state license board or another organization or agency) grants recognition that an individual has met certain criteria and, typically, passed an assessment test.

License—a permit typically issued by a state and required in order to perform certain occupational tasks.

Wayne National Forest

Polishing Skills and Moving Ahead

The previous chapter reviewed key green professional credentials such as LEED AP, NABCEP, and BPI as well as academic degree and certificate programs having a green focus. A formal credential can often provide multiple benefits including the potential for increased employability and higher wages. A recognized credential implies credibility and marketplace value. In addition, a green credential is becoming necessary for some industry personnel such as the general contractor, contract manager, job superintendent, and project manager, and for some of the major subcontractors such as electricians, plumbers, and HVAC specialists.

But not everyone may decide to make the significant time and resource commitment required to be credentialed. For these people, as well as for those holding licenses or certificates that have continuing education requirements, there are alternative approaches.

These approaches can take a variety of forms, time, and cost, ranging from short webinars and one-day workshops to conferences and blogs to academic and trade classes. Some programs include coursework and substantial academic rigor, some are quite technical and focus on a specific trade, and some look at the overall issues of green construction and the operation of high-performance buildings. Some programs are hands-on whereas others require classroom attendance. An increasing number of programs are available online.

Alternative training options are the subject of this chapter, but before moving ahead, let's review some of the reasons that enhanced technical skills and general green training are important.

The importance of green education

Previous chapters showed that several members of the design/construction team (including the general contractor and major subcontractors) require substantial training to estimate and specify, install, operate, and repair new green products and systems. But even tradespeople not directly engaged in the estimating and specifying processes may need some level of skill enhancement.[1] For example, plumbing technologies have shifted to greywater use, low-flow fixtures, and high-performance water heating systems—technologies that typically require workers to have skills beyond those required for conventional plumbing installation and repair. There are multiple other examples: painters, drywallers, masons, and insulation installers are all trades that are experiencing shifts in products, systems, and construction procedures.

US Dept. of Labor

We have learned that green and conventional projects are differentiated in several ways that directly impact workers and their roles on a jobsite. Workers are faced with changes in construction operations and practices, different site procedures, and the use of new materials and products. Cooperation among different trades is a key requirement. Maximizing building performance can be realized only when tradespeople understand the relationship between construction practices and system performance. Even a relatively minor condition such as a small hole left around pipe penetrations by one trade and not sealed by another, for example, can result in a structure failing to meet performance goals.

Because a high-performance building is concerned with a structure's context—how it impacts the environment—multiple strategies are typically required during the construction process that may be unfamiliar to many workers. The construction process might include pollution and erosion control techniques; access and heavy equipment restrictions; the reuse of on-site materials such as topsoil, asphalt, and concrete; and the management of construction activities to minimize material and resource use. No matter the trade, all workers are likely to be operating under strict recycling requirements.

Standards such as LEED, tightening codes, and owner expectations are driving the use of nontoxic products. As a result, workers need to know that even common jobsite items such as sealants, adhesives, and cleaners may have specific requirements on a green project. Workers may be required to minimize (and document) toxic ingredients. The use, installation, and waste requirements and product characteristics can be a challenge and may require specialized knowledge.

It's not enough to have trade skills alone. Successful workers on high-performance buildings are likely to have an appreciation of *why* green buildings are important. Understanding the value of sustainability (the value to the workers, to their kids, and to their community) makes it easier for workers to adopt new approaches to their work and to seek out training. Steve Lehtonen, senior director of the International Association of Plumbing and Mechanical Officials (IAPMO) believes that his experience with the Green Plumbers training program is an example of the importance of this: "We had guys that were 50, 60 years old say, 'I've changed completely! I go to a ballgame, walk around, and think they're wasting a lot of water.'"[2]

As noted, a trained work force is necessary to successfully meet project goals. For workers who do not feel they would benefit from a formal green credential, or who cannot yet make the commitment, there are various ways to enhance their skills to meet industry needs. These include:

- Classes and workshops
- Conferences
- Magazines and blogs

Classes and workshops

Non-credential classes and workshops are offered throughout the country by a variety of trainers, including nonprofit and for-profit organizations, unions and trade associations, and community colleges and technical schools. As noted, these vary tremendously in type and quality; as always, it is worth due diligence to determine value. Let's look briefly at a sampling.

Nonprofit and for-profit organizations and businesses

There are organizations—nonprofit, not-for-profit, and for-profit—all over the country that provide classes and workshops. As previously noted, these programs come in many different forms, from a couple of hours to several days. Some training providers are national organizations such as USGBC and some operate only in a single or a few states. GPRO, green professional building skills training, is an example of the latter, with programs in New Jersey, Illinois, Colorado, and Texas (*www.gpro.org*).

Local chapters of organizations such as the Construction Specifications Institute (CSI), and those identified in Chapter 11, sponsor training, as do many builders exchanges. The Valley Contractors Exchange (VCE) in Chico CA (*www.vceonline.com*), the Builders Exchange of Central Ohio (*www.bx.org*), the Builders Exchange of Kentucky (*www.bxkentucky.com*), and the North Coast Builders Exchange (*www.ncbeonline*) in Santa Rosa CA, are all examples of exchanges that have educational programs.

Other local nonprofit organizations often sponsor programs, too. Examples include: What's Working in Boulder CO (*www.whatsworking.com*), offers two-day classes in green residential projects; ImagineSolar in Austin TX (*www.imaginesolar.com*), offers classroom and online courses and workshops in solar systems; and Midwest Renewable Energy Center in Custer WI (*www.midwestrenew.org*), offers self-paced courses in solar energy and wind systems.

When searching for classes and workshops, don't forget local businesses such as home improvement stores and utility companies. The utility company Pacific Gas & Electric is an example. *The Energy Center developed by PG&E* (*www.pge.com/pec*) sponsors free lectures and classes in energy conservation

Jocelyn Augustino

and green building techniques at various locations around the San Francisco Bay Area in California. Topics include: HVAC, Industrial Systems and Technologies, Renewables and Distributed Energy, Lighting Technologies and Design, Home Energy Upgrades, High-Performance Water Systems, and Code Compliance and are typically half- or full-day programs.

There are also a growing number of for-profit training programs for builders, architects, contractors, and the general public that offer programs in various aspects of green buildings. Among them are:

- Clean Edison (*www.CleanEdison.com*)

- 411 Energy Experts (*www.411energyexperts.com*)

- Green Training USA (*www.Greentrainingusa.com*)

- Energy Conservation Training Company (*www.econtc.com*)

- *Building Performance Workshop (www.BuildingPerformanceWorkshop.com)*

- Everblue (*www.everblue.edu*)

- ConstructionPro Network (*www.constructionpronet.com*)

- AEC daily (*www.aecdaily.com*)

Private training programs offer a range of training options: hands-on, live, and online classes, and on-demand webinars. The cost and the quality of these and other programs vary and workers should review both before making a commitment. (Note: this list should not be interpreted as an endorsement of these programs.)

Unions and trade associations

Although unions are nearly nonexistent in residential construction and, in many cities, are weakened in commercial construction, too, some unions are working aggressively to train members for the move toward a green economy. Trade associations also offer classes and readers should check with their local union chapter or trade association to see what they offer. Table 12.1 lists examples of several programs.

Table 12.1 Examples of Union and Trade Association Training Programs

Organization	Comments
International Brotherhood of Electrical Workers (IBEW) *www.ibew.org*	For many years, union training facilities across the country—jointly funded by the International Brotherhood of Electrical Workers and the National Electrical Contractors Association—have been incorporating green energy into their curriculum. IBEW offers photovoltaic training and recently launched a 40-hour wind turbine "boot camp" in multiple states. The National Joint Apprenticeship Training Committee (NJATC), a collaboration between the IBEW and union electrical contractors, has a program called Working Green as part of its apprenticeship training for all levels of electrical workers.
BlueGreen Alliance *www.bluegreenalliance.org*	This alliance between unions and environmental groups includes: Service Employees International Union, United Auto Workers, United Steelworkers, Sierra Club, National Resources Defense Council, and others. The alliance offers multiple resources as well as training through the GreenPOWER program that teaches workers in the manufacturing sector about energy efficiencies, environmental awareness, and waste reduction. It also sponsors the annual Good Jobs, Green Jobs Conference, and a blog.
United Brotherhood of Carpenters (UBC) *www.carpenters.org*	The UBC offers several green training programs and its training arm, the Carpenters International Training Fund (CITF), develops curriculum for UBC members. The CITF publishes *Awareness: Green Building*, a manual that covers a broad array of topics, including components of green building, maintaining indoor environmental quality, jobsite waste reduction, and an overview of government regulations. This manual is used in a six-hour course available at any of the union's 250-plus training centers across the United States and Canada.
American Society of Heating, Refrigerating and Air Conditioning (ASHRAE) *www.ashrae.org*	ASHRAE offers several professional certificates including Building Energy Assessment and Building Energy Modeling. These certificates are designed to assess an individual's ability to audit and analyze residential, commercial, and industrial buildings and analyze energy modeling software when applied to energy performance.

There are hundreds of other trade associations, including many reviewed earlier in this text, including:

- Associated General Contractors of America (*www.agc.org*)

- Associated Builders & Contractors (*www.abc.org*)

- National Association of Home Builders (*www.nahb.com*)

- Building Trades Association (*www.buildingtrades.com*)

- National Association of Women in Construction (*www.nawic.org*)

Some associations focus on specific trades, products, or systems, such as:

- Air-Conditioning, Heating, and Refrigeration Institute (*www.ahrinet.org*)

- National Electrical Contractors Association (*www.necanet.org*)

- National Roofing Contractors Association (*www.nrca.net*)

- Solar Energy International (*www.solarenergy.org*)

- American Wind Energy Association (*www.awea.org*)

- Geothermal Energy Association (*www.geo-energy.org*)

(For a list of renewable energy trade associations by state, see *www.energy. sourceguides.com*)

Some associations sponsor green training programs for builders (for example, National Association of Home Builders, and Solar Energy International). Others, such as the International Wood Products Association, sponsor conferences and conventions. See Appendix D for an alphabetized listing of the URLS identified in this book.

Community colleges and technical schools

As discussed in the last chapter, many community colleges and technical schools around the country offer degree and certificate programs in various aspects of sustainability.

For those choosing not to matriculate, however, most schools also offer semester-length and shorter classes in different aspects of green construction. Green Renovation, Super-insulation for Zero-Energy Buildings, and Passive House Consultants Training are examples of individual courses (see Dunwoody College of Technology—*www.dunwoody.edu*—in Minneapolis MN, and Yester-morrow Design/Build School—*www.yestermorrow.org*—in Waitsfield VT).

Useful lists of colleges and technical schools

There are several websites that list colleges and technical schools including: Career Schools at *www.careerschools.org* that publishes a directory of professional, trade and vocational schools and colleges; Technical Schools Directory at *www. technical-schools-guide.com* that offers a directory of technical schools searchable by state, zip code, school name or degree program as well as online schools; *www.universities.com* that lists schools and training programs alphabetically by program of study, state or country; and the Community College Database from the University of Texas at *www.utexas.edu/world/comco/state/* that lists community colleges by state.

Training by federal and local governments

Although government agencies do not typically offer classes, they do sponsor local training initiatives. For example, a grant from the Department of Energy's Energy Efficiency and Conservation Block Fund, enabled El Paso TX, to develop its Renewable Energy Education Project. State and local governmental organizations (for example, the California Energy Commission and the Austin Energy Green Building Program) also sponsor programs. Check with your city or county for these programs.

As with credentials, not all classes and workshops are equal, and the quality and type of skills training vary tremendously. Due diligence is required to see whether training meets your goals as well as employer needs. There are multiple questions worth considering prior to making a commitment for training:

- What are the specific learning objectives for the training? Would this help you in doing your current work or seeking a new position?

- Is the training certified by a reputable organization such as the North American Board of Certified Energy Practitioners (NABCEP), the National Center for Construction Education and Research (NCCER), or USGBC, for example?

- Can you get a reference from someone who has recently completed the program you are considering?

- Can successful completion of the training add value to your resume?

In addition to classes and workshops, there are multiple other ways for workers to enhance skills, gain information and insights, and keep up with industry changes. Let's look at some of these.

Conferences and expositions

Green conferences and expositions provide a way to meet people in the industry, see new products, and attend workshops. Some are sponsored by national organizations such as trade associations or unions; some are organized by local nonprofits. The local chapter of USGBC is typically a good source for upcoming events. Table 12.2 presents a sampling of annual conferences sponsored by national organizations.

(For a comprehensive list of worldwide academic conferences that cover a wide range of topics, see *www.conferencealerts.com*, where one can view conferences by date, topic, and country and subscribe to a service that will alert you regarding conferences of interest.)

There are smaller, locally sponsored green conferences all over the country, for example:

- Plain Green Conference in Sioux Falls SD

- Greenprints conference in Atlanta GA

- Local Energy Solutions Conference in Tilton NH

- New York State Green Building Conference

- Southeast Building Conference in Florida

- Municipal Green Building Conference in Southern California

Again, your local USGBC chapter is a good resource and will have information about conferences in your area.

Table 12.2 Green Conferences and Expositions

Sponsoring Organization/ Conference	Comments
GreenBuild Conference & Exposition *www.greenbuildexpo.org*	USGBC's annual GreenBuild International Conference and Expo offers excellent educational programs. Launched in 2002, the Conference and Expo is a three-day gathering that attracts thousands of professionals from across the building industry including designers and engineers, contractors, manufacturers, academics, business and government representatives, instructors, students, and the general public. The program includes 150 different hour-long workshops in LEED and a wide range of green topics, plus plenary sessions and tours of green buildings. In addition, 2,000 exhibitors showcase innovative industry products and services. GreenBuild is held in a different city every year.
Association of General Contractors of America (AGC) Contractors Environmental Conference *www.agc.org/cs/environment*	The AGC's annual Contractors Environmental Conference provides information on multiple environmental issues. Past conferences have included topics such as green paving technologies, low-impact development, estimating and bidding green projects, and preparing a work force for green projects.
WINDPOWER Conference & Expo *www.windpowerexpo.org*	The American Wind Energy Association's annual conference and exposition includes presentations that highlight the latest industry trends, technology developments, and renewable energy policy developments. The exposition showcases vendors and their products.
GreenExpo365 *www.greenexpo365.com*	A virtual trade show and online community focused on green building, the expo sponsors "live" events multiple times a year and provides opportunities to chat live with green building professionals. Its website has useful links, blogs, and other information.
RESNET Building Performance Conference *http://conference.resnet.us*	The Residential Energy Services Network (RESNET) hosts the annual Building Performance Conference on home energy ratings, existing home retrofits, building codes and energy policy.
BlueGreen Alliance: Good Jobs Green Jobs National Conference *www.greenjobsconference.org*	Recent conference workshops at this annual conference on how to build a green economy have focused on repairing infrastructure, clean energy manufacturing and supply chain development, clean transportation alternatives, youth and environmental education and green schools, and energy efficiency.
American Society of Solar Energy (ASSE) Annual National Solar Conference *www.ases.org*	Presented by the ASSE, this annual conference covers wind, transportation, and other renewable energy issues as well as solar systems.

Publications, blogs, and other online resources

Getting information on green construction can happen right at home. In addition to online workshops and webinars, there are multiple resources easily available that focus on issues related to the green economy and sustainability. These resources include hard copy and online magazines, blogs, Q&A forums, product and material information, news, and more. Some are available simply by signing up; others are subscription-based. Some target a specific issue such as energy; others address a broad range of environmental topics. Sorting through it all can be daunting. Table 12.3 is a sampling of those the reader might find helpful.

Table 12.3 Publications and Blogs

Publication	Comments
E/The Environmental Magazine *www.emagazine.com*	Published by the Earth Action Network, *E* covers a broad range of general environmental and related topics from climate change, renewable energy, and toxins and health to where to invest responsibly and how to save energy at home. Their website includes a Q&A section (EarthTalk) plus blogs and commentaries.
Environmental Building News *www.buildinggreen.com*	This magazine from Building Green publishing offers information on a range of topics of interest to the construction industry. Recent articles include: What Makes a Building Product Green, Choosing Windows, and Healthy Insulation. The publication covers LEED, green products, case studies, news, and more.
Green Builder magazine *www.greenbuildermag.com*	This is a magazine and blog focusing on green building and sustainable development. Interesting archived articles are available online.
Home Energy *www.homeenergy.org/HETG/ index.php*	This online and print magazine provides practical information on residential energy efficiency, performance, comfort, and affordability. It has a useful website with links to training programs.
GreenSource Magazine: The Magazine of Sustainable Design *www.greensource.construction. com/zinio.asp*	This McGraw-Hill Construction publication available in hard and digital editions covers topics of specific interest to builders, including sustainable design, green building, LEED projects, and case studies. Videos, products, and features offer a substantial amount of helpful information.

Table 12.3 Publications and Blogs *(continued)*

Publication	Comments
Green Builder Insider *www.greenbuildinginsider.com*	This publication provides information on energy efficiency, certifications (LEED and more), case studies, technologies and products, reports and studies, legal matters and legislation, international happenings, and competitions and awards.
GreenBuilding Advisor *www.greenbuildingadvisor.com*	An online resource for building green homes, the website offers product guides, discussion forums, videos, and multiple blogs.
Onearth *www.onearth.org*	A subscription-based magazine published by the Natural Resources Defense Council, Onearth covers a broad range of environmental topics including cities and transportation, science and technology, and more. It offers free online newsletters, columns, and blogs.
Small Wind Energy *www.irecus.org*	Published quarterly by the Interstate Renewable Energy Institute, it features updates and news about small wind energy issues.
Greenroof.com *www.greenroofs.com*	This is an information database and clearinghouse for the green-roof movement worldwide, with news blogs, projects, and more.
Solar Today *www.ases.org/* *solar-today-magazine*	This subscription-based magazine, also available online, from the American Society of Solar Energy (ASES) has articles on the basics, buyers guides, news, and more. (ASES also sponsors an annual conference that covers wind, transportation, and other renewable energy issues as well as solar energy systems; see Table 12.2.)
CleanTechnica *www.cleantechnica.com*	This energy website offers posts on solar, wind, geothermal, and other renewables, plus reports and videos.
U.S. Green Building Council blog *www.usgbc.org/articles*	This blog on LEED features other interesting articles on green building as well.
BuildingGreen blog *www2.buildinggreen.com/blogs*	This blog offers a variety of information from different experts. Access to complete content database is by subscription.

An industry and work force that continues to change

We have seen that the construction industry is in the midst of significant changes. Our focus has been on the broad topic of green construction and

Finding work

As with conventional construction, an owner contemplating a green project or a contractor hiring a crew will expect that a potential hire will have the necessary knowledge to do the job. What sort of special questions of concern might such an employer have when interviewing contractors for a potential job? Some possibilities are:

Experience—What is the contractor's experience with green building? Can the contractor or worker point to specific projects in his or her portfolio and provide references? Does the contractor understand green products—their benefits and drawbacks, their initial and life cycle costs, their installation and operation? Can the contractor suggest local examples of high-quality green buildings? Does the contractor understand the contradictions sometimes present in green building and have an approach to dealing with these contradictions? (For example, because energy efficient windows may not be recyclable, does that make them less appropriate than using reclaimed windows?)

Credentials—What kind of specialized credential, education, or training in green building does the contractor have that could indicate a level of competency in and familiarity with the requirement of a green project?

The person's level of interest in the subject—Does the contractor's office have books, periodicals, and product information on green products and buildings? Is the contractor or worker a member of any organizations such as the U.S. Green Building Council?

Does the contractor practice what he or she preaches?—An owner contemplating hiring a general or specialty contractor for a green project is likely to be interested in how the potential hire operates his or her business. Are there green elements in the contractor's office? Examples of this might be energy-saving light fixtures or employee bicycle racks out front. Not long ago, the author interviewed a contractor for work on a green building and he arrived in a gas-guzzling Hummer. The author considered this a pretty good indicator that his heart wasn't really in it; he didn't get the job.

how the emphasis on sustainability is impacting everything from financing to job-site procedures. There are multiple other causes of change: an aging work force and shifting demographics, globalization and the consolidation of construction services, the role of technology and the development of new materials and products, increased competition due to tighter budgets, and tightening standards and codes. All will continue to exert pressures and provide both challenges and opportunities for workers.

In a shifting and increasingly competitive industry, successful workers will require skills beyond trade expertise. These skills include:

- *Adaptability* to enable workers to adjust to rapid changes in materials, products, benefits and costs, and industry procedures

- *Interdisciplinary and soft skills* to maximize effective interaction and collaboration with other trades and disciplines—one of the keys to successful high-performance buildings

- *Commitment to lifetime learning* to encourage ongoing skill enhancement, environmental literacy, and keeping up-to-date with changing codes, standards, regulations, and construction practices

As the industry changes, these core skills will be increasingly important.

Skills are not just important for individual workers and for the development of buildings that are designed to meet stringent performance goals. Skills have a strategic role to play in promoting green construction. Skill requirements change as green building technologies and practices are introduced or changed, such that previously satisfactory skills sets become inadequate. A vibrant green construction market requires a large number of well-trained, broadly informed, and collaborative workers.

How Did We Get Here? A Short History of the Green Movement

Certain characteristics of sustainable, or green, construction are not new: sensitivity to site placement, passive heating and cooling, and the use of local nontoxic materials.

Throughout history, human beings have organized their living spaces in relation to sunlight. There are multiple worldwide examples of communities that were planned in such a way that buildings faced south to allow sun penetration in winter. In North America, Native Americans made use of the heating properties of the sun through controlled orientation of their structures. As early as 500 AD, the Anasazi, of the Four Corners region in what is now the southwestern United States, lived in south-facing caves that allowed warming sunlight to heat them in winter yet offered shaded areas in summer.

National Park Service photograph

Anasazi cliff dwelling, Mesa Verde National Park

Library of Congress, Arthur C. Haskell photograph, 1936

Judge Samuel Holten House, Danvers MA, circa 1670

A more contemporary American example is the New England saltbox building design, favored by the early colonialists. Saltbox houses were oriented to the south with a two-story elevation and a north side that sloped down to a single story. Windows were concentrated on the more expansive two-story parts of the house to take advantage of solar heat gain; few windows were put in on the colder north side.

In California, Spanish colonial style homes had elongated east-west axes so that they faced the sun, with overhanging decks on the second story to shade south-facing glass in summer. Early 20th-century examples of green approaches include New York's Flatiron (1903) and New York Times (1905) buildings, each of which use deep-set windows to shade sun and regulate temperature.

This long tradition of sustainability was almost lost in the mid-20th century, however. In the period following World War II, we stopped worrying about climate and where or how we built. In addition to technological changes, the end of the war was followed by a sense of limitless possibilities: fuel was plentiful and inexpensive and, as a culture, we just didn't *think* much about what we were doing. By the 1970s, the glass box had become an American icon. The widespread use of air conditioning and glass curtain walls, along with the development of powerful (and energy-intensive) mechanical systems, meant that builders were able to use essentially the same designs in Fairbanks AK, as they did in Dallas TX, or Newark NJ.

Birth of the contemporary green movement

Although various groups and organizations in the post World War II period looked at alternative approaches to designing our communities, the current environmental movement is, in many ways, an outgrowth of the concern that was generated by the 1962 publication of Rachel Carson's *Silent Spring*.[1] This groundbreaking book exposed the hazards of the pesticide DDT and created a new public awareness that nature was often highly sensitive to human intervention, a radical thought for the time. Her primary point was that technological progress might sometimes be so at odds with natural processes that it should be curtailed. At that time in our history, few people cared much about conservation or worried about the disappearance of wilderness. The chemical threats that Carson outlined in her book, including the contamination of the food chain, cancer, genetic damage, and the deaths of entire species, horrified the public and, for the first time, large numbers of contemporary Americans began to understand and think about the relationship between human actions and the environment.

Although there were public and private efforts to shift public attitudes before the publication of *Silent Spring*, Carson's book was one of the triggers of an environmental movement that, in just a few years, began to enter mainstream culture.[2] This process was accelerated in 1970 by the success of the first U.S. Earth Day (*www.Earthday.org*). Earth Day (still celebrated around the world every April) helped solidify public interest in the environment and put it on the political agenda.

With the Arab oil embargo against the West that began in 1973, thinking shifted: natural resources and energy no longer seemed "free." Suddenly, energy use and production became powerful issues.

The 1976 presidential election of Jimmy Carter helped increase government involvement in energy efficiency as an answer to the Middle East's control over petroleum supplies. In a televised speech shortly after he took office, President Carter declared the U.S. energy situation in the 1970s to be "the moral equivalent of war" and announced goals to lower oil imports through increased fuel efficiency, as well as the goal of getting 20% of the nation's energy from renewable sources by 2000.[3] Toward this end, a variety of R&D programs and tax incentives were put in place to encourage fuel efficiency and the development and use of alternative energy sources.

In 1977, the Department of Energy (DOE; *www.doe.gov*) was created to oversee the government's role in this effort, including the development of the Solar Energy Research Institute (SERI) to research and develop solar energy and provide information to the public on existing solar technologies. SERI helped formalize the importance of alternative forms of energy. (In 1991, SERI was reformed as the National Renewable Energy Laboratory, NREL, the primary research laboratory for DOE's Office of Energy Efficiency and Renewable Energy; *www.nrel.gov*.) Other actions in the 1970s included the passage of several important pieces of environmental legislation: the Clean Air Act, the Water Pollution Control Act, the National Environmental Policy Act, and the Endangered Species Act.

There were at least two negative events in the 1970s that added to the rising concern in the United States over health and sustainability: the 1978 discovery of massive contamination at Love Canal, and the 1979 meltdown of the Three Mile Island nuclear power plant in Middletown PA. A national scandal erupted when it was revealed that, in the 1950s, Hooker Chemical Company (now Occidental Petroleum Corporation) had dumped thousands of tons of highly toxic chemicals in Love Canal, a community in upstate New York, and these chemicals were arguably causing severe health impacts including retardation, epilepsy, birth defects, and miscarriages. The poisoning of Love Canal led to passage of the Superfund Act, which holds polluters accountable for their damage.

On the heels of the public outcry over Love Canal, a core meltdown occurred at a nuclear generating station near Harrisburg PA, prompting the temporary evacuation of thousands of people from the area. Although damage was contained, the event resulted in added concerns regarding nuclear safety, which contributed to a halt in the construction of new nuclear power plants.

In the 1980s and 1990s, concern over the dwindling sources of fossil fuels and the increased dependence of the United States on oil controlled by unfriendly countries was compounded by several oil spills, especially the Exxon Valdez spill in 1989, which poured approximately half a million barrels of crude oil into Prince William Sound AK. And at the same time that scientific evidence was providing data on the potential impact of global warming on animal and human communities, other issues such as the loss of the earth's protective ozone layer and the destruction of tropical rainforests and other natural habitats were in the news.

In the 1990s several organizations were founded to provide programs and raise awareness.

The last years of the 20th Century saw the development of several influential organizations and major efforts to define the concepts of sustainability more provide programs and raise awareness among the public and professionals of the benefits of incorporating green approaches. In 1990, the first green building rating system, BREEAM (Building Research Establishment Environmental Assessment Method), was launched in Great Britain and was used as a model for the U.S. Green Building Council's influential green rating system, LEED (Leadership in Energy and Environmental Design). Green building rating systems were launched around the globe: CASBEE in Japan, Green Star in Australia and South Africa, GSAS in Qatar, and DGNB in Germany are just several.

Efforts to facilitate the adoption of sustainable approaches worldwide have been aided by the World Green Building Council (WGBC), which was founded in the 1990s and has developed into a coalition of over 90 national Green Building Councils (including the USGBC). It is the world's largest organization influencing the green building movement.[4] In part due to the contributions made by WGBC, today there are hundreds of thousands of green buildings around the globe that have been certified under a building assessment program.

In the past two decades, government actions have also contributed to an increase in the public's understanding of sustainability. These include: the strengthening of the Clean Air Act; passage of the Pollution Prevention Act, which provided incentives to corporations to reduce pollutants; launching of the Energy Star rating system by the Environmental Protection Agency (EPA) and the U.S. Department of Energy; and the introduction of the first local green building program in Austin TX, in 1992. All have contributed to a vibrant green building economy.

Today, three decades after the first Earth Day celebration, attitudes about the importance of sustainability are dramatically different in the United States. Many of the rallying points of the green movement have become ingrained into American society.

Note: Much of Appendix A is from the author's book LEED Certification: An Introduction to Certifying a Green Building, *2013.*

Our Power: Where Does It Come from and How Is It Used?

How we get our power

Fossil fuels (oil, natural gas, and coal) plus a relatively small amount from nuclear and renewable energy sources currently provide the power our buildings require, primarily for heating, cooling, and lighting.[1] Despite recent improvements in building and equipment efficiencies, overall power consumption in the building sector is growing. This is due to several factors, including the fact that an increase in the population requires more buildings to accommodate its needs. The size of our structures is also growing; houses, for example, have doubled in size since 1950.[2] Buildings are also filled with an increasing number of gadgets that get plugged in, such as computers and other electronics, refrigerators, microwaves, air conditioners, and even toothbrushes.

It's not an exaggeration to say that "cheap energy" keeps us afloat economically. But our addiction to relatively inexpensive power costs a lot: Americans pay over $1 *trillion* every year just on the direct *consumption* of energy.[3] And this doesn't take into account the multiple other costs associated with the use of fossil fuels. (As noted in Chapter 10, energy and power are not the same. The terms, however, are often used interchangeably and I will do so in this appendix.)

Low-cost power available at the flip of a switch, endless quantities of cheap consumer goods, limitless fresh water inside every home—the goodies we've come to rely on and expect—and the society they help define is a relatively new phenomenon. Our ancestors, and today almost half the world's population, derived their power primarily from wood, sun, water, animal waste, and human toil. Fossil fuel changed everything and is now continuously mined, refined, and delivered by the world's biggest corporations to every corner of the globe. This offers some of us astounding options regarding how and where we spend our time, where we live, what we do.

Energy flow charts

Where does all this power come from? The Lawrence Livermore National Laboratory at the University of California is a national research center that, among other things, works on issues around the production, development and deployment of energy resources and technologies. Every year, it publishes an energy flow chart that shows the sources of energy production, how the energy is used, and how much of it is wasted. At right is the 2014 Chart. (To see the chart in full color, go to *https://flowcharts.llnl.gov*)

As noted in the title of the chart, in 2014, total energy use in the United States was 98.3 Quads. (1 Quad equals a quadrillion BTUs and is equivalent to about 172 million barrels of oil.[4]) Along the left vertical axis of the chart are energy sources and the amount of energy each contributes to the total, starting with solar, at .427 Quads. Petroleum is the last entry on the list, and at 34.8 Quads, provides almost 35% of our energy.

The flow chart identifies other interesting data, including:

- Almost 40% of the energy we use is in the form of electricity. Electricity is a secondary form of energy, which means it is generated by conversion of primary sources of energy such as coal, natural gas, and wind. The flow chart shows the relatively modest contribution of renewable energy sources toward the generation of electric power.

- The chart details how many Quads are used in each of the residential, commercial, industrial, and transportation sectors. The commercial

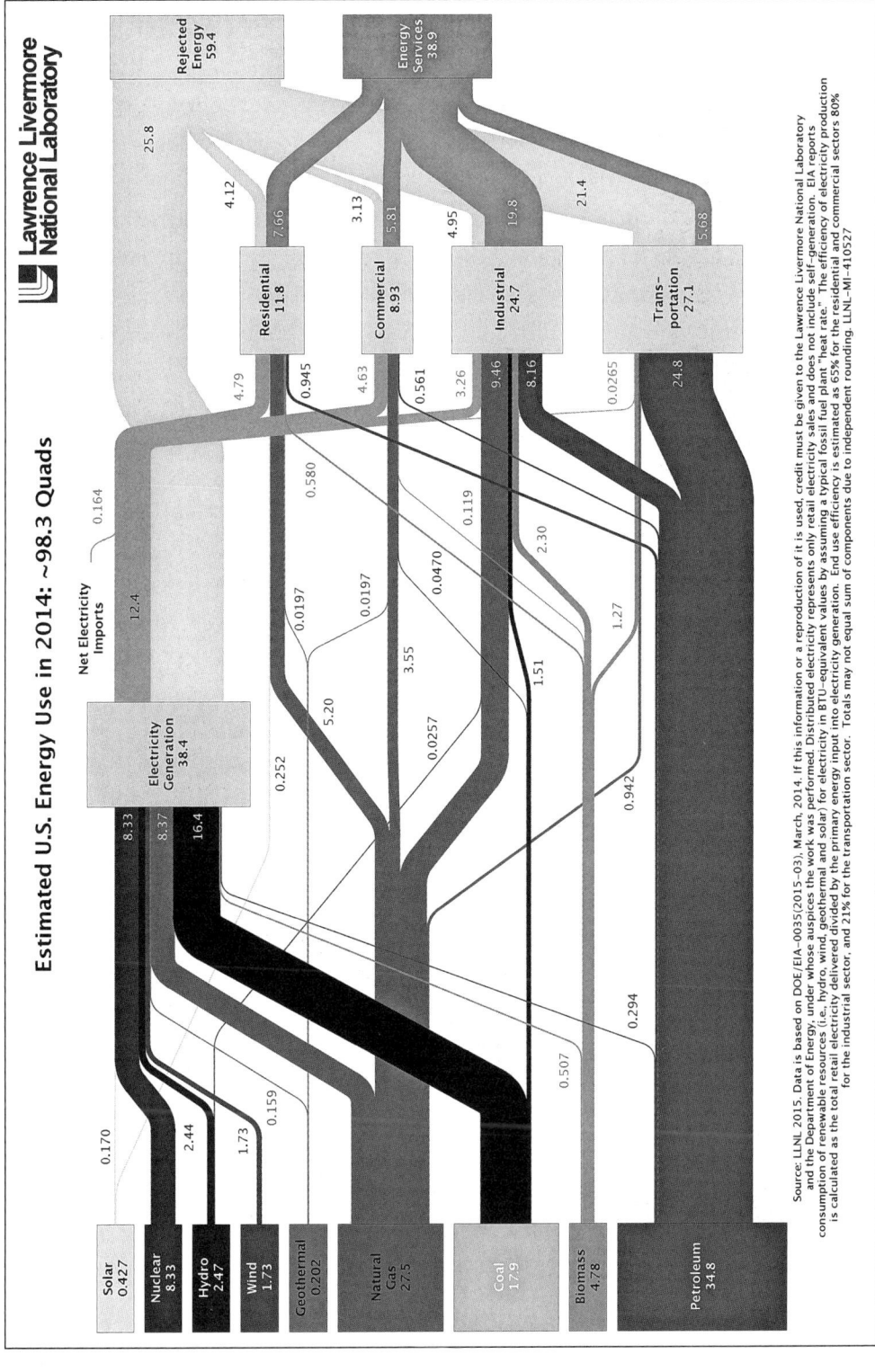

Estimated U.S. Energy Use in 2014: ~98.3 Quads

Source: LLNL 2015. Data is based on DOE/EIA-0035(2015-03), March, 2014. If this information or a reproduction of it is used, credit must be given to the Lawrence Livermore National Laboratory and the Department of Energy, under whose auspices the work was performed. Distributed electricity represents only retail electricity sales and does not include self-generation. EIA reports consumption of renewable resources (i.e., hydro, wind, geothermal and solar) for electricity in BTU-equivalent values by assuming a typical fossil fuel plant "heat rate." The efficiency of electricity production is calculated as the total retail electricity delivered divided by the primary energy input into electricity generation. End use efficiency is estimated as 65% for the residential and commercial sectors 80% for the industrial sector, and 21% for the transportation sector. Totals may not equal sum of components due to independent rounding. LLNL-MI-410527

sector consumes the least energy (8.93 Quads), and the transportation sector the most (27.1 Quads).

- The 98.3 Quads of energy used in 2014 includes both energy consumed and energy wasted (called rejected energy). On the upper right side of the chart, the reader can see that waste equals 59.4 Quads, or almost 40% of the total energy used in the United States. Electricity is the biggest culprit and almost 70% of the electricity that is converted from other forms of energy is lost as waste, due primarily to inefficiencies in production and distribution systems. According to the Environmental Protection Agency, fossil-fuel-based electric power plants in the United States are only about 33% efficient, and "two-thirds of the energy in the fuel is lost—vented as heat."[5]

A great idea—body heat as an energy source

As we go about our lives—sitting, walking, exercising, sleeping—each of us gives off energy in the form of heat. One may ask, "Why waste it?" In Paris, architects designed a system that captures the heat generated by subway commuters and uses it to radiantly heat 17 nearby apartments. A similar project in Stockholm's Central Rail Station harnesses the heat from 250,000 daily commuters. The station's ventilation system captures the body heat, which it uses to heat water in underground tanks. From there, the hot water is pumped to the heating pipes of a nearby office building, saving it 25% on its annual energy costs.[6]

How to Get a Building LEED Certified™

To receive LEED certification, building projects satisfy prerequisites and earn points to achieve different levels of certification. Prerequisites and credits differ for each rating system within LEED, and the owner (often working with his or her team of designers, builders, and consultants) chooses the best fit for the project. Here are, briefly, the five steps required to get a project LEED certified. Additional details and resources are available at *http://www.usgbc.org/certification*

▶ **Certification Step 1**

Verify minimum project requirements (MPRs) and select correct rating system.

▶ **Certification Step 2**

Register the project with Green Building Certification Institute (GBCI).

▶ **Certification Step 3**

Identify credits with points sufficient to meet desired level of certification.

▶ **Certification Step 4**

Fulfill prerequisites and selected credits; document as required by the rating system.

▶ **Certification Step 5**

Apply to GBCI for review and certification.

Let's look at each of these steps.

▶ Certification Step 1
Verify minimum project requirements (MPRs)
and select the appropriate rating system

Not all projects are eligible to be LEED-certified. There are baseline minimum project requirements (MPRs) that must be met and that define the types of projects that LEED was designed to evaluate. The latest version of LEED (v4) identifies three MPRs. Projects that do not meet these requirements do not qualify to apply for certification. What are these MPRs?

- *MPR #1: The project must be in a permanent location on existing land.*

  A significant portion of LEED requirements depends on the project's location. Therefore, it is important that LEED projects are evaluated as permanent structures. Typically, any structure that might move during its lifetime, such as a mobile home, is not eligible for LEED certification. Locating projects on existing land is important to avoid artificial landmasses that have the potential to displace and disrupt ecosystems.

- *MPR #2: The project must use reasonable boundaries.*

  The LEED rating system is designed to evaluate buildings, spaces, or neighborhoods, and all environmental impacts associated with those projects. Defining a reasonable boundary (for example landscaping, parking, and sidewalks) ensures that the project is accurately evaluated.

- *MPR #3: The project must comply with size requirements.*

  Projects can't be too small. Most projects must be at least 1,000 square feet, although for commercial and retail interiors, the figure is much smaller. LEED's five rating systems differ in size and acreage requirements and the project team will verify that the project meets specific MPR #3 requirements.

As noted in Chapter 4, LEED recognizes that different project types require different design approaches and requirements. Therefore, LEED offers a suite of rating systems, based on various construction types and usage. Once the project team determines that the project satisfies the MPRs, it must choose which rating system to adopt. Certification is awarded to a project based on the team's ability to satisfy the multiple prerequisites specific to that rating system plus the completion or incorporation of a minimum number of performance credits (see the following).

The five LEED green rating systems are:

- **Building Design and Construction (LEED® BD+C)** for buildings that are being newly constructed or are going through major renovation. LEED BD+C includes 10 building/project types, including new construction and major renovations, core and shell development, schools, retail, and others.

- **Interior Design and Construction (LEED® ID+C)** for projects that are a complete interior fit-out (the process of making interior space suitable for use). This category includes commercial, retail, and hospitality project types.

- **Building Operations and Maintenance (LEED® O+M)** for buildings that are undergoing improvement work or little to no construction, including existing buildings, data centers, warehouses, and more.

- **Neighborhood Development (LEED® ND)** for new land development projects or redevelopment projects containing residential uses, nonresidential uses, or a mix. Projects can be at any stage of the development process, from conceptual planning to construction.

- **Homes Design and Construction (LEED® Homes)** for single-family homes, low-rise multi-family (one to three stories), or mid-rise multi-family (four to six stories).

Alta Vista multi-family housing: LEED for Homes Plantinum

Abode Communities

Every project team that decides to pursue LEED certification must select one of these rating systems and follow its individual requirements. Because not all projects fit neatly into a single system (but must commit to only one), the USGBC has developed the *Rating System Selection Guidance* to help project teams select the most appropriate system. (The *Guidance* is available to download at *http://www.usgbc.org/articles/rating-system-selection-guidance*)

▶ Certification Step 2
Register the project with the Green Building Certification Institute

Once the rating system has been selected, the team registers the project with the Green Building Certification Institute (GBCI). Ideally, registration occurs early in the planning or design phase, and involves the completion of an online questionnaire.

Registration provides notice of an owner's intent to seek certification for a project and provides GBCI with general information such as project owner, location, square footage, and general project timeline. In addition, registration establishes the project team's administrator.

Selection of a rating system and registration with GBCI enables the project team to move ahead with the next step in the certification process.

When a project is registered (and a fee is paid), access is provided to online resources that can assist the team in completing the certification process. The project is also listed in the online LEED project directory at *http://www.usgbc.org/projects*

▶ Certification Step 3
Identify credits with points sufficient to meet desired level of certification

After selecting a rating system, the project team determines which level of certification it hopes to earn (in ascending order: Certified, Silver, Gold, or Platinum) and how it intends to do so. Each certification level requires that the project earn a minimum number of points by completing credits. It is up to the team to determine which combination of credits it will pursue in order to meet this minimum.

In addition to required prerequisites, all LEED rating systems (except for Neighborhood Development) identify eight credit categories:

1. **Sustainable sites**

   This credit category focuses on the environment surrounding the building: restoring project site elements, integrating the site with local and regional ecosystems, and preserving the biodiversity upon which natural systems rely.

2. **Water efficiency**

   Indoor and outdoor water use, specialized uses, and metering systems.

3. **Energy & atmosphere**

   Energy use reduction, energy-efficient design strategies, and renewable energy sources.

4. **Materials & resources**

   Minimizing the embodied-energy and other impacts associated with the extraction, processing, transport, maintenance, and disposal of building materials.

5. **Indoor environmental quality**

   Indoor air quality, and thermal, visual, and acoustic comfort.

6. **Location and transportation**

   Site location and access: compact development, the use of previously used or disadvantaged sites, alternative transportation, and connection with amenities such as restaurants and parks.

7. **Innovation**

   This category is designed to recognize projects for innovative building features and sustainable building practices and strategies that exceed those identified by LEED.

8. **Regional priority**

   Points are earned for approaches that address regional environmental priorities and concerns.

Each of these categories is further subdivided into credits that are assigned point values depending upon their anticipated impact. Although credits and points are distributed slightly differently according to which rating system is being used, all projects must be awarded at least 40 points of a possible 100 to be certified.

Let's take another look at Table 4.2 (reprinted here) to review credits and points. This table identifies the Energy & Atmosphere credit category for the LEED Building Design & Construction rating system. The first four credits

Credits and Points: Energy and Atmosphere for the LEED Building Design and Construction Rating System (LEED BD+C)

Credit	Possible Points	Focus
Fundamental commissioning/ verification	This is a required prerequisite	Project team must follow ASHRAE guidelines for commissioning services
Minimum energy performance	Required prerequisite	Must exceed an ASHRAE energy benchmark (based on performance projections)
Building-level energy metering	Required prerequisite	Must install metering devices to enable post-occupancy energy consumption for five years
Fundamental refrigerant management	Required prerequisite	No use of chlorofluorocarbon (CFC)–based refrigerants or complete a phase-out plan for existing equipment
Enhanced commissioning	Maximum 6 points	Commissioning beyond what is required as a prerequisite
Optimize energy performance	Maximum 18 points	Energy performance beyond what is required as a prerequisite
Advanced energy metering	Maximum 1 point	More detailed metering than what is required as a prerequisite
Demand response	Maximum 2 points	Project reduces energy demand during certain periods
Renewable energy production	Maximum 3 points	Project meets a percentage of energy use through renewable sources
Enhanced refrigerant management	Maximum 1 point	Select refrigerants that minimize ozone depletion
Green power and carbon offsets	Maximum 2 points	Actions that reduce greenhouse gas emissions

listed in the left column are mandatory prerequisites and therefore are not awarded points. Each of the other credits is assigned a possible maximum point value and the project team determines which credits to include in the project.

If the project team chooses to fulfill each credit, the maximum possible points will be 33. Not every credit needs to be addressed to qualify for certification and during this step in the process, the project team determines which level of certification (Gold, Platinum, etc.) they will pursue and which credits, in which credit categories, they will satisfy to meet the minimum threshold for that level of certification. (It should be noted that there are also opportunities for projects to earn up to 10 bonus points for going beyond the performance requirements or addressing specific regional concerns.) The number of points a project earns determines the level of certification the project will receive:

- LEED Certified = 40+ points

- LEED Silver = 50+ points

- LEED Gold = 60+ points

- LEED Platinum = 80+ points

Once the project team determines the LEED certification level for which it wishes to apply, design plans are developed, and the team makes preparations for fulfilling documentation and other verification requirements. Typically, at the conclusion of Step 3, the project team will have a road map for fulfilling all prerequisites and the selected credits, and they're ready to move on to Step 4: completion of the work, verifications, and documentation in preparation of an application for certification.

▶ Certification Step 4

Fulfill prerequisites and selected credits; document as required
by the rating system

In Step 4, the physical work to fulfill the prerequisites and the credits selected for the project are completed. Project teams need to do more than complete the work; as part of the certification process, verification must be provided to GBCI to show that all prerequisites have been met and calculations are completed for the credits the team has chosen to pursue. Although documentation requirements vary somewhat between different rating systems, they all share the following characteristics:

- Declarations that the project meets certain criteria

- Narratives providing brief overviews of strategies for meeting credit requirements

- Calculations/tables that demonstrate compliance and identify points earned against a baseline

- Documents such as drawings (which are uploaded to LEED Online: *http://www.leedonline.com*)

- Required signatures on certain forms and proof of professional exemption for any streamlined documentation compliance paths (available for certain credits within certain rating systems)

The team may make adjustments to its design plan as work proceeds: documentation will be adjusted and revised as necessary. As we'll see in the next step, the required documents may be submitted during design for preliminary review or all together at the completion of the work.

▶ Certification Step 5

Apply to GBCI for review and certification

In addition to managing the development of LEED updates and providing tools and resources to assist project teams in completing the certification process, the USGBC develops the requirements for certifying projects. As previously noted, it is the third-party Green Building Certification Institute that reviews projects, administers the process, and determines the level of certification. All documentation must be submitted to GBCI for review.

When does the team submit the documentation to formally apply for review and certification? There are two paths:

1. Standard Review, in which all documentation is submitted at the completion of construction

2. Split Application, which provides an opportunity for the team to receive preliminary review feedback from GBCI during the design phase of a project

Typically, projects can choose either the standard review or the split application path. (Some project types are required to follow the standard review process.) Completion of documentation by the project team can take weeks or months, depending upon project complexity. The application of documents for certification may be submitted up to two years following substantial completion of construction.

Certain aspects of the application process have implications for the composition of the project team and its strategy for completing program requirements. For example, some credits provide for a streamlined compliance path and others require sign-offs from professionals (such as engineers, architects, or LEED credentialed professionals).

Upon receipt of an application for certification, plus payment of a fee based on square footage and documentation, GBCI initiates a formal review process. In 25 days, a preliminary review is issued to the project team, identifying credits as "anticipated," "pending," or "denied." The team may accept the findings or, if unsatisfied with the findings, may choose to provide revised documentation or information. A final report is then issued, with a declaration of points awarded and level of certification achieved.

GBCI has a formal appeal process for all disputed reports, and certification is not granted until all appeals have been resolved.

Certified projects receive a certificate and brass plaque, along with a media kit and the promise of exposure on the USGBC website and in the trade press. Perhaps as important from a marketing standpoint, LEED projects may display the LEED logo on their building. Projects are included in the LEED Project Directory (*http://www.usgbc.org/projects*), which contains basic project details, a project overview or summary of what a project team accomplished, and the credits met. If desired, the project may also be listed in the Department of Energy High Performance Buildings Database (*http://buildingdata.energy.gov*).

Helpful Web Addresses

apps2.eere.energy.gov/wind/windexchange – U.S. Department of Energy WINDExchange—provides publications, webinars, podcasts, maps of wind resources, and a locator map of wind education and training programs in the United States.

www.azbex.com/category/green-renewable-energy – Arizona Builders Exchange compilation of green and renewable energy news

http://conference.resnet.us – Residential Energy Services Network (RESNET) Building Performance Conference on home energy ratings, existing home retrofits, building codes, and energy policy.

www.greenadvantage.org – Green Advantage—an ANSI-approved training and certification for green builders and remodelers that is unaffiliated with a trade association and not linked to its own building rating system.

http://greenspec.buildinggreen.com – BuildingGreen—publishes the GreenSpec Directory listing of green products with manufacturer's information, sponsors Environmental Building News, which features articles, product reviews, and other information.

www.nfrc.org – National Fenestration Rating Council (NFRC)—a nonprofit organization that provides energy performance information, education, and certified ratings.

https://www.kaplancleantech.com – Kaplan—for-profit training programs in clean energy.

www.earthday.org – Earth Day Network (EDN)—works with over 50,000 partners in 192 countries to broaden, diversify, and mobilize the environmental movement; Earth Day is the largest civic observance in the world.

www.greenJobs.net – Green Jobs Network—a job search engine that links workers up with environmental or social responsibility jobs.

www.greentrainingusa.com – Green Training USA—a for-profit training program that offers online programs.

www.NAHBgreen.org – National Association of Home Buildings (NAHB)—green building, remodeling, and development training programs to prepare builders for work in green construction.

www.rateitgreen.com – Rate It Green—a directory, network, and resource for green builders.

www.aament.org – American Architectural Manufacturers Association (AAMA)—a trade association for the fenestration industry: windows, doors, skylights, and curtain walls.

www.abc.org – Associated Builders and Contractors (ABC)—a trade organization that represents open-shop (merit/non-union) construction firms that work primarily in the industrial and commercial sectors.

www.sfi.program.org – Sustainable Forest Initiative (SFI)—a nonprofit organization responsible for maintaining, overseeing, and improving the Sustainable Forestry Initiative program.

www.acca.org – Air-Conditioning Contractors of America (ACCA)—a trade association for individuals and businesses in heating, ventilation, and air conditioning (HVAC).

www.aecdaily.com – AEC Daily—a developer of free online education, building product information, and industry news.

www.aeecenter.org – Association of Energy Engineers (AEE)—an international membership organization with 95 chapters in the United States; sponsors multiple training programs and certificates in various aspects of green construction.

www.agc.org – Associated General Contractors of America (AGC)—a membership organization for contractors working in the commercial sector of the industry; they have over 90 chapters around the country and offer training and a Green Contractor Certification (see *www.greenconstructionatwork.com*).

www.agc.org/cs/environment – Association of General Contractors of America (AGC) Contractors Environmental Conference—provides information on multiple environmental issues; past conferences have included topics such as green paving technologies, low impact development, estimating and bidding green projects, and preparing a work force for green projects.

www.ahrinet.org – Air-Conditioning, Heating, and Refrigeration Institute (AHRI) trade association.

www.ahridirectory.org – Directory of Certified Product Performance—developed by the Consortium for Energy Efficiency (CEE) and Air-Conditioning Heating and Refrigeration Institute (AHRI); a listing of residential and small commercial mechanical equipment.

www.airbarrier.org – Air Barrier Association (ABAA)—an association that provides information on air barriers and building envelopes.

www.ases.org – American Solar Energy Society (ASES), affiliated with the International Solar Energy Society (ISES; see *www.ises.org*)—provides information on renewable energy issues worldwide, has a network of student and young professional ISES members, publishes a scientific journal (Solar Energy) and issues reports and newsletters on the industry; has independent chapters (e.g., NorCal Solar *www.norcalsolar.org*).

www.ases.org/solar-today-magazine – Solar Today—subscription-based magazine also available online, from the American Solar Energy Society (ASES).

www.ashrae.org – American Society of Heating, Refrigerating and Air-Conditioning Engineers (ASHRAE)—a source of technical standards for the HVAC industry.

www.astm.org – ASTM International (formerly American Society for Testing and Materials)—develops standards for a wide range of products including its list of Sustainability Standards.

www.awci.org – Association of the Wall and Ceiling Industry (AWCI)— trade association for wall and ceiling contractors, manufacturers, suppliers, and distributors that offers resources including magazines, newsletters, and product catalogs.

www.awea.org – American Wind Energy Association (AWEA)—national trade association that provides information on wind energy, publishes a membership directory, and hosts the annual WINDPOWER conference.

www.bacweb.org – International Union of Bricklayers and Allied Craftworkers (BAC)—a union representing bricklayers, stone and marble masons, cement masons, plasterers, tile-setters, terrazzo and mosaic workers, and pointers/cleaners/caulkers.

www.biomasscenter.org – Biomass Energy Resource Center (BERC)—a nonprofit organization that works to advance community-scale biomass, whose website includes a resource library and an extensive glossary.

www.bls.gov – Bureau of Labor Statistics (BLS)—part of the U.S. Department of Labor; includes information on renewable energy and job opportunities in the field.

www.bluegreenalliance.org – BlueGreen Alliance—an association between unions ("blue collar") and environmental ("green") groups, offering multiple resources and training through the GreenPOWER program; sponsors the annual Good Jobs, Green Jobs Conference.

www.bpi.org – Building Performance Institute (BPI)—develops standards for home energy retrofit projects and offers credentials from entry-level to skilled.

www.buildinggreen.com – Building Green—a membership organization that offers news (Environmental Building News), a blog, a product database, and more.

www.buildingtrades.com – Building Trades Association—provides various services for contractors such as online job postings, insurance, and a directory of contractors.

www.builditgreen.org – Build It Green—a nonprofit membership organization in California that sponsors a system for assessing and verifying green residential buildings; provides professional certification training.

www.bx.org – Builders Exchange of Central Ohio.

www.bxkentucky.com – Builders Exchange of Kentucky.

www.c2ccertified.org – Cradle to Cradle Products Innovation Institute—a nonprofit organization that manages the Cradle to Cradle Certified Product Standard, which provides criteria and requirements for products.

www.carpenters.org – United Brotherhood of Carpenters (UBC)—large building-trades unions, with a green training program; see its website to locate regional councils and training centers.

www.carpet-rug.org – Carpet and Rug Institute (CRI)—a trade association for the carpet industry, offers education and resources, testing, and labeling for carpet products.

www.careerschools.org – Careers Schools—directory of professional, trade, vocational schools, and colleges. Users can browse by state or by program of study.

www.cfinstallers.com – Certified Floorcovering Installers Association (CFI)—a trade association for floor installers, offering professional certifications and hands-on training courses.

www.cleantechnica.com – CleanTechnica—an energy website with posts on solar, wind, geothermal, and other renewables, plus reports and videos.

www.conferencealerts.com – Conference Alerts—a comprehensive list of worldwide academic conferences, where one can view conferences by date, topic, and country and subscribe to a service to receives alerts regarding conferences of interest.

www.constructionpronet.com – ConstructionPro Network—a for-profit training company.

www.contractorcollege.org – Painting and Decorating Contractors of America's Contractor College—an industry training center offering green training; see also *www.pdca.org*

www.csinet.org – Construction Specifications Institute (CSI)—membership organization that develops standards and formats for managing construction information, and offers professional education and certification; chapters are nationwide.

www.doe.gov – U.S. Department of Energy (DOE)—provides information on green construction, including information on energy incentive programs in each state (see also *www.energy.gov*).

www.dsireusa.org – Database of State Incentives for Renewables & Efficiency (DSIRE)—an excellent source of information on state, local, federal, and utility financial and other incentives that promote renewable energy and energy efficiency.

www.econtc.com – Energy Conservation Training Company—a for-profit training program in green building.

www.emagazine.com – E/The Environmental Magazine—published by the Earth Action Network, covering a broad range of environmental and related topics.

www.energy.gov – U.S. Department of Energy (DOE)—information on energy incentive programs in each state; see also *www.doe.gov*

www.energy.gov/eere/geothermal – U.S. Department of Energy Geothermal Technologies Office.

www.energy.sourceguides.com – Energy Source Guides—a list of renewable energy trade associations by state.

www.energystar.gov – Energy Star—a program of the U.S. Environmental Protection Agency (EPA) that helps consumers identify energy-efficient products, such as washing machines and dryers.

www.energystar.gov/buildings – Energy Star Certified Buildings and (Industrial) Plants—the U.S. government's energy rating program for residential and commercial buildings, developed by the Department of Energy and the EPA; includes an online tool that focuses on energy performance.

www.epa.gov – U.S. Environmental Protection Agency (EPA)—sponsors the Energy Star and WaterSense programs; its website has a map with links to local EPA activities.

www.epa.gov/watersense – EPA WaterSense—labels products that conserve water (such as low-flush toilets and motion-activated faucets) and seeks to educate consumers about water efficiency.

www.everblue.edu – Everblue—a for-profit training program in green building.

www.fcica.com – Flooring Contractors Association (FCICA)—a trade association representing the commercial floor covering industry; provides newsletters, magazine, webinars, and floor covering training.

www.fscus.org – Forest Stewardship Council (FSC)—a third-party certification program in sustainable forestry, including ecological functions, old-growth forests, plantations, restoration, native habitat, indigenous people's rights, and sound management for timber production.

www.geo-energy.org – Geothermal Energy Association—a trade association of companies supporting the expanded use of geothermal energy, with a list of member companies, with addresses and contact names.

www.geoexchange.org – Geothermal Heat Pump Consortium—a trade association that promotes the manufacture, design, and installation of geothermal systems; its website offers a directory of contractors/service providers by state.

www.gpro.org – Green Professional (GPRO)—offers training in green professional building skills, with programs in several states.

www.green-colleges.com – Making a Difference College Guide—provides information on green classes and degrees.

www.greenbuildermag.com – Green Builder—magazine and blog focusing on green building and sustainable development; interesting archived articles are available online.

www.greenbuildexpo.org – GreenBuild Conference & Exposition—USGBC's annual GreenBuild International Conference and Expo.

www.greenbuildingadvisor.com – GreenBuilding Advisor—online resource for building green homes; its website offers product guides, discussion forums, videos, and multiple blogs.

www.greenbuildinginsider.com – Green Builder Insider—provides information on energy efficiency, certifications including LEED, case studies, technologies and products, reports and studies, legal matters and legislation, international happenings, and competitions and awards.

www.greenconstructionatwork.com – Green Contractor Certification program of the Associated General Contractors (see *www.agc.org*).

www.greenexpo365.com – GreenExpo365—a virtual trade show and online community focused on green building, sponsoring "live" events, opportunities to chat live with green building professionals; its website has useful links, blogs, and other information.

www.greenhomeguide.org – Green Home Guide—a site sponsored by the U.S. Green Building Council that enables the user to ask questions and get opinions from others in the industry.

www.greenjobsconference.org – Good Jobs Green Jobs National Conference—annual conference sponsored by the Blue Green Alliance Foundation.

www.greenplumberstraining.org – GreenPlumbers—part of the International Association of Plumbing and Mechanical Officials (IAPMO), a training and accreditation program that promotes the use of energy efficient and water-saving technologies; see also *www.iampo.org*

www.greenroofs.org – Green Roofs for Healthy Cities (GRHC)—a trade association that offers a range of services and information on green roofs and courses in over 30 cities nationwide.

www.greenroofs.com – Green Roofs—an online news media organization focusing on green roofs.

www.greenseal.org – Green Seal—a third-party certifier of a variety of building products (paints, adhesives, lamps, chillers, windows, cleaners, and more), considering product impacts over the entire life cycle of a product.

www.greensource.construction.com – GreenSource Magazine: The Magazine of Sustainable Design—a publication available in hard and digital editions, covering topics of interest to builders including green building, LEED projects, case studies, and more; videos, products, and features offer a substantial amount of helpful information.

www.gwec.net – Global Wind Energy Council (GWEC)—members include all major wind turbine manufacturers; provides news, information, publications, and job listings for wind farm and wind energy jobs worldwide.

www.hbi.com – Home Builders Institute (HBI)—an organization associated with the National Association of Home Builders (NAHB; see *www.nahb.org*).

www.healthybuilding.net – Healthy Building Network (HBN)—an organization founded to reduce the use of hazardous chemicals in buildings; provides research and information on materials and sponsors the Pharos Project database that identifies health hazards in building materials (see also *www.pharosproject.net*).

www.homeenergy.org/HETG – Home Energy—online and print magazines providing practical information on residential energy efficiency, performance, comfort, and affordability. It has a useful website with links to training programs.

www.homeinnovation.com – Home Innovations Research Labs—associated with National Association of Home Builders (NAHB; see *www.nahb.org*).

www.hydro.org – National Hydro Association (NHA)—a nonprofit working to develop hydropower.

www.hydropower.org – International Hydropower Association (IHA)—created under the auspices of UNESCO, IHA advocates for sustainable hydropower; its blog has up-to-date information on what's happening around the world in hydro.

www.hydroreform.org – Hydropower Reform Coalition—information on how dams and hydropower projects can be operated differently to reduce their adverse impacts.

www.iampo.org – International Association of Plumbing and Mechanical Officials (IAMPO)—publishes the Uniform Plumbing Code (UPC), Uniform Mechanical Code (UMC), and Uniform Solar Energy Code (USEC); offers the Green Plumbing and Mechanical Code Supplement, a model code developed to standardize sustainable residential and commercial plumbing and mechanical systems; see also GreenPlumbers training and accreditation (*www.greenplumberstraining.org*).

www.ibew.org – International Brotherhood of Electrical Workers (IBEW)—a trade union that represents several hundred thousand workers; it provides green training, credentialing, and a jobs board.

www.iccsafe.org – International Green Construction Code (IgCC)—developed by the International Code Council (ICC) and National Association of Home Buildings (NAHB) and adopted by many state and municipal governments for the establishment of minimum design and construction requirements for energy efficiency for homes, schools, and commercial buildings.

www.ieci.org – Independent Electrical Contractors Association (IEC)—a trade association for "merit shop" (non-union) electrical and systems contractors, with almost 3,000 member companies in 60 chapters throughout the United States; provides training, apprenticeships, and credentialing.

www.ies.org – Illuminating Engineering Society of North America (IES)—a trade organization of manufacturers of lighting products, lighting designers, electricians, building contractors, and individuals working in affiliated lighting fields; sponsors conferences and seminars and has a scholarship program.

www.igshpa.okstate.edu – International Ground Source Heat Pump Association (IGSHPA)—a nonprofit group supporting the ground-source heat pump industry with publications, information, research, and more.

www.imaginesolar.com – ImagineSolar—classroom and online courses in Austin TX.

www.indeed.com – Indeed—a job search engine.

www.insulate.org – Insulation Contractors Association of America (ICCA)—a trade organization for residential and commercial insulation installers.

www.insulation.org – National Insulation Association (NIA)—a trade association representing both union and non-union contractors, distributors, and manufacturers primarily in commercial and industrial construction; sponsors annual conventions and training programs; website has links to insulation associations around the country.

www.insulators.org – International Association of Heat and Frost Insulators and Allied Workers (AWWIU)—a trade association with updated apprenticeship training and information on green construction.

www.irecusa.org – Interstate Renewable Energy Council (IREC)—a nonprofit that provides links to helpful databases, training providers, available incentives, and publishes multiple publications; in partnership with the American National Standards Institute (ANSI), provides standards for solar and renewable energy training programs.

www.ises.org – International Solar Energy Society (ISES)—largest international solar organization, with members in more than 110 countries; advocates for the solar industry and provides education and outreach.

www.living-future.org – Living Building Challenge (LBC)—developed by the International Living Future Institute (previously called the International Living Building Institute).

www.makanipower.com – Makani Airborne Wind Turbine (AWT)—develops energy kites; owned by Google X.

www.mcaa.org – Mechanical Contractors Association of America (MCAA)—a trade organization for firms working in heating, air conditioning, refrigeration, plumbing, piping, and mechanical service; includes Mechanical Service Contractors of America, the Plumbing Contractors of America, the Manufacturer/ Supplier Council, the Mechanical Contracting Education and Research Foundation, and the National Certified Pipe Welding Bureau.

www.mcaa.org/green – Mechanical Contractors Association of America (MCAA) Green Education—offers hour-long webinars for contractors working in green and sustainable mechanical construction, service, and plumbing.

www.midwestrenew.org – Midwest Renewable Energy Center—a nonprofit offering self-paced courses in solar energy and wind systems.

www.monster.com – Monster—a job search engine.

www.nabcep.org – North American Board of Certified Energy Practitioners (NABCEP)—offers professional certification in small wind Installation.

www.nahb.org – National Association of Home Builders (NAHB)—a trade and membership association that helps promote housing policies, with more than 100,000 members, and provides green training through some of its local builders associations.

www.nahb.org/local_association_search_form.aspx – National Association of Home Builders (NAHB)—search form for local builders associations.

www.naima.org – North American Insulation Manufacturing Association (NAIMA)—a trade association with a useful website and information on sustainability and energy efficiency.

www.nawic.org – National Association of Women in Construction (NAWIC)—a membership organization that provides mentoring, technical information, education, and more to women involved in the construction industry.

www.ncbeonline.com – North Coast Builders Exchange, Santa Rosa, CA—a builders exchange with educational programs related to green construction.

www.nccer.org – National Center for Construction Education and Research (NCCER)—educational affiliate of the Associated Builders and Contractors (ABC; *www.abc.org*), provides work-force development, including green technology credentialing.

www.necanet.org – National Electrical Contractors Association (NECA)—a trade association providing advocacy, education, research, and standards development; with 119 chapters, NECA offers a variety of training and apprentice opportunities.

www.norcalsolar.org – NorCal Solar—Northern California chapter of American Solar Energy Society (ASES; *www.ases.org*).

www.nrca.net – National Roofing Contractors Association (NRCA)—a nonprofit association that represents all segments of the roofing industry; sponsors EnergyWise Roof Calculator Online, to evaluate thermal performance and energy costs; offers classes in rooftop photovoltaic systems.

www.nrdc.org – National Resources Defense Council (NRDC)—an environmental action group that, among other services, provides useful information on renewable energy systems; also see its Onearth magazine (*www.onearth.org*).

www.nrdc.org/energy/renewables/biomass.asp—NRDC website section on biomass.

www.nrel.gov – National Renewable Energy Laboratory (NREL)—the primary research laboratory for DOE's Office of Energy Efficiency and Renewable Energy, and a good source of technical information and data on renewable energy.

www.nrel.gov/biomass – NREL bioenergy research program—research program on bioenergy, produces biomass energy maps.

www.nrep.org – National Registry of Environmental Professionals (NREP)—an organization of affiliates that provide professional training and recognition.

www.onearth.org – Onearth—a subscription-based magazine published by the Natural Resources Defense Council (NRDC; *www.nrdc.org*), covering a broad range of environmental topics including cities and transportation, science and technology, and more; offers free online newsletter, columns, and blogs.

www.passivehouse.us – Passive House Institute US (PHIUS)—a nonprofit organization that offers building and professional certifications; see also *www.Phius.org*

www.pdca.org – Painting and Decorating Contractors of America (PDCA)—a trade association for the coating and wall covering industry with standards, training, and advocacy; Contractor College is its training center and offers multiple programs on green aspects of the trade (see *www.contractorcollege.org*).

www.pge.com/pec – Pacific Gas & Electric (PG&E) Energy Center—sponsors free lectures and classes in energy conservation and green building techniques at various locations around the San Francisco Bay Area in California.

www.pharosproject.net – Pharos Project—a database from the Healthy Building Network (HBN) on the health and environmental hazards of building products and materials; its website lists products and rates product certifications.

www.phccweb.org – Plumbing-Heating-Cooling Contractors National Association (PHCC)—a trade association representing more than 3,500 contractor members; provides training opportunities and more.

www.princetonreview.com/green.aspx – Princeton Review—provides information on green college classes and degrees.

www.regreenprogram.org – Green Residential Remodeling Program (REGREEN)— a resource for green home remodeling, developed by USGBC and the American Society of Interior Designers (ASID); offers a REGREEN Trained Certificate.

www.resnet.us – Residential Energy Services Network (RESNET)—a nonprofit organization that developed the Home Energy Rating System (HERS) that measures and rates a home's energy efficiency; trains energy raters and auditors.

www.resnet.us/energy-rating – Home Energy Rating System (HERS)—developed by the nonprofit Residential Energy Services Network (RESNET), HERS is used to measure and rate the energy efficiency of a home.

www.rfci.com – Resilient Floor Coverings Institute (RFC)—a trade association of resilient flooring manufacturers and suppliers.

www.scsglobalservices.com – SCS Global Systems—a third-party certification program that certifies a wide range of products from textiles to construction products; its website has a helpful list of certified products; certifies FloorScore (see *www.rfci.com*) and indoor air quality performance under the Indoor Advantage label.

www.seia.org – Solar Energy Industry Association (SEIA)—a trade association with news, a job board, information regarding legislation, training opportunities, certifications, and more; its National Solar Database provides comprehensive information on solar companies operating in the United States.

www.sierraclub.org/sierra/coolschools-2014 – Sierra Club—a program sponsored by the nonprofit organization that provides information on colleges with green classes and green degrees.

www.simplyhired.com – Simply Hired—a job search engine.

www.smacna.org – Sheet Metal and Air Conditioning Contractors' National Association (SMACNA)—an international association of union contractors in heating, ventilating, and air conditioning; sheet metal; energy management and maintenance and more.

www.solar-rating.org – Solar Rating & Certification Corporation (ICC-SRCC)— a nonprofit organization whose primary purpose is the development and implementation of national rating standards and certification programs for solar energy equipment.

www.solarenergy.org – Solar Energy International (SEI)—a nonprofit educational organization that provides technical training and expertise in renewable energy.

www.spri.org – Single Ply Roofing Industry (SPRI)—a trade association representing sheet membrane and component suppliers to the commercial roofing industry.

www.stars.aashe.org – Sustainability Tracking, Assessment & Rating System (STARS)—provides information on colleges with green courses and green degrees.

www.sustainabilityprofessionals.org – International Society of Sustainability Professionals (ISSP)—a nonprofit educational organization that offers workshops, information, and links to local professionals.

www.thegbi.org – Green Building Initiative (GBI)—a nonprofit building-rating organization that administers the Green Globes building rating system and provides professional certifications (see *www.thegbi.org/professional-certification*).

www.tile-assn.com – National Tile Contractors Association (NTCA)—a trade association for installers of ceramic tile and natural stone. It focuses on education and training and offers a variety of resources.

www.trade-schools.net – Trade Schools, Colleges, and Universities—a directory of trade schools organized by academic programs, trade, or location; includes construction, building, carpentry, welding, and plumbing schools, and provides information profiles for each trade school.

www.technical-schools-guide.com – Technical Schools Guide—a listing of 495+ schools with more than 2,510 campus locations across that United States and Canada.

www.ua.org – United Association (UA)—union of plumbers, welders, pipefitters, and service techs; provides training in green skills, including the Green Systems Awareness program.

www.ul.com – Underwriters Laboratories (UL)—writes testing standards and certifies products for safety; includes UL Environment and Greenguard, which provides third-party certification for low-chemical-emitting products; certified products are subject to a review of the manufacturing process and routine testing to ensure minimal impact on the indoor environment.

www.universities.com – Universities.com—a directory of universities, colleges, vocational schools, training centers, and learning programs alphabetically, by program of study, by U.S. state, or, for international schools, by country; provides school information and Web links.

www.usgbc.org – U.S. Green Building Council (USGBC)—a member of the International Green Building Council and the primary green organization in the United States. USGBC developed the LEED green building rating systems; there are chapters around the country (see *www.usgbc.org/chapters).*

www.usgbc.org/articles – USGBC blog on LEED, and other interesting articles on green building.

www.usgbc.org/articles/rating-system-selection-guidance – USGBC Rating System Selection Guidance

www.usgbc.org/chapters – USGBC list of individual chapters, which sponsor meetings and educational workshops.

www.usgbc.org/LEED – USGBC Leadership in Energy and Environmental Design (LEED)—a voluntary green building certification program, developed by the U.S. Green Building Council and administered by the Green Building Certification Institute, that recognizes best-in-class building strategies and practices. LEED includes a suite of green building rating systems as well as programs for professional accreditation.

www.usgbc.org/projects – LEED project directory—a publically accessible and searchable directory of LEED projects, organized by building type.

www.utexas.edu/world/comco/state – University of Texas Community College Database—lists community colleges by state.

www.vceonline.com – Valley Contractors Exchange (VCE) in Chico, CA—a builders exchange that offers educational programs locally.

www.wdma.com – Window & Door Manufacturers Association (WDMA)—an industry association that provides information, advocacy, and product certification for window and door manufacturers.

www.windpowerexpo.org – WINDPOWER Conference & Expo—American Wind Energy Association's annual conference and exposition.

www.411energyexperts.com – 411 Energy Experts—a for-profit training program in green building.

Glossary

2030 Challenge—a call to the design and construction communities that all new and renovated buildings will be zero net energy by 2030.

Academic degree—a post-secondary credential offered by colleges and universities.

Air changes—how much air circulates in and out of a room.

Air quality—a measurement of the pollutants in the air.

ANSI (American National Standards Institute)—certifies standards developed by other organizations.

Architect—see Designer.

ASHRAE (American Society of Heating, Refrigerating and Air-Conditioning Engineers)—a source of technical standards for the HVAC industry.

ASTM International (formerly American Society for Testing and Materials)—develops standards for a wide range of products, materials, and systems.

Authority Having Jurisdiction (AHJ)—an agency such as a city's building department with jurisdiction over a project.

Biomass—any organic matter that can be burned for energy.

Bioswales—vegetation-filled depressions used to manage runoff.

Blackwater—wastewater that includes human waste.

BREEAM (Building Research Establishment Environmental Assessment Method)—developed in 1990 by the Building Research Establishment in

Great Britain, a design and assessment method for sustainable buildings; it was the model for LEED.

Brownfield—a site that has hazardous substances, pollutants, or contaminants from an earlier use.

BTU (British thermal unit)—a unit of energy equivalent to the heat produced by a single lit kitchen match and measured in watts.

Building assessment program—an evaluation tool for measuring the qualities and nature of a building; often used interchangeably with building rating system.

Building codes—mandatory requirements that promote safe practices in the design and construction of buildings.

Building envelope—the physical separators between the parts of a building that are heated and cooled (conditioned) and those parts that are not.

Building Information Modeling (BIM)—a process of gathering and managing information that uses 3D virtual models as a tool for design, construction, and facilities management.

Building-integrated photovoltaics (BIPVs)—systems that integrate photovoltaic solar cells directly into building materials.

Building rating system—an evaluation tool for measuring the qualities and nature of a building; often used interchangeably with building assessment program.

Built environment—human-made buildings and parks, transportation systems, energy and water infrastructure, and all the other constructed components that form our surroundings.

CALGreen—California's statewide building energy standards code.

Capacity—the amount of heating or cooling a piece of HVAC equipment can provide under optimum conditions.

Certificate—a voluntary non-degree credential.

Certification—a document used to demonstrate that a product, system, or building has met certain performance criteria.

Closed shop—a place of work where the employer agrees to hire union members only.

Close-out—the process of completing the terms of a contract; includes completion of the physical work (construction close-out), completion of fulfilling the terms of the construction contract (contract close-out), and final evaluations by the contractor (contractor close-out). On a green project, close-out includes submittal of required documentation.

Codes—laws put into place to promote safe practices in design and construction; compliance is enforced through whichever agency has jurisdiction over the project.

Commercial sector—a sector of the construction industry that includes offices, large apartment complexes, theaters, schools, hospitals, and other such facilities.

Commissioning—a process of verifying that building systems and equipment are installed as specified and the building is operating at optimal performance. Commissioning can occur during design, construction, and operation.

Commissioning agent—member of the project team who coordinates the commissioning process.

Compliance—conformity in fulfilling official requirements.

Concentrating photovoltaic (CPV) systems—systems that generate electric power by concentrating sunlight or thermal energy on photovoltaic cells. Not to be confused with concentrating solar power (CSP) systems.

Concentrating solar power (CSP) systems—systems that use a mechanism to reflect sunlight onto a focal point to create heat or steam. Not to be confused with concentrating photovoltaic (CPV) systems.

Conservation—the act of trying to protect or preserve something or the limiting of how much of a resource is used.

Construction—the execution of physical work as outlined in contract documents.

Construction and demolition (C&D) waste—the materials that are discarded from the renovation of existing buildings, the demolition of old buildings, and the construction of new buildings and infrastructure.

Construction industry—the sector of the economy that is engaged with the construction, alteration, maintenance, and repair of systems, buildings, structures, infrastructure, and other real property.

Construction management—the process of coordinating, monitoring, evaluating, and controlling a construction project; not to be confused with the specific delivery method known as construction management project delivery.

Construction management project delivery—a delivery method in which a contract manager is hired early in the process and acts as the owner's representative. During construction, the contract manager may either manage (but not physically complete the work) or perform as a general contractor.

Contract documents—the drawings and other written, printed, or electronic matter that make up the contractor's legal agreement with the owner.

Contract manager—an individual or firm, hired as an owner's representative during preconstruction under a Construction management project delivery method; the contract manager typically coordinates completion of the physical work.

Contractor (also called constructor or builder)—an individual or firm that agrees to construct a project in accordance with contract documents (the drawings and other written, printed, or electronic matter that make up the contractor's legal agreement with the owner).

Conventional buildings—a building that meets but does not exceed basic code requirements.

Credential—recognition by a qualified agent that an individual has met certain criteria and passed an assessment in a subject.

Credentialing—the umbrella term used to describe a process whereby a qualified agent (such as a state license board or another organization or agency) grants recognition that an individual has met certain criteria and, typically, passed an assessment test.

Decommissioning—the process of taking something (such as a building) out of service.

Deep-green retrofits—efforts that result in energy savings of 50% or more, as measured against a pre-renovation baseline.

Delivered energy—the amount of energy consumed at an end point.

Delivery method—the organizational structure for completing a project; also called project delivery.

Demand—the amount of heating or cooling a building needs; also called "load."

Design-bid-build delivery method—a system of organizing a project in which a general contractor is hired on a lump-sum-bid basis after design is complete; also called a traditional/lump-sum delivery method.

Design-Build delivery method—a system of organizing projects marked by the owner hiring a single firm to provide both design and construction services.

Designer—an individual or firm that provides planning, design, and construction administration services to a project; they are typically licensed architects or engineers.

Developer—a private owner who coordinates the tasks required to create a project.

Drip irrigation—systems that slowly deliver water directly to the root zone of a plant, with almost no water loss through surface runoff or evaporation.

Dual-flush toilets—toilets that are based on the standard toilets but have two buttons that allow for different flushing options.

Durability—a measure of the anticipated useful life of a system or product before it must be removed and replaced.

Efficient—see Energy efficiency.

Electrical energy—the energy made available by the flow of a charged particle through a conductor.

Embodied energy—the energy required to extract, process, manufacture, transport, and install a material or product.

Energy—the ability to do work. Different forms of energy can be converted to other forms, but the total amount of energy remains the same.

Energy consumption—the amount of energy used by a product, process, or system.

Energy efficiency—the percentage of total energy consumed in useful work (and not wasted) relative to the amount of energy supplied.

Energy infrastructure—facilities required to turn raw ingredients into useful forms of power and deliver it to users, including the pipes, trucks, and rail lines that transport oil and natural gas, and the transmission lines that move electricity.

Energy Star—an energy-rating program for residential and commercial buildings developed by the U.S. Department of Energy and the U.S. Environmental Protection Agency.

Environmental product declaration (EPD)—a detailed report developed by a manufacturer that lists product ingredients and environmental impacts that occur over the entire life cycle of a product.

EPA (U.S. Environmental Protection Agency)—an agency of the federal government whose mission is to protect human health and the environment.

Evacuated tube collectors—solar thermal systems that use glass tubes surrounded by absorber plates.

Facility manager—employed by the owner to ensure that all systems are operated and maintained properly in a building, plant, or complex after occupancy.

Fenestration—the arrangement of windows and doors on the elevation of a building.

Finish materials—materials such as drywall, wallpaper, paints, and so on that are used to form decorative and protective coatings.

Flat plate PV system—a group of solar photovoltaic panels connected together.

Foreman—an individual who is responsible for direct supervision of the contractor's workers.

Fossil fuels—non-renewable forms of energy that were formed hundreds of millions of years ago and including coal, oil, and natural gas; carbon is their basic element.

Fracking—the process of injecting water and sand at high pressure into shale rock in order to release gas and oil.

General contractor (GC)—an individual or firm hired by and responsible to an owner for coordinating the completion of a project. The GC hires subcontractors and suppliers.

Geothermal heat pump—a system that uses the earth (and its constant temperature) as a giant heat exchanger; more accurately termed a ground-source heat pump.

Geothermal systems—systems that produce energy using the heat of the earth.

Green—the ability of something to contribute to long-term environmental and social endurance. In construction, sustainability, high-performance, and green are often used interchangeably.

Green Building Initiative—a nonprofit organization that administers professional certification and the Green Globes building assessment and certification in the United States.

Green building materials and products—an imprecise term that describes materials and products that have certain efficiency and other attributes.

Green construction—a process for creating and operating buildings and communities that strives to reduce their environmental impact and maximize social and economic value.

Green documentation—verification that a building and its materials, products, and systems meet green program requirements.

Green Globes—building assessment programs for new and existing buildings, distributed and managed by the Green Building Initiative.

Green infrastructure—the use of vegetation, soils, and systems that mimic natural processes to manage excess runoff, and then infiltrate it into the ground, evaporate it into the air, or slowly discharge it.

Green products—see Green building materials and products.

Green rating systems—programs designed to measure the environmental and social impact of products, systems, and buildings.

Green roof—a roof that is partially or completely covered with vegetation; also called a living roof.

Greenwashing—the practice of misrepresenting or "spinning" the environmental benefits of a product (or structure).

Greywater—wastewater that has not been generated by toilets or urinals.

Ground-source heat pump—a system that uses the earth (and its constant temperature) as a giant heat exchanger for heating and cooling; often inaccurately referred to as a geothermal heat pump.

Health Product Declaration (HPD)—a standard format for reporting product content and associated health information for building products and materials.

Heating and cooling loads—the amount of heating or cooling a building needs; also called "demand."

Heavy metals—metallic elements such as lead, mercury, and chromium, among others.

High-performance building—a building that optimizes energy efficiency, is durable, meets high-performance standards throughout its life (from the extraction of materials through decommission), and contributes toward occupant productivity. Many sources, including this book, use the terms "green," "sustainable," and "high-performance" interchangeably.

Home Energy Rating System (HERS)—a residential energy-use index developed by Residential Energy Services Network (RESNET).

HVAC(R)—heating, ventilating, air conditioning (refrigeration).

Hydropower—systems that use the energy in moving water to do mechanical tasks or to produce electricity.

ICC (International Code Council)—an association that develops coordinated building safety and fire prevention model codes and standards, including the International Green Construction Code (IGCC).

Industrial sector—a sector of the construction industry that includes refineries, electrical stations, chemical processing plants, factories, and similar facilities.

Infill development—the placement of a new development on a previously under-used or abandoned parcel.

Infrastructure—a sector of the construction industry that includes transportation and service projects such as roads, tunnels, ferries, water collection and distribution, and waste management systems that are required to keep our communities functioning.

Insulation—a material or product that prevents the transfer of heat (or sound).

Integrated Project Delivery (IPD)—a project delivery system that is based on a highly collaborative approach to project design and construction.

Interior fit-out—the process of making interior space suitable for use (also called build-out).

Job superintendent—person on a jobsite responsible for coordinating and managing the work. Also called construction superintendent.

Jurisdiction—see Authority having jurisdiction (AHJ).

Kilowatt—a measurement of the rate at which electricity flows (equal to 1,000 watts).

Labor union—an organized group of workers who collectively use their strength to have a voice in their workplace; also called a trade union.

LED light—LEDs, or light-emitting diodes, are semiconductor devices that produce visible light very efficiently when an electrical current passes through them.

LEED (Leadership in Energy and Environmental Design)—a voluntary green building certification program developed by the U.S. Green Building Council and administered by the Green Building Certification Institute that recognizes best-in-class building strategies and practices. LEED includes a suite of green building rating systems as well as professional accreditation.

License—a permit typically issued by a state and required in order to perform certain occupational tasks.

Life-cycle assessment (LCA)—an analysis of the environmental impacts of a product over its entire lifetime.

Life-cycle costing (LCC)—an analysis of costs over the entire life of a product.

Living Building Challenge—building certification programs developed by the International Living Future Institute.

Living roof—a roof that is partially or completely covered with vegetation; also called a green roof.

Load calculations—the process used to determine heating and cooling demand.

Low-E glass—glass with a coating that reflects long-wave heat energy and improves insulating characteristics.

Lump-sum delivery method—a system of organizing a project in which a general contractor is hired on a lump-sum-bid basis after design is complete; also called a traditional/design-bid-build delivery method.

MasterFormat—an organizational tool developed by the Construction Specifications Institute.

Material—a substance that serves as the raw matter from which a product is made (e.g., silicon is a raw material of PV cells); see Products.

MEP—an acronym standing for the mechanical, electrical, and plumbing trades or services.

Merit shop (open shop)—a firm or organization that pays workers according to the laws of the state and federal government and the individual's abilities; workers are not required to be in a union or pay the union dues.

Metered-valve faucets—fixtures that use a predetermined amount of water.

Motion energy—the energy something possesses due to its movement.

NAHB (National Association of Home Builders)—a trade and membership association that helps promote housing policies; developed National Green Building Standards for residential construction.

National Green Building Standard—a point-based rating system for green residential construction, remodeling, and land development developed by the National Association of Home Builders and the International Code Council and ANSI-approved.

Natural ventilation—the process of supplying and removing air through an indoor space by natural means, without the use of a fan or other mechanical system.

Net-metering—the practice of using a single meter to measure consumption and generation of electricity by a small generation facility (such as a house with a wind or solar photovoltaic system); the net energy produced or consumed is, respectively, sold to or purchased from the power provider.

Nontoxic materials and products—those that are not harmful to people and animals.

Off-gassing—the emission of noxious gases, as from building materials.

Operations & Maintenance (O&M) Manual—A manual provided to the owner at the completion of the work that gives critical operation, maintenance, repair, and replacement information.

Orientation—the way a building is situated on a site and the positioning of windows, rooflines, and other features.

Owner—an individual or entity that comes up with a project concept or idea, establishes the time and budget constraints, provides the site, figures out how to pay for the project, and hires many of the people who will help make it happen; owners may be private or public entities.

Performance—the capabilities of something (e.g., a building) under operation. In construction, performance refers to resource use and other building operations and impacts.

PHIUS+—an energy rating system primarily for residential projects, developed by the Passive House Institute US.

Photovoltaic array—a group of solar photovoltaic modules connected together; also called flat plate PV panels.

Photovoltaic panel (also called a flat plate PV panel)—an arrangement of photovoltaic cells mounted on a rigid flat surface with the cells exposed freely to incoming sunlight and a transparent top.

Photovoltaic (PV) systems—systems that use semiconductors to convert the sun's energy directly into electricity.

Photovoltaic (solar) cell—treated semiconductor material that converts solar energy to electricity.

Plug-load—the energy drawn by unregulated appliances and products.

Polyurethane—a manufactured material that comes in different forms and is resilient, flexible, and durable. Polyurethane is found in rigid foam, coatings and paints, adhesives, sealants and elastomers (such as wood sealers and caulks), window treatments, resin flooring, gaskets, and other thermoplastics.

Post-occupancy—the period following construction when a building is used for its intended purpose.

Power—the rate at which energy is produced or consumed; it is measured in watts. See Energy; power and energy are often mistakenly used interchangeably.

Power plant—an installation where electricity is generated for distribution.

Prime contractor—anyone with a direct contract with the owner, typically the general contractor.

Procurement—the process of obtaining goods and services.

Products—goods that are manufactured or refined and typically comprised of raw materials (e.g., PV cells are products that are made, in part, from the raw material silicon). See Materials.

Project—a unique activity that has a beginning and an end, uses resources, is not routinely done, and requires managing.

Project delivery—the organizational structure for completing a project; also called delivery method.

Project manager (PM)—an individual who is typically responsible for the business end of a construction project, in contrast to the job superintendent who is responsible for production.

Radiant energy—the energy that is transmitted by waves, especially electromagnetic waves. Light is a form of radiant energy.

Rainwater harvesting—the process of intercepting rainwater from a roof or other surface and putting it to beneficial use.

Rebound effect—the condition whereby green building performs poorly due to human actions.

Red list—a list of 13 toxic chemicals and materials commonly found in building materials today, which are not allowed in projects seeking certification under the Living Building Challenge.

Renewable energy—fuels that are not diminished when they are used, such as solar, wind, geothermal, and others.

Renewables—energy generated from continually replenishing natural sources.

Residential sector—a sector of the construction industry that includes both new construction and renovation of single- and multi-family properties such as houses, condominiums, and apartments.

R-value—a measure of resistance to heat flow; the higher the R value the greater the insulating value.

Solar farm—multiple solar panels that are grouped together into a single power plant to generate electricity

Solar heat gain—the increase in temperature in a space, object or structure that results from solar radiation.

Smart building—a building that uses technology to integrate its systems to optimize services, costs, and operation.

Smart technology—systems equipped with or using electronic controls.

Solar flat plate thermal collectors—panel systems that use the sun's energy to heat a fluid or air.

Specialty trade contractor—a contractor who is an expert in a specific area of construction.

Specifications—written descriptions of the work that define the materials, the processes, and the quality of products and systems.

Standards—guidelines developed as a way to measure the quality or characteristics of something. Standards may be adopted as mandatory codes.

Stormwater—an abnormal quantity of surface water arising from rain or snow.

Subcontractor—an individual or firm that has a contract with another contractor. In construction, subcontractors are typically specialty trades.

Sustainability—the ability of something to contribute toward long-term environmental and social endurance. In construction, sustainability, high-performance, and green are often used interchangeably.

Systems—in construction, systems are the elements that make up a structure and include the skin (e.g., the roof and exterior walls), the structure (e.g., framing), the heating/cooling/ventilating/lighting assemblies, and the furniture and equipment. Green buildings assume that the systems are integrated with one another in order to optimize efficiency and comfort. See Whole building design.

Thermal bridging—a heat-loss situation that occurs when one area has significantly higher heat transfer capability than the surrounding area.

Thermal energy—energy in the form of heat.

Third-party certifiers—independent product evaluators.

Tight building—a building with an envelope designed to greatly restrict air, heat, and moisture flow from conditioned to unconditioned spaces.

Trade association—an organization founded and funded by businesses that operate in a specific industry.

Trade union—an organized group of workers who collectively use their strength to have a voice in their workplace; also called a labor union.

Traditional delivery method—a general contractor is hired on a lump-sum-bid basis after design is complete. Also called a Design-Bid-Build or Lump-Sum delivery method)

UL (Underwriters Laboratories)—an organization that writes testing standards and certifies products for safety.

U.S. Environmental Protection Agency (EPA)—an agency of the federal government whose mission is to protect human health and the environment.

USGBC (U.S. Green Building Council)—a membership-based nonprofit organization that promotes sustainability in how buildings are designed, built, and operated; developed the LEED rating systems.

Vinyl chloride—a chemical component used primarily to make polyvinyl chloride (PVC) pipes, vinyl siding, vinyl flooring, and other products.

Volatile organic compounds (VOCs)—elements that contain carbon and can vaporize at normal temperatures and enter the air. VOCs lead to the formation of air pollution.

Waste management—the processes of dealing with and controlling construction and demolition debris.

Wastewater—any used water as well as runoff from streets.

Waterless toilets—toilets, including composting toilets and urinals, that use no water.

Wetland—an area that is regularly saturated by surface water or groundwater with vegetation that is adapted to these conditions

WGBC (World Green Building Council)—a worldwide network of green building councils, including the U.S. Green Building Council.

Whole building design—a design approach that analyzes system interdependencies and how they can be leveraged for maximum benefit.

Wind farm—multiple wind turbines that are grouped together into a single power plant.

Wind powered systems—systems that take the kinetic energy present in wind and convert it into mechanical or electric energy.

Zero net energy (ZNE) building—a building that produces, on average, as much energy as it uses.

Zoning ordinances—regulations that determine how a site can be used.

Bibliography

American Society of Interior Designers and U.S. Green Building Council. *REGREEN Residential Guidelines*, 2nd Edition. Washington, DC: 2008.

Arup and WBCSD. *Material Choice for Green Buildings.* London, UK: Arup and World Business Council for Sustainable Development (WBCSD), 2012.

Jeffrey Beard. *A Study of Comparative Sustainability Construction Costs/ Green Rating System Cost Comparison Study: LEED and Green Globes.* Philadelphia, PA: Drexel University, 2014.

Jared O. Blum. "Impact of Advancements in Model Energy Codes." *Construction Specifier,* January 2014.

Build It Green. *New Home Construction: Green Building Guidelines.* Oakland, CA: 2007.

Lane Burt and Duane Desiderio. *A New Retrofit Industry.* USGBC and the Real Estate Roundtable, June 13, 2011.

Peter Calthorpe. *Urbanism in the Age of Climate Change.* Washington, DC: Island Press, 2011.

Rachel Carson. *Silent Spring.* Boston: Houghton Mifflin, 1962.

Jim Cassio & Alice Rush. *Green Careers: Choosing Work for a Sustainable Future.* Gabriola Island, BC, Canada: New Society Publishers, 2009.

CBRE Group. *National Green Building Adoption Index 2014.* Los Angeles, CA: CBRE, 2014

Daniel D. Chiras. *The Solar House: Passive Heating and Cooling.* White River Junction, VT: Chelsea Green, 2002.

Construction Specifications Institute. *The CSI Sustainable Design and Construction Practice Guide*. Hoboken NJ: John Wiley, 2013.

Paul Crabtree. *Principles of Green Infrastructure*. CNU Rainwater-in-Context-Initiative, Congress for the New Urbanism. *www.cnu.org*.

Jesse Dean, Otto VanGeet, Scott Simkus, and Mark Eastment. *Design and Evaluation of a Net Zero Energy Low-Income Residential Housing in Lafayette, Colorado*. Golden, CO: National Renewable Energy Laboratory, 2012.

Alison Dykstra. *Construction Project Management: An Introduction*. San Francisco, CA: Kirshner Books, 2011.

Alison Dykstra. *LEED Certification: An Introduction to Certifying a Green Building*. San Francisco, CA: Kirshner Books, 2013.

Energy Information Administration, U.S. Department of Energy. *Annual Energy Outlook 2014*, Dec. 2013 preview. Washington, DC.

Gene Farmer. *Contractor's Guide to LEED-Certified Construction*. Clifton Park, NY: Delmar, 2012.

Kathryn Ferbholz, Jim Bowyer, Sarah Stai, Steve Bratkovich, and Jeff Howe. *Differences between the Forest Stewardship Council (FSC) and Sustainable Forestry Initiative (SFI) Certification Standards for Forest Management*. Minneapolis, MN: Dovetail Partners, 2011.

Monika Freyman. "Hydraulic Fracturing and Water Stress: Water Demand by the Numbers." *Ceres*, February 2014.

Thomas L. Friedman. *Hot, Flat and Crowded: Why We Need a Green Revolution and How It Can Renew America*. New York: Picador, 2009.

Lynn Froeschle. "Environmental Assessment and Specification of Green Building Materials." *Construction Specifier*, October 1999.

Geothermal Energy Association. *2014 Annual U.S. and Global Geothermal Power Production Report*. Washington, DC.

Peter Gevorkian. *Alternative Energy Systems in Building Design*. New York: McGraw-Hill, 2010.

David Gissen, Editor. *Big and Green: Toward Sustainable Architecture in the 21st Century*. New York: Princeton Architectural Press/National Building Museum, 2002.

Thomas E. Glavinich. *Contractor's Guide to Green Building Construction: Management, Project Delivery, Documentation and Risk Protection.* Hoboken, NJ: John Wiley, 2008.

Mike Guertin. *Green Applications for Residential Construction.* Clifton Park, NY: Delmar, 2011.

James Hamilton. *Careers in Solar Power.* Washington, DC: U.S. Bureau of Labor Statistics, 2011.

Stuart Hand. "LEED vs. Green Globes: How to Choose." *Daily Journal of Commerce,* February 27, 2014.

EC Harris. *Global Built Asset Wealth Index Report 2013.* London, UK: EC Harris Built Asset Consultancy.

Holly Henderson. *Becoming a Green Building Professional.* Hoboken NJ: John Wiley, 2012.

ILO Skills and Employability Department, European Union. *Skills and Occupational Needs in Green Building.* Geneva, Switzerland: 2011.

David Johnston and Scott Gibson. *Green from the Ground Up: A Builder's Guide.* Newtown, CT: Taunton Press, 2008.

David Johnston and Scott Gibson, *Green from the Ground Up: Sustainable, Healthy, and Energy-Efficient Home Construction.* Newton CT: Taunton Press, 2008.

David Johnston and Scott Gibson. *Toward a Zero Energy Home: A Complete Guide to Energy Self-Sufficiency at Home.* Newtown, CT: Taunton Press, 2010.

Van Jones. *The Green Collar Economy.* New York: HarperCollins, 2008.

Greg Kats. *Greening Our Built World: Costs, Benefits and Strategies.* Washington, DC: Island Press, 2010.

Joseph F. Kennedy, Michael G. Smith, and Catherine Wanek. *The Art of Natural Building: Design, Construction, Resources,* 2nd Edition. Gabriola Island, BC, Canada: New Society Publishers, 2015.

Charles J. Kibert. *Sustainable Construction: Green Building and Design.* Hoboken, NJ: John Wiley, 2005.

Catharine Killian. *Deep Green Renovation: Broad Scale Strategies for Achieving Deep Energy Savings in Existing Buildings.* 2011 AIAS/AIA COTE Research Fellowship.

Jong-Jin Kim and Brenda Rigdon. *Qualities, Use, and Examples of Sustainable Building Materials.* University of Michigan, National Pollution Prevention Center for Higher Education, December 1998.

Sharon Kooman Harmon and Katherine E. Kennon. *The Codes Guidebook for Interiors,* 5th Edition. Hoboken, NJ: John Wiley, 2011.

Abe Kruger and Carl Seville. *Green Building: Principles and Practices in Residential Construction.* Clifton Park, NY: Delmar, 2013.

Sam Kubba. *Handbook of Green Building Design and Construction: LEED, BREEAM, and GREEN Globes.* Waltham, MA: Butterworth-Heinemann, 2012.

Norbert Lechner. *Heating, Cooling, Lighting: Sustainable Methods for Architects,* 4th Edition. Hoboken NJ: John Wiley, 2015.

Barry B. Lepatner. *Broken Buildings, Busted Budgets: How to Fix America's Trillion-Dollar Construction Industry.* Chicago: University of Chicago Press, 2007.

Amory Lovins, Paul Hawken, and L. Hunter Lovins. *Natural Capitalism.* New York: Little Brown, 1999.

Amory Lovins and Rocky Mountain Institute. *Reinventing Fire: Bold Business Solutions for the New Energy Era.* White River Junction, VT: Chelsea Green, 2011.

Donald Martin, Stevan Vinci, and Dan Prows. *Green Globes for New Construction: Building Better Science for Better Results,* May 2013. Retrieved from: *http://www.thegbi.org/content/misc/White_Paper_for_an_Overview_of_Green_Globes_New_Construction.pdf*

William McDonough and Michael Braungart. *Cradle to Cradle: Remaking the Way We Make Things.* New York: North Point Press, 2002.

McGraw-Hill Construction. *SmartMarket Report: Construction Industry Workforce Shortages—Role of Certification, Training and Green Jobs in Filling the Gap.* Bedford, MA: McGraw-Hill Construction, 2012.

Ian L. McHarg. *Design with Nature,* 25th Anniversary Edition. Hoboken NJ: John Wiley, 1992.

William McKibben. *The End of Nature.* New York: Random House, 2006.

R. S. Means. *Green Building: Project Planning and Cost Estimating,* 3rd Edition. Hoboken NJ: John Wiley, 2011.

Molly Miller. *Integral: Revolutionary Engineering.* Portland, OR: Ecotone, 2013.

Peter Morris and Lisa Fay Matthiessen. *The Cost of Green Revisited: Reexamining the Feasibility and Cost Impact of Sustainable Design in the Light of Increased Market Adoption.* San Diego, CA: Davis Langdon (now known as AECOM), 2007.

Natural Resources Defense Council. *Energy Down the Drain: The Hidden Costs of California's Water Supply.* Oakland, CA: NRDC Pacific Institute, 2004.

New Buildings Institute. *Core Performance Guide: A Prescriptive Program to Achieve Significant, Predictable Energy Savings in New Commercial Buildings.* Vancouver, WA: NBI, 2007.

New Buildings Institute. *NEEA Study: Examples of Deep Energy Savings in Existing Buildings.* Vancouver, WA: NBI, 2011.

David W. Orr. *Design on the Edge: The Making of a High-Performance Building.* Cambridge, MA: MIT Press, 2008.

Ron Pernick and Clint Wilder. *The Clean Tech Revolution.* New York: HarperCollins, 2008.

Peterson's. *Green Careers in Building and Landscaping.* Lawrenceville, NJ: Peterson's, 2011.

Peterson's. *Green Careers in Energy.* Lawrenceville, NJ: Peterson's, 2010.

Peterson's. *Green Jobs for a New Economy.* Lawrenceville, NJ: Peterson's, 2009.

Stephanie S. Pincetl. *Transforming California: A Political History of Land Use and Development.* Baltimore, MD: Johns Hopkins University Press, 1999.

Linda Reeder. *Guide to Green Building Rating Systems.* Hoboken NJ: John Wiley, 2010.

Hegazy Rezk and Abou Hashema M. El-Sayed. Sizing of a stand alone concentrated photovoltaic system in Egyptian site. *International Journal of Electrical Power and Energy Systems*, Vol. 45, Issue 1, February 2013.

David Riley, Kim Pexton, and Jennifer Drilling. *Defining the Role of the Contractor on Green Building Projects.* State College, PA: Pennsylvania State University, 2003.

William Souder. *On a Farther Shore: The Life and Legacy of Rachel Carson.* New York: Crown, 2012.

Ross Spiegel and Dru Meadows. *Green Building Materials: A Guide to Product Selection and Specification.* Hoboken, NJ: John Wiley, 2012.

J. William Thompson and Kim Sorvig. *Sustainable Landscape Construction: A Guide to Green Building Outdoors,* 2nd Edition. Washington, DC: Island Press, 2008.

Union of Concerned Scientists. *Production Tax Credit for Renewable Energy.* January 4, 2013. *xucsusa.org*

U.S. Department of Energy/Building Technologies Program, Energy Efficiency and Renewable Energy. *Buildings Energy Data Book 2011.* Washington, DC: 2012 (Metadata updated August 28, 2015).

U.S. Energy Information Administration. *Annual Energy Outlook 2010 With Projections to 2035.* Washington, DC: Office of Integrated Analysis and Forecasting, U.S. Department of Energy, 2010.

U.S. Energy Information Administration. *Annual Energy Outlook 2013 Early Release Overview* (with projections through 2040). Washington, DC: Office of Integrated Analysis and Forecasting, U.S. Department of Energy, 2013.

U.S. Environmental Protection Agency, Office of Wetlands, Oceans and Watersheds. *Case Studies Analyzing the Economic Benefits of Low Impact Development and Green Infrastructure Programs.* Washington, DC: 2013.

U.S. Green Building Council. *Green Jobs Study.* McLean, VA: Booz Allen Hamilton, 2012.

U.S. Green Building Council. *LEED Core Concepts Guide,* 3rd Edition. Washington, DC: USGBC, 2014.

Sim Van der Ryn. *Design for an Empathetic World; Reconnecting People, Nature, and Self.* Washington, DC: Island Press, 2013.

Sim Van der Ryn and Stuart Cowan. *Ecological Design,* 10th Anniversary Edition. Washington, DC: Island Press, 2007.

Rob Watson. *Green Building: Market and Impact Report 2011.* Oakland, CA: GreenBiz Group, 2011.

Sarah L. White. *U.S. Skill Formation: Towards a Greener Future.* Greenforce
    Initiative: Advancing Greener Careers and Campuses. Merrifield, VA:
    National Wildlife Foundation, October 20, 2011.

World Commission on Environment and Development. *Our Common Future.*
    Oxford, England: Oxford University Press, 1987.

World Green Building Council. *Annual Report 2012/2013. www.worldgbc.org*

World Green Building Council. *The Case for Green Building: A Review of the
    Costs and Benefits for Developers, Investors and Occupants.* WBG, 2013.
    www.worldgbc.org

Jerry Yudelson. *Green Building A to Z.* Gabriola Island, BC, Canada: New Society
    Publishers, 2007.

Jerry Yudelson. *The Green Building Revolution.* Washington, DC: Island
    Press, 2008.

Jerry Yudelson. *Green Building Through Integrated Design.* New York: McGraw-
    Hill, Greensource Books, 2009.

Jerry Yudelson. *Green Building Trends: Europe.* Washington, DC: Island
    Press, 2009.

Endnotes

INTRODUCTION

1   McGraw Hill Construction, "Green Building Outlook Strong for Both Non-Residential & Residential Sectors Despite Soft Economy, Says New Report from Dodge," *Press Release*, November 15, 2012.

2   President Obama's "New Energy for America" program aims to achieve 25% of our energy from renewable sources by 2025. This program was reinforced by the $787 billion 2009 stimulus package which devoted billions toward energy efficiency and conservation, the development of renewable energy sources and transmission, and workforce training. At the same time the Federal Departments of Energy and Transportation, the Environmental Protection Agency and states developed programs to reinforce these goals.

CHAPTER 1

1   E. C. Harris, *Global Built Asset Wealth Index 2013*.This is a very interesting report that attaches a dollar value to the built assets of various countries. Built asset wealth value includes all the public and private property and infrastructure in a country—all of its residential and commercial office space, its transport infrastructure such as roads and rail, airports, plus power plants, water networks, and so on. At almost $40 trillion in 2012 (and expected to rise to more than $47 trillion by 2022), the United States had the greatest share of built asset wealth in the 30 countries included in this study. (On a wealth *per person* basis, Singapore is the wealthiest.) *http://www.echarris.com/pdf/ GlobalBuiltAssetWealthIndexReport2013.pdf*

2   Tony Reaves, "Casino Developers not pursuing green certification," Oxford Hills Sun Journal, January 15, 2011.

3 The British Thermal Unit (BTU) is a measurement of heat (1 barrel of crude oil, 42 gallons, is equal to 5,800,000 BTUs.) A Quad = 10^{15} BTUs and is equivalent to approximately 170 million barrels of crude oil. The United States uses over 90 Quads of energy every year of which around 40% is used by the building sector. For more see Appendix B in this book. For comprehensive data on energy use, sources, and more see the U.S. Department of Energy, Energy Information Administration at *www.eia.gov*

4 Ibid.

5 Lawrence Livermore National Laboratory, *Estimated U.S. Energy Use in 2013*. *www.lini.gov*

6 Booz Allen Hamilton, *Green Jobs Study*, prepared for the U.S. Green Building Council, January 2012.

7 U.S. Census Data, Characteristics of New Housing, 2012.

8 U.S. Energy Information Agency *www.eia.gov/tools/faqs/faq.cfm?id=727&t=6*

9 Amory Lovins and Rocky Mountain Institute, *Reinventing Fire: Bold Business Solutions for the New Energy Era*, White River Junction, VT: Chelsea Green Publishing, 2011, p. 6.

10 Matthew L. Wald, "Fossil Fuels' Hidden Cost Is in Billions, Study Says," *New York Times*, October 19, 2009.

11 Monika Freyman, Ceres research paper, *Hydraulic Fracturing & Water Stress: Water Demand by the Numbers—Shareholder, Lender & Operator Guide to Water Sourcing*, Ceres: Boston, MA, February, 2014.

12 Charles J. Kibert, *Sustainable Construction: Green Building Design and Construction*, 3rd Edition, Hoboken NJ: John Wiley, 2013.

13 Brett Walton, "Price of Water 2014: Up 6 Percent in 30 Major U.S. Cities; 33 Percent Rise Since 2010 ," Circle of Blue, *www.circleofblue.org/waternews/2014, May 4, 2014.*

14 Water Sense/U.S. Environmental Protection Agency, *Fix a Leak Week, www.epa.gov/ WaterSense/pubs/fixleak.html* (accessed August 22, 2014).

15 U.S. Dept. of Energy, Energy Efficiency & Renewable Energy.

16 Claudia Copeland, *Energy-Water Nexus: The Water Sector's Energy Use*, August 28, 2013, p. 2, Congressional Research Service.

17 U.S. Geological Service, *Total Water Use in the United States, 2005*, Circular 1344.

18 The Nature Conservancy, *www.nature.org*

19 Southern Environmental Law Center, *Tri-State Water Wars*, May 2013.

20 U.S. Environmental Protection Agency, *Buildings and Their Impact on the Environment: A Statistical Summary*, revised April 22, 2009.

21 U.S. Department of Labor, OSHA, *Toxic Metals, www.osha.gov/SLTC/metalsheavy*

22 U.S. Environmental Protection Agency, "Hazard Summary—Vinyl Chloride," revised January 2000. *www.epa.gov/ttnatw01/hlthef/vinylchl.html*

23 *http://water.epa.gov/drink/info/well/health.cfm*

24 Charles J. Kibert, p. 424.

25 Booz Allen Hamilton, *RCRA Solid Waste Programs,* for the EPA, June 1999.

26 U.S. Environmental Protection Agency *http://cfpub.epa.gov/eroe/index.cfm?fuseaction=list.listBySubTopic&ch=48&s=225*

CHAPTER 2

1 Architecture 2030, *A Historic Opportunity, http://architecture2030.org/the_solution/buildings_solution_how*

2 Ibid.

3 McGraw-Hill Construction, SmartMarket Report 2013, p. 40.

4 Don Prowler, FAIA, *Whole Building Design*, Whole Building Design Guide (WBDG), Revised and updated by Stephanie Vierra, March 22, 2012.

5 *http://brownfieldaction.org/brownfieldaction/brownfield_basics*

6 Harvey M. Bernstein, "World Green Building Trends," *Smart Market Report,* McGraw-Hill Construction, 2013.

7 Booz Allen Hamilton, *Exhibit 2-1: Green Construction Market Value, Green Jobs Study*, prepared for the U.S. Green Building Council, January 2012.

8 *Energy Policy Act of 2005 (Public Law 109-058), Section 914. Building Standards.*

9 Pacific Gas & Electric, *Zero Net Energy Pilot Program, www.pge.com*

10 Greg Kats, *Greening our Built World: Costs, Benefits, and Strategies*, Washington, DC: Island Press, 2010, p. 22. This is a very helpful book for anyone interested in deconstructing the economics behind green building.

11 Living Building Challenge, certification case studies.

12 David Kaneda, Integral Group, Construction Specifications Institute seminar, Santa Rosa, CA, March 5, 2015.

13 Mike Rovito," Rethinking the Incremental Cost Equation," *Getting to Zero National Forum*, August 15, 2013.

14 Matthew Kotchen, "Beware of the Rebound Effect," *New York Times,* March 20, 2012.

15 Catharine Killian, 2011 AIAS/AIA COTE Research Fellowship, *Deep Green Renovation: Broad Scale Strategies for Achieving Deep Energy Savings in Existing Buildings. http://www.aia.org/aiaucmp/groups/aia/documents/pdf/aiab092925.pdf*

16 Ibid.

17 Prepared for BetterBricks, an initiative of Northwest Energy Efficiency Alliance (NEEA) by the New Buildings Institute, *NEEA Study: Examples of Deep Energy Savings in Existing Buildings*, July 2011.

18 For a very interesting discussion on alternative systems engineering, the reader is referred to the Rocky Mountain Institute's 2011 paper *Big Pumps, Small Pipes.* This paper is a case study of a carpet company that used non-conventional pipe layout and design to dramatically improve energy efficiencies. See the Rocky Mountain Institute, *www.rmi.org*

19 Claudia Copeland, *Energy-Water Nexus: The Water Sector's Energy Use*, Congressional Research Service, August 28, 2013, p. 2.

20 CBS Los Angeles, "Santa Monica, Other Cities Seek Water Independence," March 16, 2014.

21 U.S. Geological Survey, Rain and Precipitation, *https://water.usgs.gov/edu/earthrain.html*

22 Ibid.

23 U.S. Environmental Protection Agency, Water Sense, *Outdoor Water Use in the United States.*

24 City of Baltimore, Healthy Harbor, *Managing Stormwater*, *www.healthyharborbaltimore.org/healthy-harbor-plan/managing-stormwater*

25 US Environmental Protection Agency, *What is Green Infrastructure? http://water.epa. gov/infrastructure/greeninfrastructure/gi_what.cfm*

26 Environmental Services, City of Portland, Oregon, Programs, *Sustainable Stormwater Management.*

27 United Nations General Assembly, March 20, 1987. *Report of the World Commission on Environment and Development: Our Common Future;* Transmitted to the General Assembly as an Annex to document A/42/427, *Development and International Co-operation: Environment; Our Common Future, Chapter 2: Towards Sustainable Development*, paragraph 1. This report is often referred to as the Brundtland Report, named for the commission that authored the report and was tasked with developing information to encourage sustainable development around the globe.

CHAPTER 3

1 Rob Watson, *Green Building Market and Impact Report 2011*, Executive Summary, GreenBiz group, 2011. *www.GreenBizGroup.com*

2 Christopher Nutter, "Emerging Risks in the Design and Construction of Green Buildings," *American Bar Association, Construction Litigation*, April 11, 2012.

3 Booz Allen Hamilton, *Exhibit 2-1: Green Construction Market Value, Green Jobs Study*, prepared for the U. S. Green Building Council, January 2012.

4 McGraw-Hill Construction press release, "Green Building Outlook Strong for Both Non-Residential & Residential Sectors Despite Soft Economy, Says New Report from Dodge," November 15, 2012.

5 Christopher Nutter, "Emerging Risks in the Design and Construction of Green Buildings", *American Bar Association, Construction Litigation,* April 11, 2012.

6 General Services Administration, *FY 2011-2016 Strategic Sustainability Performance Plan, www.gsa.gov/graphics/ogp/SSPP.pdf*

7 Gideon Fink Shapiro, "Building Bytes," *Architect Magazine,* July 2014.

8 Christopher Nutter, "Emerging Risks in the Design and Construction of Green Buildings."

9 Stuart Kaplow, Green Building Law Update, *Lawsuit over LEED Documentation,* July 27, 2014.

CHAPTER 4

1 International Code Council, *www.icc.org*

2 "Why 189.1 Is Important, Industry News", *ASHRAE Journal,* March 2010, *www.ashrae.org*

3 NAHB, *http://www.nahb.org/page.aspx/generic/sectionID=2510*

4 *http://sefaira.com/resources/us-energy-codes-could-surpass-leed/*

5 University of California, Berkeley, Center for the Built Environment, *Simulated and Actual Energy Use: The Role of Plug Loads,* May 7, 2014.

6 *www.gbci.org*

7 *http://www.usgbc.org/profile*

8 *http://www.usgbc.org/articles/infographic-leed-world*

9 Rick Fedrizzi, "*The Oldest LEED-certified Building in the World,*" USGBC, June 25, 2013, *http://www.usgbc.org/articles/oldest-leed-certified-building-world*

10 Paula Melton and Tristan Roberts, *LEED vs GREEN GLOBES: A Definitive Analysis,* GreenBuilding, 2014. *www2.buildinggreen.com*

11 Jerry Yudelson, written comments to the author, January, 2015

12 *http://www.usgbc.org/credits/new-construction/v2009*

13 Ibid.

14 Paula Melton and Tristan Roberts, *LEED vs GREEN GLOBES: A Definitive Analysis.*

15 International Living Future Institute, *http://living-future.org/ilfi/about-international-living-future-institute*

16 Bullitt Foundation, Denis Hayes, *Better, Faster, More: Toward Sustainable Cities,* 2013,

http://www.bullittcenter.org/vision/message-from-denis-hayes/

17 Bullitt Center, Living Proof Blog, *Bullitt Center Earns Living Building Certification*, April 1, 2015.

18 Home Research Labs, NGBS certified homes, *www.homeinnovation.com/green*

19 *Green Buildings: Building and Energy Codes*, 2012 Pacific Southwest Region 9, EPA, *www.epa.gov/region9/greenbuilding/building-codes.html*

20 *Building the Future: A Builder's Personal Dream* (Part 1), *Energy Design Update*, Vol. 34, No. 8, August 2014.

21 *http://www.sustainableinfrastructure.org/awards/index.cfm*

22 Richard Reed, Anita Bilos, Sara Wilkinson, and Karl-Werner Schulte, "International Comparison of Sustainable Rating Tools," *Journal of Sustainable Real Estate*, Vol. 1, No. 1, 2009, Clemson University, Clemson, SC.

23 For information on the World Green Building Council and its members and activities, see *www.worldgbc.org*

CHAPTER 5

1 Ross Spiegel and Dru Meadows, *Green Building Materials: A Guide to Product Selection and Specifications*, Hoboken, NJ: John Wiley, 2012, p. 16.

2 Ibid., p. 9.

3 John Guill, DTR Consulting, Comments to author, March 4, 2015.

4 Alison Dykstra, *Construction Project Management: A Complete Introduction*, San Francisco, CA: Kirshner Books, 2011.

5 Spiegel and Meadows, p. 50.

6 Bruce King, Comments to author, February 15, 2015.

7 The Pharos Project, *http://www.pharosproject.net/product_category/show/id/5*

8 Charles J. Kibert, *Sustainable Construction: Green Building and Design*, Hoboken, NJ: John Wiley, 2005, p. 353.

9 John Guill, Comments to author, February, 2015

10 Spiegel and Meadows, p. 98.

11 HPD Collaborative, *http://hpdcollaborative.org/use-the-hpd/faq*

12 International Living Future Institute, *http://declareproducts.com/for-consumers*

13 Blaine Brownell, "Visible Green: New material Opportunities in Sustainable Design," *ECOBUILDING Pulse, Materials + Products*, a publication of American Institute of Architects, October 20, 2014. *http://www.ecobuildingpulse.com/vision-2020/materials-products/material-products_o*

CHAPTER 6

1 McGraw-Hill Construction, "Green Building Outlook Strong for Both Non-Residential & Residential Sectors Despite Soft Economy, Says New Report from Dodge," November 15, 2012.

2 Ibid.

3 Ibid.

4 Booz Allen Hamilton, *Green Jobs Study*, prepared for the U.S. Green Building Council, January 2012. p. 21. This report looks at the economic impacts of green buildings in general and LEED-certified buildings in particular.

5 Bureau of Labor Statistics, U.S. Dept. of Labor, *Employment in Green Goods and Services—2011*, March 2013.

6 Ibid. Note that green job figures come primarily from the U.S. Bureau of Labor Statistics. On March 1, 2013, President Obama ordered into effect the across-the-board spending cuts (commonly referred to as sequestration) required by the Balanced Budget and Emergency Deficit Control Act, as amended. Under the order, the Bureau of Labor Statistics (BLS) must cut its current budget by more than $30 million, 5% of the current 2013 appropriation, by September 30, 2013. In order to achieve these savings and protect core programs, the BLS will eliminate two programs and all "measuring green jobs" products. These products include: data on employment by industry and occupation for businesses that produce green goods and services, data on the occupations and wages of jobs related to green technologies and practices, and green career information publications. This is the last scheduled release of new data on employment by industry for businesses that produce green goods and services.

7 Jonathan A. Lesser, *Gresham's Law of Green Energy*, Cato Institute, *Resolution Magazine*, Winter 2010–2011.

8 Jorge Madrid and Adam James, Bureau of Labor Statistics, U.S. Dept. of Labor, *Bureau of Labor Statistics Reports 3.1 Million U.S. Green Jobs: Top 5 Takeaways*, March 23, 2012.

9 Ibid.

10 Turner Construction Company, *2012 Green Market Barometer*, p. 3.

11 Ibid., p. 1

12 Charles J. Kibert, *Sustainable Construction: Green Building and Design*, Hoboken, NJ: John Wiley, 2005, p. 61.

13 Amory Lovins, Paul Hawken, and L. Hunter Lovins, *Natural Capitalism*, New York: Little Brown, 1999, p. 114.

14 Booz Allen Hamilton, *Green Jobs Study*, p. 4.

15 Greg Kats, *Greening Our Built World: Costs, Benefits and Strategies*, Washington, DC: Island Press, 2010.

16 U.S. Environmental Protection Agency, *http://www.epa.gov/greenbuilding/pubs/faqs.htm#13*

17 World Green Building Council, The Business Case for Green Building: A Review of the Costs and Benefits for Developers, Investors and Occupants, 2013 *www.wgbc.org*

18 Bruce King, Comments to the author February 15, 2015.

19 Mountain Institute, *Factor 10 Engineering Design Principles, Version 1.0*, 2010, p. 6.

20 U.S. Energy Information Administration, U.S. Department of Energy, *http://www.eia.gov/totalenergy/data/annual/pdf/sec3_11.pdf*

21 Kibert, pp. 400–401.

22 U.S. Department of Energy, *Frequently Asked Questions: Lighting Choices to Save You Money, www.Energy.gov*

23 Tom Javits, Vice President for Construction, Metropolitan Museum of Art, interview with author, October 2014.

24 U.S. Environmental Protection Agency, *http://www.epa.gov/watersense/commercial/docs/factsheets/offices_fact_sheet_508.pdf*

25 Brett Walton, *Price of Water 2014: Up 6 Percent in 30 Major U.S. Cities; 33 Percent Rise Since 2010*, Circle of Blue, *www.circleofblue.org/waternews/2014*, May 4, 2014.

26 Ibid.

27 Booz Allen Hamilton, *Green Jobs Study*, p. 3.

28 Randyl Drummer, CoStar, "Case for Green Buildings Grows Stronger for Owners, Occupants," March 9, 2011, *http://www.costar.com/News/Article/Case-for-Green-Buildings-Grows-Stronger-for-Owners-Occupants/127092*

29 National Association of Insurance Commissioners, *Climate Change and Risk Disclosure*, July 18, 2014, *http://www.naic.org/cipr_topics/topic_climate_risk_disclosure.htm*

30 *http://www.triplepundit.com/2013/11/climate-change-insurance-industry*

31 World Green Building Council, *Health, Productivity, and Well-being in Offices, http://www.worldgbc.org/files/6314/1152/0821/WorldGBC_Health_Wellbeing_productivity_Full_Report.pdf*

32 Heschong Mahone Group, *Windows and Offices: A Study of Performance and the Indoor Environment* and *Daylight and Retail Sales—CEC Pier 2003, http://www.h-m-g.com/projects/daylighting/summaries%20on%20daylighting.htm*

CHAPTER 7

1 USGBC, Green Building Facts, February 23, 2015.

2 McGraw-Hill Construction, Harvey Bernstein, *SmartMarket Report*, 2013, Introduction.

3 Charles J. Kibert, *Sustainable Construction: Green Building and Design,* Hoboken, NJ: John Wiley, 2005, p. 193.

4 Ibid., p. 194.

5 Scott McLeod, Comments to author, March, 2015

6 David Riley, Kim Pexton, and Jennifer Drilling, *Defining the Role of the Contractor on Green Building Projects,* State College, PA: Pennsylvania State University, 2003.

7 A. Frattari, M. Dalprà, and G. Salvaterra, "The Role of the General Contractor in Sustainable Green Buildings," *International Journal for Housing Science,* Vol. 36, No.3, pp. 138–148.

8 Institute for Building Efficiency, *www.institutebe.com/smart-grid-smart-building/ What-is-a-Smart-Building.aspx*

CHAPTER 8

1 BLS, *http://www.bls.gov/iag/tgs/iag23.htm*

2 Peterson's, *Green Careers in Building and Landscaping,* Lawrenceville, NJ: Peterson's, 2011.

3 Rob Bolin, "HVAC Integration of the Building Envelope," *Whole Building Design Guide* December 1, 2009, *https://www.wbdg.org/resources/env_hvac_integration. php?r=env_bg_slab*

4 P. C. Thomas and Steven Moller, *HVAC System Size: Getting It Right: Right-Sizing HVAC Systems in Commercial Buildings,* CRC Construction Innovation, 2007.

5 Boris Kingma and Wouter van Marken Lichtenbelt, "Energy consumption and female thermal demand," *Nature Climate Change,* August 3, 2015.

6 Exploratorium press release, *Exploratorium's Net-Zero Energy Goal for New Waterfront Home 2013,* September 19, 2012.

7 M. Frankel, M. Heater, and J. Heller, *Sensitivity Analysis: Relative Impact of Design, Commissioning Maintenance and Operational Variables on the Energy Performance of Office Buildings,* New Buildings Institute, August 2012.

8 Peterson's, *Green Careers in Building and Landscaping.*

9 Houston Neal, "The Coming Renaissance of Electrical Contracting," *Software Advice,* February 10, 2010.

10 Elisa Wood, *Lighting Standards: DOE's Final Act of 2014 to Save Office Buildings and Schools $15 Billion,* January 5, 2015, *http://energyefficiencymarkets.com/ final-act-2014-save-office-buildings-schools-15-billion*

11 Tom Javits, Interview.

12 Ibid., p. 60.

13 Kurtis Elton and S. E. Wolfe, "Water Efficiency and the Professional Plumbing Sector: How Capacity and Capability Influence Knowledge Acquisition and Innovation," *Water Resources Management,* Vol. 26, No. 2, pp. 595–608.

CHAPTER 9

1   National Resources Defense Council, *http://www.nrdc.org/enterprise/greeningadvisor/aq-low_voc.asp*

2   Martin Solomon, "Gypsum Board: Are Our Walls Leaching Toxins?" *Building Green,* March 2012, *http://greenspec.buildinggreen.com/blogs/gypsum-board-are-our-walls-leaching-toxins*

3   U.S. Environmental Protection Agency, *Vinyl chloride, Hazard Summary*, revised January 2000.

4   National Resources Defense Council, Smarter Living: Energy, *Energy Out the Window?* November 2011, *http://www.nrdc.org/living/energy/energy-out-window.asp*

5   Empire State Building information, Sustainability, *www.esbnyc.com/esb-sustainability/project*

6   Greenbuilding.com, *Insulating Choices and Strategies—Zero Energy Home.*

7   *www. energy.gov/energysaver/articles/insulation*

8   Michael Russo, "Minimizing Risks with Solar Roofs," *Construction Specifier,* August 2014, p. 29.

9   Climate Protection Partnership, U.S.Environmental Protection Agency, Office of Atmospheric Programs, *Reducing Urban Heat Islands: Compendium of Strategies—Green Roofs,* www.epa.gov/heatisland/Resources:/pdf/GreenRoofsCompendium.pdf

10 "New LIC Coffee Shop Serves up Goodies from Brooklyn Grange," *New York Neighborhood News,* October 18, 2012, *DNAinfo.com*

11 Green Roofs for Healthy Cities, *Green Roofs Offer Many Public, Private, and Design-Based Benefits,* www.greenroofs.org/index.php/about/greenroofbenefits

12 AFL-CIO Department of Government Affairs, *Union Involvement in Green Jobs and Sound Environmental Policy*, February 2009, p. 13.

13 Charles J. Kibert, *Sustainable Construction: Green Building and Design*, Hoboken, NJ: John Wiley, 2005, p. 450.

CHAPTER 10

1   Doug McKenzie, *NorCalSolar.org*, Interview with the author, August 26, 2015.

2   Jeff Tsao (U.S. Department of Energy, Office of Basic Energy Science), Nate Lewis (California Institute of Technology), George Crabtree (Argonne National Laboratory), *Solar FAQs*, 2005, p. 10. The figures quoted are from 2001. *http://www.sandia.gov/~jytsao/Solar%20FAQs.pdf*

3   Rhone Resch, Solar Energy Industries Association, *http://cleantechnica.com/2011/10/20/texas-solar-energy-hitting-state-in-1-month-all-energy-texas-oil-gas-industry-has-ever-produced*

4   Energy Information Administration, *Monthly Energy Review, April 2015,* Table 1.3, *http://www.eia.doe.gov/emeu/mer/pdf/pages/sec1_7.pdf*

5   U.S. Energy Information Agency, *Annual Energy Outlook 2015*, Executive Summary. The EIA is part of the U.S. Federal Statistical System and releases regular data on energy sources and uses. In their 2015 Outlook, by making certain assumptions regarding oil prices and demand, they anticipate that renewable electricity generation will increase by 72% from 2013 to 2040, accounting for more than one-third of new generation capacity. Wind and solar generation will account for nearly two-thirds of the increase in total renewable generation. For historical, future, and current data, see their website at *www.eia.gov*

6   Ibid., *Renewables Meet Much of the Growth in Electricity Demand.*

7   Royal Society of Chemistry, *http://www.rsc.org/campaigning-outreach/ global-challenges/energy/#solar*

8   James Hamilton, *Careers in Solar Power*, U.S. Bureau of Labor Statistics, June 2011.

9   Charles J. Kibert, *Sustainable Construction: Green Building and Design*, Hoboken, NJ: John Wiley, 2005, p. 285.

10 Silvia Martinez Romero, World Bank, Energy Sector Management Assistance Program, *Concentrating Photovoltaic* presentation, May 2014, *www.esmap.org/sites/esmap.org/ files/ESMAP_SAR_EAP_Renewable_Energy_Resource_Mapping_CPV_Martinez.pdf*

11 Martin Holloday is a skeptic about solar thermal systems (at least for residential applications). See his blog (Musings of an Energy Nerd) and informative articles on renewable energy systems. For a comparison of thermal flat plate and PV systems, see his December 26, 2014, article titled "Solar Thermal is Really, Really Dead" *at www. GreenBuildingAdvisor.com*

12 Bright Source, *World's Largest Solar Thermal Power Project at Ivanpah Achieves Commercial Operation*, February 13, 2014, *http://www.brightsourceenergy.com/ ivanpah-achieves-commercial-operation#.VL62Dkt6eFI*

13 *http://cleantechnica.com/2012/08/17/construction-of-worlds-largest-concentrating-solar-power-plant-reaches-halfway-mark*

14 Office of Energy Efficiency and Renewable Energy (EERE), *How Do Wind Turbines Work? http://energy.gov/eere/wind/how-do-wind-turbines-work*

15 Brian Smith, NREL, Interview with the author, September 1, 2015.

16 *www.bls.gov/green/wind_energy/#manuphase*

17 *American Wind Farms*, National Resources Defense Council, September 2012, p. 6.

18 James Hamilton and Drew Liming, U.S. Department of Labor, Bureau of Labor Statistics, *Careers in Wind Energy, http://www.bls.gov/green/wind_energy*

19 Brian Smith interview.

20 Liza Featherstone, "Help Wanted for Green Jobs," *Nation,* January 2009.

21 Ibid.

22 American Wind Energy Association, *Third Quarter 2012 Market Report. http://www. awea.org/Resources/Content.aspx?ItemNumber=4599*

23 American Council On Renewable Energy, *The Outlook for Renewable Energy in America, 2014*, p. 7.

24 "Citi, Google to Finance Terra-Gen Power's Alta Wind Energy Center in California: Nation's First Gigawatt-Scale Wind Center to Have 1020 MW Online by Year's End," Terra-Gen Power, *News,* May 24, 2011, *www.terra-genpower.com/News.aspx*

25 Amy Harder, "When Energy Isn't Popular—Anywhere," *National Journal,* April 27, 2012.

26 Brian Smith interview.

27 U. S. Department of Energy, Wind Vision Report, *Wind Vision: A New Era for Wind Power in the United States*, March 2015. This is a very comprehensive review of the costs, benefits, challenges, and opportunities for wind power in the United States. The Executive Summary may be downloaded at: *http://energy.gov/sites/prod/files/2015/03/ f20/wv_executive_summary_overview_and_key_chapter_findings.pdf*

28 Makani Power, Inc., Alameda, CA. Founded in 2006, Makani Power was purchased by Google in May, 2013, as part of the Google X research program.

29 Diane Cardwell, "Tax Credit in Doubt, Wind Power Industry Is Withering," *New York Times,* September 20, 2012.

30 Ben Adler, "Why Congress Needs to Extend the Wind Energy Tax Credit," *Grist,* December 9, 2013.

31 California Energy Commission, "Types of Geothermal Power Plants," *Energy Almanac, http://energyalmanac.ca.gov/renewables/geothermal/types.html*

32 Geothermal Energy Association, *2014 Annual U.S. & Global Geothermal Power Production Report*, April 2014, p. 16.

33 California Energy Commission, California Geothermal Energy Statistics & Data, *http:// energyalmanac.ca.gov/renewables/geothermal/index.php*

34 Ibid., p. 4.

35 Ibid.

36 Allison A. Bailes, PhD, Interview with author, August 2, 2015.

37 Allison A. Bailes, PhD, "Is a Ground-Source Heat Pump a Renewable Energy System?" *Green Building Advisor,* July 24, 2012, *http://www.greenbuildingadvisor.com/blogs/dept/ building-science/ground-source-heat-pump-renewable-energy-system*

38 NRCD, *http://www.nrdc.org/energy/renewables/geothermal.asp*

39 Drew Liming, U.S. Bureau of Labor Statistics, *Careers in Geothermal Energy, http://www.bls.gov/green/geothermal_energy/geothermal_energy.htm* The BLS has lots of helpful information on renewable energy systems and overviews of careers and job trends. On March 1, 2013, President Obama ordered into effect the across-the-board spending cuts (commonly referred to as sequestration) required by the Balanced Budget and Emergency Deficit Control Act, as amended. Under the order, the Bureau

of Labor Statistics (BLS) must cut its current budget by more than $30 million. As a result, the BLS has eliminated all data on employment by industry and occupation for businesses that produce green goods and services, data on the occupations and wages of jobs related to green technologies and practices, and green career information publications. For more information regarding the sequestration at BLS, see *http://www.bls.gov/bls/sequester_info.htm*

40 US Geological Society, *http://water.usgs.gov/edu/hydroadvantages.html*

41 *Grand Coulee Dam Visitors Guide, http://www.gcdvisitor.com/grand-coulee-dam-facts*

42 Ibid.

43 *www.pbs.org/itvs/greatwall/dam1.html*

44 Energy.gov, *http://energy.gov/energysaver/articles/microhydropower-systems*

45 U.S. Department of Energy, *2014 Hydropower Market Report Highlights,* April 2015. DOE/Energy Efficiency and Renewable Energy put out extensive reports. To download a summation of the 2015 report, see: *http://energy.gov/sites/prod/files/2015/04/f22/Hydropower-Market-Report-Highlights.pdf*

46 Energy.gov, *Hydropower Still in the Mix*, April 27, 2015, *http://energy.gov/eere/articles/hydropower-still-mix*

47 DOE, *2014 Hydropower Market Report Highlights.*

48 Jeff Opperman, "Sustainable Hydropower: Are Small Dams Really Better for the Environment?" *Smarter by Nature,* March 17, 2014.

49 National Hydropower Association, *http://www.hydro.org/tech-and-policy/technology/marine-and-hydrokinetic*

50 Federal Energy Regulatory Commission, *Issued Hydrokinetic Preliminary Permits,* updated January 2015.

51 This information is from *Estimated U.S. Energy Use 2013,* developed by Lawrence Livermore National Laboratory.

52 Biomass Power Association, U.S. Biomass Facilities, *http://www.usabiomass.org/docs/biomass_map.pdf*

53 Kendric Wait, *Biomass Power, Colorado Forest Health and Water Resources,* prepared for the Joint Senate/House Water Resources Review Committee, October 10, 2013. *http://www.colorado.gov/cs/Satellite?blobcol=urldata&blobheader=application%2Fpdf&blobkey=id&blobtable=MungoBlobs&blobwhere=1251895860366&ssbinary=true*

54 National Resources Defense Council, "Biomass Energy and Cellulosic Ethanol," *http://www.nrdc.org/energy/renewables/biomass.asp*

55 Mary Booth and Edward Miller, *Trees, Trash, and Toxics: How Biomass Energy Has Become the New Coal,* Partnership for Policy Integrity, April 2014.

56 U.S. Energy Information Administration, *Energy in Brief, http://www.eia.gov/energy_in_brief/article/renewable_electricity.cfm*

CHAPTER 11

1   Mickie S. Rops and Associates, "Credentialing, Licensure, Certification, Accreditation, Certificates: What's the Difference?" 2002–2007. *http://msrops.blogs.com/akac/files/Credentialing_Terminology.pdf*

2   USGBC, "Exploding Demand for LEED Credentials among Employers," June 26, 2014. *www.usgbc.org/articles/exploding-demand-leed-credentials-among-employers*

3   McGraw-Hill Construction, *SmartMarket Report: Construction Industry Workforce Shortages: Role of Certification, Training and Green Jobs in Filling the Gap*, 2012. This report is available through USGBC: *www.usgbc.org/sites/default/files/ConstructIndWorkforceShort.pdf. Note that the construction industry, in general, faces work-force shortages. These shortages have a variety of causes: during the recession the industry lost many workers and they have not returned, there has been a downward trend in construction attracting new young workers, and, consequently, the workforce is aging and retiring and there are insufficient numbers of young workers in the pipeline. The industry and the federal government are dealing with this problem through increased apprenticeship opportunities and the 2014 Workforce Innovation & Opportunity Act (WIOA). For additional information, see http://www.doleta.gov/wioa*

4   Association of Energy Engineers, *Energy Management Jobs Report: Relevant Trends, Opportunities, Projections and Resources*, 2013. *http://www.aeecenter.org/files/reports/2013%20Energy%20Mgt%20Jobs.pdf*

5   McGraw-Hill Construction, *SmartMarket Report.*

CHAPTER 12

1   U.S. Department of Labor, Employment and Training Administration, *The Greening of Registered Apprenticeship: An Environmental Scan of the Impact of Green Jobs on Registered Apprenticeship and Implications for Workforce Development*, June 2009.

2   Ibid.

APPENDIX A

1   Rachel Carson, *Silent Spring,* Boston: Houghton Mifflin, 1962.

2   During the 1940s and 1950s, the United States was undergoing a considerable transformation in its energy situation. Prior to and during World War II, the country was virtually self-sufficient in petroleum. But the enormous growth in the number of automobiles over that decade, as well as the explosive growth of other uses of

petroleum, resulted in the United States becoming a consistent net importer by the end of the 1940s. By 1960, the United States was importing almost one-fifth of its petroleum consumption (Arjun Makhijani and Scott Saleska, *The Nuclear Power Deception: US Nuclear Mythology from Electricity "Too Cheap to Meter" to "Inherently Safe" Reactors,* Apex Press, 1999). On November 20, 1952, a blue-panel commission appointed by President Truman and headed by William Paley, released *Resources for Freedom: Foundations for Growth and Security,* which detailed the increasing dependence of the United States on foreign sources of natural resources, and argued for the necessity to transition to renewable energy. This document was one of the first to argue both for the dire need for Americans to stop their reliance on oil and for the potential of solar energy as a solution.

3   *www.pbs.org/wgbh/americanexperience*

4   World Green Building Council, *http://www.worldgbc.org/worldgbc/about*

APPENDIX B

1   U.S. Department of Energy, *Buildings Energy Data Book, 2011.*

2   Karen Long, "Ranch Homes Then and Now," *JCCC Honors Journal,* Vol. 4, No. 2, Spring 2013.

3   U.S. Energy Information Agency, *Consumer Expenditure Estimates for Energy by Source, 1970–2010, http://www.eia.gov/totalenergy/data/annual/pdf/sec3_11.pdf*

4   Dennis Silverman, *Energy Units and Conversions,* University of California Irvine, Physics and Astronomy, *http://www.physics.uci.edu/~silverma/units.html*

5   Randy Sandoval, Environmental Defense Fund, "Why you only get 25% of the electricity you pay for," May 27, 2014, *https://www.edf.org/blog/2014/05/27/why-you-only-get-25-electricity-you-pay*

6   Diane Ackerman, "The Power of a Hot Body," *New York Times,* December 30, 2012.

Index

About the author

Alison Dykstra has a masters degree in architecture from the University of Colorado and has been a licensed architect since 1983. She is a member of the American Institute of Architects, the Construction Specifications Institute, from which she received her CDT certification in construction documents technology, and her local chapter of the US Green Building Council. Her work with and commitment to the issues of renewable energy started at the Farallones Institute in the 1970s, where she worked on passive solar systems, alternative construction technologies, and integrated community design systems.

Dykstra has been an adjunct faculty member at Santa Rosa Junior College since 1992 and was inspired to write this book by her students. "How do we get started in green construction?" was a common refrain even among students skeptical of environmentalism. This book is a first step in answering that question.